MINOR MONUMENTS

SELECTED

ESSAYS BY

HOWARD

MOSS

The Ecco Press

NEW YORK

First published by The Ecco Press in 1986
18 West 30th Street, New York, N.Y. 10001
Published simultaneously in Canada by
Penguin Books Canada Ltd.
2801 John Street
Markham, Ontario, Canada L3R 1 B4

Library of Congress Cataloging-in-Publication Data
Moss, Howard, 1922–
Minor monuments.
1. Literature, Modern—19th century—History and
criticism—Addresses, essays, lectures. 2. Literature,
Modern—20th century—History and criticism—Addresses,
essays, lectures. I. Title.
PN761.M638 1986 809 85-20413
ISBN 0-88001-089-4
ISBN 0-88001-104-1 ppb.
Publication of this book was made possible
in part by a grant from The National Endowment
for the Arts.

Acknowledgments on p. 337 constitute an extension of the copyright page

For Edward Parone

CONTENTS

PART FIVE

The critical work selected here ranges in time from the late 50's to the present day. Collections of essays and reviews are usually prefaced by an apology: despite the look of a miscellany, the taste and sensibility of the author unites them all. While I hope that holds true of *Minor Monuments*, something else links these pieces together — they are all forays into alien territory, into the terra incognita of prose, and each was, for me, in one way or another, a struggle to master the demands of fact, coherence, and style.

One other thing may need to be said: For a poet, the preponderance of critical essays on prose writers may seem somewhat odd. Because I have been the poetry editor of *The New Yorker* since 1950 — and still am, as of this writing — I learned to avoid speaking of the very writers I was editing. Of the five poets discussed here at some length, three — Whitman, Cavafy, and Auden — were dead at the time I wrote about them, and therefore outside the limit of my proscription. The two who were exceptions, Elizabeth Bishop and James Schuyler, may require some explanation. My enthusiasm for the late Miss Bishop's work is no secret and I think at the time I wrote the first of the three Bishop pieces collected here, "All Praise," she was living in Brazil and seemed remote and foreign and far away enough to make her permissible to discuss. An excuse, perhaps, but one I seized upon. James Schuyler had a view of nature so similar to my own and yet so differently expressed (and was so knowledgeable about flowers) that I began to write notes to myself about him. They eventually grew into an essay, and since I could find no critical discussion of him elsewhere I considered valuable, I undertook a layman's journey of my own, and finally decided to publish it.

Four pieces here have never before been collected: the review of Chekhov's early stories; another of Elizabeth Bishop's fiction; the essay on Flaubert; and, finally, the one on Eileen Simpson's *Poets in Their Youth*, whose subjects were not only writers I admired but people I knew, and whose text brought up issues I thought important.

November, 1985

Time which antiquates antiquities,

and hath an art to make dust of all things,

hath yet spared these minor monuments.

—from "Urne Burial" by Sir Thomas Browne

PART ONE

Hingley's Biography

READING the biographies of great writers, one gets the impression that literature is mainly the occupation of mistreated children — those preoccupied with being unloved or being unable to return love. These deficiencies branch out into all sorts of tributaries: anger, shyness, aggression, despair. We admire and analyze the products of these disorders as if unhappiness were an oyster exuding pearl after pearl. And we should feel guilty — we probably do — once we know this secret of art. For aren't we in the uncomfortable position of welcoming bad news? Where would we be if Proust's mother had kissed him good night? If Beethoven's nephew had been a little nicer? If Chekhov — in this case — had been treated with the affection he claims he missed during a childhood of enforced churchgoing, shopkeeping (his father was a grocer), and schoolwork? We are given enigmas — the artist's way of handling the impossible — and the biographer, confronted with enigmas, becomes obsessed by fact. *This* explains *that*, he keeps telling us, with a certain amount of rueful hope.

But sometimes it is in the nature of the artist to accomplish the opposite, to give us work that takes on the illusion of fact — photographs snapped without filters, perfectly clear, without affectation — and to save the real enigma for the life itself. And Chekhov would seem to be a case in point, for literary criticism has never been able to make him one of its martyrs — about a certain kind of excellence there is little to say — and, of all writers, he strikes us as the least neurotic, the one least having us on, the man who has nothing to hide.

Yet reading Ronald Hingley's *A New Life of Anton Chekhov* (1976) — "new" because he wrote an earlier biography in 1950 — one realizes that the more we know of Chekhov the less apt any of the standard portraits seem: the gray patriarch of twilight Russia, black coat buttoned to the neck, pince-nez and cane, gloomily tracing the decline of an attractive but listless gentry; its counterimage — the lively and witty host, always surrounded by people, teaser of women, doctor, builder of schoolhouses, planter of trees; the elegant Chekhov, staring with just a bit of world-weariness straight into the camera, perhaps recalling the gambling tables of Monte Carlo, the palm-lined boulevards of Nice; the adventuresome loner, crossing the five thousand miles of Siberian wasteland (before the construction of the Trans-Siberian Railroad) by horse and buggy, flatboat and steamer, to take a census of the exiled prisoners on remote Sakhalin Island; and the official Soviet version, hand to dedicated breast, gazing off into a revolutionary future.

The blurred outlines of all these pictures must have some

truth, for we are dealing, after all, with the same man, and one who lived only to the age of forty-four. Mr. Hingley goes to great lengths to take down these well-worn icons. What he puts in their place is a rational metamorphosis, the transformation of the grandson of a freed serf into the most admired short-story writer and playwright of his day — and of this century.

A spirited and humorous child, Chekhov was filled with contradictions from the beginning. Like Keats, he studied medicine, became a writer, contracted tuberculosis, died young, and became celebrated for a posthumous body of work, the letters. Hingley doesn't tell us anything new, really — that is, about the life itself — but he manages to add enough detail to make the truth more believable. Chekhov was that paradoxical creature in whom subtlety and honesty were mixed in equal parts — uncomfortable bedfellows. He saw more than anyone around him and what he saw was either ludicrous or painful. But the pain was not only outside. An ironic man, he seems to have known everything about love but how to feel it, or — if that seems an unfair description of someone who has taught us so much about it — at least how to express it. For what amazes one reading any Chekhov biography, including this one, are two basic facts: everyone adored him; no one felt close to him. He was a moral man and a free one, and, though he eventually married — very late — marriage, perhaps intimacy of any kind, were not freedom's noteworthy ingredients. Story after story, play after play make the same point: if life is a disappointment, love is the biggest disappointment in it. Behind every social failure — of class, illusion, accomplishment — there lies an unconnected couple.

5

And that may be why Hingley spends a bit too much time on Chekhov's "loves," a subject he feels he neglected in the earlier biography. Chekhov's attitude toward sex was surprisingly prudish; on the other hand, many examples are quoted from his correspondence with Alexander and Nicholas, his older brothers, and, in their cases, prudishness may have been the other side of caution. Both brothers were charming, alcoholic, and self-destructive. Hingley's insistence on delving into Chekhov's love life makes the biographer seem sometimes like a high-wire artist balancing on a wire that isn't quite there. Gossip is never teased into fact; still, Hingley overdoes it, for in a biography, any conjecture is easily confused with history, and very little in the area of passion can be pinned down. Even if it were, with someone as elusive as Chekhov, its significance would remain in doubt. The man who invented a way of revealing everything about character through the seeming miracle of making character inarticulate surely was on to the trick himself, and it was a technique that could easily be reversed.

If there were no great loves, there were flirtations and romances, and we know most about the one with Lika Mizinova because Chekhov made the most use of it. Lika, in love with Chekhov for many years, was tolerated, indulged, but not wildly encouraged, and she finally ran off with Potapenko, a Ukrainian writer. Potapenko and his amour were trailed across Europe by his ferocious wife, Mariya Andreyevna, who was good at making scenes. Potapenko, a tower of Jell-O, abandoned the pregnant Lika in Paris and the Potapenkos departed for Italy. Lika appealed to Chekhov for help; he was polite but not cooperative, and, as Hingley points out, if she had read "A Dreary Story," published five years earlier, where a similar appeal goes unanswered, she might have saved herself the trouble. Chekhov had once before exploited the lives of his friends in the story "The Butterfly," but Lika and the Potapenkos turned up, all too visibly, as Nina, Trigorin, and Arkadina in *The Seagull*.

Chekhov was not quite the traditional angel of legend; he could be two-faced and insensitive, and manipulated people for his own ends. Not many occasions present themselves to support these assertions, but Hingley is fair in pointing them out, and he does so almost gratefully, as if thankful for the few shreds of evidence that might rescue Chekhov from the danger of becoming a plaster saint.

Illness and impotency — a frequent complaint — must have had their psychological effects. But circumstances may have been crucial in Chekhov's reluctance to form any sort of permanent relationship. He was the third child in a family of six children; his father left Taganrog — Chekhov's provincial birthplace — bankrupt, stealing off into the night to avoid his creditors; and by the time Chekhov arrived in Moscow to study medicine, he was not only the center of a family struggling for survival but its openly acknowledged head.

From the age of twenty, Chekhov was in varying degrees, and at various times, responsible for a family of from four to eight people. It was not the kind of situation, even if he were the kind of man, to make marriage attractive. His younger sister, Masha, remained a spinster, and it is clear from Hingley's account that every time she made a bid for freedom, Chekhov, through the simple expedient of withholding emotional support, made a difficult decision impossible. Until Chekhov married the Moscow Art Theater actress Olga Knipper, Masha was his housekeeper, hostess, companion, and nurse.

If Hingley doesn't quite solve the ambiguities of Chekhov's

emotional life, he does something more important. He provides a coherent structure for a body of work that has floundered in confusion from the beginning. American readers, in particular, are bedeviled by edition after edition in which the stories appear haphazardly, where no attempt is made to arrange the contents chronologically (Robert Payne's *The Image of Chekhov* is an exception), and we are given, willy-nilly, early and late work thrown together, no corresponding Russian titles, and no dates of composition or publication. Something called "Grief," about a horse, in one paperback, turns up as "Misery" in another, but then, there is "Grief" again, which turns out to be another story entirely, about a bishop, something we had formerly known under the title of "Anguish."

Hingley redresses all these wrongs: first, in his admirably translated and edited Oxford *Chekhov*, a nine-volume chronological edition of the plays and stories, and in this biography, where, dividing Chekhov's work into two main categories, he allows the second to be the period of the major stories and plays, dating from 1888 with the publication of "The Steppes."

The first category, the more or less immature work — there are early masterpieces, genius not fitting easily into grooves — is subdivided into four distinct periods, the earliest being that of the skits, jokes, one-liners, puns, and sketches Chekhov turned out for the humor magazines of the day under the pseudonym of Antosha Chekonte to help support himself while studying medicine. The three remaining periods simply correspond to whichever magazine Chekhov happened to be publishing in most frequently at the time: *Splinters*, *The Petersburg Gazette*, or *New Time*.

There are overlappings and problems — one-act plays were hammered out of stories, early work was revised to surface again, the most notable being the transformation of the middling *The Wood Demon* into *Uncle Vanya* — but in the main the method works, and, for the first time, all of Chekhov's writing falls into place as if, at last, an extraordinarily complex series of facts were reduced to basic propositions. Even tables in an appendix, forbiddingly academic and scientific elsewhere, are helpful and illuminating here. Hingley has created order out of a mess, and the whole hodgepodge of Chekhov's fiction is put into clear relief, the Russian compositions matched with their English equivalents.

Certain Chekhovian stereotypes are abandoned or corrected. Chekhov and Stanislavsky had a running battle in regard to the production of the plays. But though Stanislavsky may have been heavy-handed, and given to a naturalism the plays made obsolete, in one way he was right. Chekhov claimed Stanislavsky's interpretations had made "cry-babies" out of his plays, but to call *The Cherry Orchard* a comedy is to be disingenuous. Hingley thinks Chekhov, trying to assure a certain "lightness" of tone, used the word "comedy" as a signpost, a guarantee against heaviness. Perhaps so. But the result has been a series of productions of the plays veering sharply toward melancholy — or, as an antidote, the bucolic. In any case, who but a madman would leave a performance of *The Seagull* laughing?

Gorky called Chekhov the only free man he knew. Immune to cant at a time when the air was practically solid with it, Chekhov was able to resist the deadliness of prescribed truths, whether of the left or of the right. Even his admiration and love of Tolstoy didn't blind him to the inan-

ities of Tolstoy's theories. Chekhov made his position — or
non-position — unequivocal: "I am not a liberal. I am not a
conservative. I am not an advocate of moderate reform. I am
not a monk. Nor am I committed to non-commitment. I
should like to be a free artist, that's all."

Chekhov had — still has — a way of surprising his readers
by not raising his voice to denounce the lazy, the sexually
loose, the ne'er-do-well, or to praise the philanthropist, the
samaritan, and the morally correct. The moral complexity of
the stories and plays stems from this undercurrent of ambiguous sympathy, this withholding of judgment. In "The
Duel," Layevsky, the sloppy adulterer, is more congenial
than Von Koren, the enlightened Darwinian. Motive counts
more than action because motive ultimately reveals itself.
What Chekhov hated most was rigidity, authoritarianism,
and hypocrisy. He saw little difference between the dead
hand of the imperial censor and the pernicious overseers of
the liberal press; he was hounded equally from both sides.
Chekhov once said, "Morals do not purify plays any more
than flies purify the air," and felt that fanaticism of any
stripe was the ultimate danger. And in denouncing the editors of *Russkaya mysl*, a liberal paper (one he later published
in), he made a prediction:

Just you wait. . . . Under the banner of learning, art and per-
secuted freedom of thought Russia will one day be ruled by
such toads and crocodiles as were unknown even in Spain under
the Inquisition. . . . Narrow-mindedness, enormous pretensions, excessive self-importance, a total absence of literary or
social conscience: these things will do their work [and] will
spawn an atmosphere so stifling that every healthy person will

be . . . nauseated by literature, while every charlatan and wolf in sheep's clothing will have a stage on which to parade his lies. . . .

And Chekhov was right to distrust the mind devoted to one idea. Governments are more easily changed than cultural climates; the imperial censors of Czarist Russia have their Soviet counterparts. And Soviet editors (not necessarily willingly) have bowdlerized Chekhov's correspondence. An incorrect political opinion or a sexual reference — prudery and repression going hand in hand — is expunged from the text or given the usual three-dot treatment. In the present and forthcoming Soviet edition of *Works and Letters*, 1974–1982, replacing the earlier edition of 1944–1951, some progress has been made (in the few early volumes Hingley has been able to examine). But it is progress of a dubious kind. The word "Yid," for instance, is now printable. But whether this is a relaxation of censorship or a footnote to unofficial anti-Semitism remains moot. According to Hingley, the word was less pejorative in Chekhov's time than it is now. But it was always condescending, if not worse, and disheartening coming from Chekhov. He was hardly an anti-Semite, having been engaged to a Jewish girl, come to the defense of a Jewish student denied entrance to his school under the quota system, and taken up the cause of Dreyfus. Still, there it is.

Where Hingley is most original is in tracing the growth of Chekhov's fiction. He distinguishes the finest work — "Ward Number Six," "A Dreary Story," "The Kiss," and so on — from the very good work, separating the cream from the cream. And he deplores the botched ending of "The Duel," a flawed masterpiece, which resolves itself in an atypically sentimental manner in its last pages. One goes back to that story, and others, with a new eye. They are mentioned by Hingley in passing, for he insists this book, unlike the earlier one, is purely biographical. The panorama of the whole is laid before us, the ups and downs, the hills and the valleys; and if Hingley's perspective somehow manages to go flat on heights and to skim some depths, we understand the relation of the stories to the life and the times, to each other, and, to a lesser degree, to the plays. Hingley also points out what may be either a repetitive subject or merely a technical device in the more structured stories and the plays: the opposition of two male characters in basic philosophical or emotional conflict: Treplev and Trigorin, Von Koren and Layevsky, Serabryakov and Vanya.

Many Chekhovs appear in Hingley's biography: the natural mimic, got up in dark glasses and fur coat, sneaking into the balcony of Taganrog's theater; the writer at one summer dacha or another, fishing, hunting, mushroom-gathering; the estate owner at Melikhova, planting his orchards, running a small medical clinic; the famous playwright uncomfortably taking his bows after the premiere of *The Cherry Orchard;* the friend of Bunin, Gorky, Tolstoy; and finally the celebrated exile dying in Yalta of tuberculosis, a disease he couldn't or wouldn't diagnose for over ten years, in spite of his medical training.

Confronted with all this documentation, the most complete ever assembled in an examination of Chekhov's life, why is it that the man who so convincingly coalesces into a single portrait in the letters eludes a biographer as knowledgeable as Hingley? It is partly, I think, Chekhov's ability to hold two things at once in suspension: the sensitivity and

the candor, the "poetry" of the plays and their clear-headed-
ness, the scientific discipline of the doctor and the imaginative freedom of the writer. We have in Chekhov someone
contradictory but completely trustworthy, someone devoted
to truth by temperament rather than by doctrine.

It takes a superb writer to make discordant notes sound
like a single tone. And Hingley is not a superb writer;
in fact, he is often a dull one, given to odd grammatical
quirks, an occasionally highfalutin vocabulary ("subven-
tion," "swived," "equipollent"), and a style sometimes too
sprightly, as if to counteract the drugs of academe. And he
makes one brave but classic misjudgment, in my opinion, in
preferring *Ivanov* to *The Seagull.* Hingley has written the
most informative biography of Chekhov we have, the one
based on the most recent evidence, the most advanced scholarship. But somehow the right tone is never struck, the man
we get to know so much about dips under the net and, with
a little smile, a wave of the hand, disappears. We are in-
debted to Hingley in a thousand ways: for rescuing us from
inflated translations, for putting work in its proper sequence,
for correcting the record where Soviet censorship has inter-
vened. But for the live Chekhov, flesh and blood, the letters
are still the richest source.

Early Chekhov

Our view of Chekhov as a fiction writer has been a matter of luck — haphazard glimpses proffered at the whim of this or that translator and publisher. Chekhov wrote 588 stories; the mature work — some sixty pieces — appeared between 1888 and 1904. That leaves "528 items" (according to the introduction to this book) not quite accounted for, and the vagueness of that statement is typical of our relationship to Chekhov in English.

No complete chronological edition of the stories is available. Ronald Hingley's Oxford Chekhov, for which there were such high hopes, turned out to be a disappointment.[1] Hingley confined himself to the plays and the later fiction, and though he has provided the reader with the most extensive apparatus on Chekhov in English — revisions, alternate ver-

[1] *The Oxford Chekhov*, translated by Ronald Hingley (Oxford University Press, 9 vols., 1968–1980).

sions, the publication history of each story, and considerable background on the writing — his translation steers a rocky course between the colloquial and the academic. The truth is, Hingley, invaluable as a Chekhov commentator, has a tin ear. Though we are heavily in debt to him we pay a high price for the loan. Chekhov's early stories come to us piecemeal — some in the Constance Garnett versions (all thirteen volumes about to be reissued by Ecco Press), and in sundry collections over the years.[2]

And so we have more reasons than usual to be grateful to Patrick Miles and Harvey Pitcher for these thirty-five early stories, known and unknown, arranged chronologically over a period of six years. They are smoothly readable for the most part, but the phrasing is sometimes relentlessly British or merely odd. Would anyone, even in England, say "Read it out" when they meant "Read it aloud"? Or "sneaking on people" when the sense conveys either "snitching on people," in colloquial American, or "sneaking up on people," in plain English?

The reprinting of any early work by Chekhov can be justified as representing the kind of thing he was grinding out as a medical student to make money. It is hard, though, to admire so fragmentary and lifeless a caricature as "Rapture," the opening story of the book, where a young officer wakes his parents to share his newfound notoriety in the press — he has merely been apprehended for being drunk. In fact, it

---

[2] *Selected Stories*, translated by Ann Dunnigan (New American Library, 1960); *The Unknown Chekhov*, translated by Avrahm Yarmolinsky (Noonday Press, 1954); *St. Peter's Day, and Other Tales*, translated by Frances H. Jones (Capricorn Books, 1959); *The Image of Chekhov: Forty Stories*, translated by Robert Payne (Knopf, 1963); *Late-Blooming Flowers and Other Stories*, translated by I. C. Chertok and Jean Gardner (McGraw-Hill, 1964); and others.

takes ten stories before we arrive at "The Huntsman," of 1885, and are steeped in the special mixture that is ultimately to become the Chekhovian potion.

In it, a handsome young huntsman meets the peasant wife he deserted and has been avoiding ever since he married her in an alcoholic stupor years before. Now he belongs to the manor house, a favorite of the owner. He and his wife have been mismatched from the beginning — woods are not fields nor forests farms. Though the story consists mainly of dialogue, we feel the impact of the woods; they are the huntsman's world and allow for sudden appearances and disappearances, for silences and murders. The huntsman is as much a part of the woods as the game he stalks. Yet in spite of his commitment to something larger than himself — the skill of the hunt — he is incapable, in his ignorance, of devoting himself to anything else. In him, something of the poetry of civilization and the savagery of the barbarian are imperfectly mixed. An animal barely awakened to a moral sense, he finally hands his wife a ruble and vanishes, slowly but conclusively, into the woods.

By the time we finish the story, our moral judgment is shaded. It is a Chekhovian subtlety to suggest that the huntsman lives by a set of values we might just possibly not be aware of. Like all of Chekhov's best stories, this one leaves us uneasy. Taken for granted assumptions are subtly undermined. No matter how many realities there are, none can be generalized without risking the truth. Deep down in the well, complication flavors the drinking water with an oddly different taste.

Chekhov's tales vary widely in quality as they do in the kind of character they take up — an immense mix of people surprising in their diversity as well as in the authority with which Chekhov handles them — English governesses, Russian boys, fishermen, bass fiddlers, lawyers, government officials, painters, ferrymen, actors, merchants, cab drivers, writers, chorus girls, shepherds, monks, railway officers, priests, peasants, landed gentry, self-made men — nothing fazes him. What fazes *us* is the extraordinary leap from the hardly worth reprinting "Rapture" to something as extraordinary as "The Kiss" four years later. And in Chekhov's case, development was more complicated than usual.

It could have taken a hundred years or never to get from "Rapture" to "The Kiss," and the signposts on the way aren't helpful. They range from the hackneyed to the sublime, and in no particular order. The tiny *frisson*, the easy irony typical of the early stories, dooms many of them to the academic cupboard. And yet there are a hundred charms along the way. (There are early stories like "Late-Blooming Flowers," from 1883, that seem to me more worth reprinting than "Rapture.") But another piece from 1883, "The Death of a Civil Servant," can stand for a whole category of early Chekhov stories that depend on the stupidities of class and rank: a civil servant sneezes at the theater, spraying the man in front of him, who turns around. The civil servant realizes his fellow theatergoer is a general, a "Number 2 in the Ministry of Communications." His guilt becomes obsessive, and he pursues the general for days to apologize further, to explain, to qualify, to make certain the general understands no insult was intended. Finally, the enraged general rebuffs him decisively and the civil servant goes home and dies. Funny, limited, a small, extended joke, the story is a farcical comment on toadying. Like so many of its counterparts, it leans heavily on the obvious and is meant to titillate the coarsest of palates. As distinguished from a superb story like "Easter Night," it is a potboiler serving up its single grain of truth.

The largest sampling of these stories were written in 1886, and here they begin to be remarkable, to have that special originality we now think of as Chekhovian. What does it consist of? In part, a deceptive simplicity. We are lured onto the field before we realize what peculiarly dangerous territory it is. The poetry of everyday life reaches its exact level; it is never falsified by naturalism or mannered by heightening. There is almost a rule of thumb by which we can judge the excellence and profundity of Chekhov's stories: the less drama the more revelation. And that is true even of the plays. The firing of a gun, so necessary to the muted but highly dramatic ending of *The Seagull,* to the farcical but lethal confrontation scene in *Uncle Vanya,* and to the ultimate sentence passed on Irena, Olga, and Masha in *The Three Sisters,* can be dispensed with in *The Cherry Orchard.* One needs to bring to the stories and the plays, in spite of their seeming simplicity, a knowledge of life rarely demanded of either audiences or readers. The plays do not resound for the inexperienced; they do not pander or preach. Devoid of easy sentiment, even the so-called comedies end up being pessimistic. Chekhov's lightness can be acidly satirical; his darkness is a darkness never seen before, and the one that haunts everyone — the darkness of what is not being said.

Chekhov's characters commonly reveal themselves without appearing to, and they speak in a new language, a language somewhat analogous to the one Mozart made up for the characters in his operas — where the words and their sounds are allied to a convention while at the same time freeing them-

selves from it. There is nothing "advanced" about Mozart or
Chekhov; they are the least self-conscious of innovators. They
used conservative vocabularies, and, because they did, their
true originality escaped immediate detection. Chekhov's depth,
reaching through a seeming convention, is what is new. Chekhov's plays, for instance, fit nicely into a realistic tradition.
But when one tries to pin down the "poetry" of his theater — often mentioned but rarely discussed — words become
blurred and meaningless. Chekhov at his best, which is most
often, evokes emotional effects not easily explained. There is
an alchemy at work that cannot be traced to subject, style,
or profundity of thought. We are being talked to in the most
natural way imaginable by the most natural of writers, whose
ultimate triumph of style was to seem to have none.

Chekhov's genius was something like a darkroom chemical
that could develop even the chanciest of negatives. The quality of his work doesn't depend on syntax and rarely on metaphor. His natural descriptions, often extremely beautiful, are
brief. In that way, he is like a poet; compression is the heart
of the matter. One image describes a sunset in a winter
woodland, not two. Chekhov is after character — what people are really like. And he knew them amazingly well.

There is another reason for Chekhov's position in modern
letters: the accuracy of his psychological insights. He ex-
plored the unconscious without formulating it as a concept.
And then, both as a man and as a writer, he has come to represent objectivity — the observer above the battle, the recorder free of partisanship. This view of him is only partly
true. He was, by every standard we can think of, an extraordinarily moral man, but he was also a man who could spot
humbug a mile away and was as sensitive to the fake philan-

thropy of the do-gooder as he was to the evil of the landlord, the military leader, or the estate owner who made doing good necessary in the first place. He had a cool eye, a large brain, and a heart that went out toward individual people, not movements.

He saw how contaminated dedication could be, both on the left and on the right, and yet was troubled at the same time by the notion that, without commitment, nothing important might be accomplished at all. In short, he was of particular interest because, in him, we actually see a great writer wrestling with the problem of how art and politics should or should not be joined. He was *forced* to wrestle with the problem, rather, because he was so often accused of not having a philosophical or political point of view. His conclusion is Chekhovian — inconclusive, which is not at all the same as being evasive. He seemed to distrust political commitment, detested moral preaching, and suspected the grand overall view of man that was considered the mark of a great nineteenth-century Russian writer.

Chekhov's early stories often turn on misunderstood circumstances as well as the absurdities of status. The later stories take up more complicated relationships and larger issues on wider canvases. The immoderate and the fantastic have yet to raise their heads (though "The Witch" is a precursor to "Ward Six"), partly because these early stories have less to do with middle-class neurotics, professional people, and the gentry, and partly because the editors are overly insistent on our seeing the comic side of Chekhov's talent, as if to redress a false emphasis. (It is not reassuring to discover that Mr. Pitcher coauthored a book called "Chuckle with Chekhov" in 1975.)

Miles and Pitcher retranslate "The Kiss," from 1887. And here, eleven years before what is generally considered the period of Chekhov's major work, we have a story that will never be surpassed. What might have been a novel in other hands is condensed into a few miraculous pages, in which the execution is as remarkable as the conception.

The story is simple enough: a battery officer, Staff-Captain Ryabovich, arriving in an unfamiliar town, is invited with other members of his company to the district manor for dinner. Once arrived, the officers are treated with exemplary politeness but transparent falseness — the kind of superficial good manners one might find on a more extended level at one of Proust's marathon dinners. The ballroom provides the setting for a dance. Ryabovich, "a short, round-shouldered officer in spectacles and with whiskers like a lynx's," ashamed of his ugliness and painfully shy, wanders off with a group to the billiard room. To get there, they pass through many strange, dimly lit rooms. The officers playing billiards ignore him. And so he decides, eventually, to wander back. On the way, he gets lost in a vast labyrinth of rooms. Opening doors, trying to find his way, he stumbles into a room completely dark; a chink of light through a distant door illuminates the room beyond. Suddenly, he hears a rustle, and a woman says, "At last!" and kisses him on the cheek. Then she cries out in horror, realizing her error; they are both terrified. She runs out. He wanders back and eventually regains the ballroom where he finds himself talkative, genial, even possibly charming. He tries to figure out which of the women present could have kissed him — none seems likely.

The evening ends; the battery leaves the next morning. But the kiss has utterly transformed Ryabovich. Some composite

version of the women present begins to haunt him. He has
fallen in love. He thinks of nothing else and begins to dream
of a new life; the woman who kissed him becomes his wife;
they have a family. He has been awakened to the notion of
the ideal.

That awakening destroys him in time because, like so many
illusions, it is based on absolutely nothing. "The Kiss" is a
story of how the imagination engages hope, how fantasy
nourishes desire, how romance is fostered by less than the
merest suggestion. If, as Eliot said, "human kind cannot bear
very much reality," it is also true that man can invent perverse and delusive versions of it. Romantic and terrible, "The
Kiss" is a kind of Frankenstein story that requires no electric
apparatus or sputtering wires. A mistake brings a man to life;
the resurrection makes life impossible to bear. "The Kiss" ex-
plores an enlargement of the self, touched into being by accident, and becomes a total revelation for the reader. The
borderline between ordinariness and fantasy suggests another, never broached in the story: the borderline between
fantasy and madness. The first is to be crossed, time and time
again, in the plays; the second to become a country of its own
in "The Black Monk" and "Ward Six."

There is another noteworthy aspect to "The Kiss," a kind
of infrastructure supporting its theme — the world of the ar-
tillery officers described with exactitude. The requirements
of cannon, the male camaraderie of the officers form an opposing current to the feminine strategies of the manor house.
The story's technical details have the authority of the hospital in "Ward Six," the grocery store in "In the Ravine," the
warehouse in "Three Years," and the railroad in "My Life."

The difficulty of seeing Chekhov's fiction as a whole is not
only a matter of chronology; it is also a matter of form and

substance. It is clear, now, by hindsight, that Chekhov managed to create an epical canvas made up of large and little masterpieces, the stories, the plays, and several short novels still classified as "stories" — "Three Years," "The Duel," "In the Ravine," "My Life" — filled with event and incident and the recording of changes that overtake a large cast of leading characters over a period of time. In each, a full-scale drama is acted out to its conclusion. They are not "stories" in the sense that "The Kiss" is a story, where a single wave forms offshore and finally breaks on the sand.

As for substance, Edmund Wilson, in his preface to his selection of Chekhov's stories called *Peasants*,[3] made some necessary distinctions:

> In the later years . . . Chekhov . . . was occupied mainly with a series of works, plays as well as stories, that were evidently intended to constitute a kind of analysis of Russian society, a miniature *Comédie Humaine*. [These stories] tend to be studies of milieux — . . . the new factory owners in "A Woman's Kingdom"; the old Moscow merchant class in "Three Years"; in "The Murder," the half-literate countrymen, fundamentalist and independent . . . the Tolstoyan intelligentsia in "My Life"; the lowest stratum of the peasantry in "Peasants"; the new class of engineers in "The New Villa"; the Kulaks, in "In the Ravine," on their way to the commercial middle class; the professional churchmen in "The Bishop"; and in "Betrothed," the old-fashioned provincial household and the revolt against it of the new generation.

Yet "My Life," to take an example, is more than a study of "the Tolstoyan intelligentsia"; it is a black comedy of ex-

---

[3] Doubleday/Anchor, 1956.

uberant malice, in which a narrator, far more intelligent than he should be, in a series of reversals exposes the whole social fabric of a town, and finally decides to become a house painter. Wilson's description of the stories is sociologically accurate and illuminating — the conjunction of the stories themselves a brilliant stroke — but, as often in Chekhov, we are, again, left uneasy. If these stories are sociological, we still have to deal with the stories of "ideas": the conflict between a "superfluous man" and a neo-Darwinian scientist in "The Duel"; the opposition of a paranoid with insight and his passive doctor, who participates in evil, in "Ward Six"; and that harrowing tale of fame and death, posed against a tenuous duality of art and science, "A Boring Story."

Chekhov was a revolutionary writer, but one without a thesis. In fact, that is exactly what is revolutionary about him. Tangible, precise, real, he remains, nevertheless, elusive. Theory — though he was attracted to it at one point in his life — never meant much to him. He had no panaceas for the human condition. His sympathies lay, obviously, with the oppressed, the underdog, the peasant — he was not very far from being one himself. Of the work as a whole these thirty-five stories, welcome as they are, provide the merest clue. In the end, we are still left in the position of putting Chekhov together.

ANTON CHEKHOV

Three Sisters

"Loneliness is a terrible thing, Andrei."

IN *Three Sisters*, the inability to act becomes the action of the play. How to make stasis dramatic is its problem, and Chekhov solves it by a gradual deepening of insight rather than by the play of event. The grandeur of great gestures and magnificent speeches remains a Shakespearean possibility — a diminishing one. Most often, we get to know people through the accretion of small details — minute responses, tiny actions, little gauze screens being lifted in the day-to-day pressure of relationships. In most plays, action builds toward a major crisis. In *Three Sisters*, it might be compared to the drip of a faucet in a water basin; a continuous process wears away the enamel of the façade.

Many stories are being told simultaneously: the stories of the four Prozorov orphans — three girls, one boy, grown up in varying degrees — living in one of those Chekhovian provincial towns that have the literal detail of a newspaper story but keep drifting off into song. There is the old drunken doctor, Chebutykin, once in love with the Prozorovs' mother. There is a slew of battery officers stationed in the town — one of them, Vershinin, a married man, falls in love with the already-married middle-sister, Masha; another proposes to the youngest, Irena; and still a third, Soliony, also declares his love for her. There is Olga, the oldest sister, and Kulighin, Masha's awkward schoolteacher husband. And there is Natasha, the small-town girl who sets her heart on Andrei, the brother. It is Natasha's and Andrei's marriage that provides the catalyst of change. Each of these characters might be conceived as a voice entering the score at intervals to announce or to develop its subject, to join and part in various combinations: duets, trios, and so on. *Three Sisters* is the most musical in construction of all of Chekhov's plays, the one that depends most heavily on the repetition of motifs. And it uses music throughout: marching bands, hummed tunes, "the faint sound of an accordion coming from the street," a guitar, a piano, the human voice raised in song.

Yet too much can be made of the "music" of the play at the expense of its command of narrative style. Private confrontation and social conflict are handled with equal authority, and a symbolism still amateur in *The Seagull*, written five years earlier, has matured and gone underground to permeate the texture of the work. No dead bird is brought onstage weighted with meaning. No ideas are embalmed in objects. What we have instead is a kind of geometric structure, one angle of each story fitting into the triangular figure of another, and, overlaying that, a subtle web of connected images and words. Seemingly artless, it is made of steel. In a letter to his sister, Chekhov complained, "I find it very difficult to write *Three Sisters*, much more difficult than any of my other plays." One can well believe it.

Because immobility is the subject — no other play catches hold of the notion so definitively, with the exception of *Hamlet* — secondary characters carry the burden of narration forward. Natasha and Andrei establish the main line of construction; their marriage is the network to which everything else attaches. Yet Andrei never spins the wheels of action. That task is left to Natasha, a character originally outside the immediate family, and to another stranger to the domestic circle, Soliony. One a provincial social climber, the other a neurotic captain, each takes on, in time, an ultimate coloration: Natasha, the devouring wife; Soliony, the lethal friend.

Natasha's motives are obvious enough to be disarming — disarming in its literal sense: to deprive one of weapons. No one need *suspect* her of the worst; her lies are so transparent that every civilized resource is called upon to deal with the transparency rather than the lie.

Soliony lacks accessible motivation but is easily recognizable as a true creature from life. Panicky and literal, he is repellent — one of the few repellent characters Chekhov ever created. If Soliony is shy, shyness is dangerous. Instinct, not insight, leads him to the weak spot in other people. A deeply wounded man who has turned into a weapon, he is a member of a species: the seducer-duelist, a nineteenth-century stock character Chekhov manages to twist into a perverse original.

When Irena rejects him, he says he will kill anyone who wins her; and in the name of affection, he makes good his threat. Ironically, Irena's halfhearted relationship to Tuzenbach becomes the fatal rivalry of the play; Tuzenbach has won Irena's hand but not her heart. Moreover, Soliony is introduced into the Prozorov circle by Tuzenbach, who therefore begins the chain of events leading to his own death.

Nothing redeems Soliony except the barbarity of his manner, a symptom of an alienation deep enough, perhaps, to evoke pity. A person who cannot feel pleasure and destroys everyone else's, his touchy uneasiness is irrational, the punishment it exacts inexhaustible. Unwilling to be mollified by life's niceties or won over by its distractions, he is a definite negative force in a play in which a lack of energy is crucial. Natasha turned inside-out, a killer without her affectations and pieties, he is, if never likable, at least not a liar. He tells us several times that, even to him, the scent he uses fails to disguise the smell of a dead man. That stench rises from a whole gallery of literary soldiers. No matter how heroic a military man may be, he is, functionally, a murderer. Soliony reminds us of that easily forgotten fact; he is the gunman of the play.

And the gunshot in *Three Sisters* is fired offstage — a shot heard before in *Ivanov*, *The Seagull*, and *The Wood Demon*. In *Uncle Vanya*, the shots occur *on*stage; half-farcical, they are not without psychological danger. Vanya shoots out of humiliation; his failure to hit anything only deepens it. The offstage gunshot in *Three Sisters* does more than end Tuzenbach's life and destroy Irena's marriage. A final fact, it leaves in its wake a slowly emerging revelation, the dark edge of an outline: the black side of Irena.

In the scene just preceding the shot, Tuzenbach makes a crucial request. Irena has described herself earlier as a locked piano to which she has lost the key.

TUZENBACH: I was awake all night. Not that there's anything to be afraid of in my life, nothing's threatening. . . . Only the thought of that lost key torments me and keeps me awake. Say something to me. . . . (*A pause.*) Say something!
IRENA: What? What am I to say? What?
TUZENBACH: Anything.

Tuzenbach, about to fight a duel with Soliony, needs Irena's reassurance. Forced to obscure a fact while trying to express an emotion, he says ". . . nothing's threatening." He is telling a lie, and, unaware of his true situation, Irena can hardly be blamed for not understanding its desperateness. There is something odd about Tuzenbach's request in the first place: he already knows Irena doesn't love him and is hoping against hope for a last reprieve. The inability to bare or face emotional realities — a favorite Chekhovian notion — is only partly in question here; here there is something worse: to feel the demand but not the attraction. For even if Irena understood Tuzenbach's request, her response, if honest, would have to be equivocal. They are both guilty; he for demanding love where he knows it doesn't exist, she for not loving. He is asking too much; she is offering too little.

Tuzenbach's request echoes almost exactly the one Katya makes to the Professor at the end of "A Dreary Story," where it is met with the same failure:

"Help me, help me!" she begs. "I can't stand anymore . . ."
"There's nothing I can say, Katya . . ."
I am at a loss, embarrassed, moved by her sobbing, and I can hardly stand.
"Let's have lunch, Katya," I say with a forced smile. "And stop that crying. I shall soon be dead, Katya." I at once add in a low voice.

"Just say one word, just one word!" she cries, holding out her hands.

Katya seems as impervious to the Professor's death sentence as he is to her despair. Each is too full of his own suffering. The characters in *Three Sisters*, like Katya and the Professor, do not hear each other's pleas, partly out of selfishness — other people's troubles are boring — partly out of self-protection. If they *did* hear them, what could they do?

Needs, revealed but never satisfied, drive Chekhov's characters toward two kinds of action: the deranged — Vanya's hysterical outbursts, Treplev's suicide — or flight. They desert each other — as Katya deserts the Professor half a page after the dialogue above, and as Trigorin abandons Nina in *The Seagull*. Nothing could be more Chekhovian than the last sentence of "A Dreary Story." The Professor, watching Katya go, wonders if she'll turn around and look back at him for the last time. She doesn't. Then he says to himself "Goodbye, my treasure" — end of story. But those three words are endlessly and ambiguously illuminating. Does he love Katya? Is she his treasure because this is the last feeling he will ever have? Is this final desertion the one symptom of his being human? Is there a tiny sarcastic twinge to "treasure"? In regard to people, every credible truth is only partial.

The inability to respond evokes responses: coldness, hatred, contempt. Loneliness can be viewed as humiliation and misfortune as insult. What cannot be given is interpreted as being withheld. The wrong people always love each other — bad luck or the telltale sign of a fundamental incapacity to love. The typical Chekhovian character longs for what he can neither express nor have, and each unrequited wish is one more dream in a universal nightmare. If the great treachery lies in the disparity between what we feel and what we say, between what we want and what we get, do we have — through an unconscious perversity — a vested interest in disparity itself? Proust, the ultimate dissector of jealousy, thought so, and it is odd to think that Chekhov, working with such different material and in such a different way, may have come to a similar conclusion. The truth is that what is interesting about love is how it doesn't work out, and Proust and Chekhov saw that truth and that interest from different angles. Surprisingly, like Proust in *Remembrance of Things Past*, who provides us with not one example of a happy marriage in over four thousand pages, Chekhov offers us none either.

And both Proust and Chekhov concern themselves with a social class that is about to be overwhelmed by forces rising from below. In Proust, the class distinctions are clear; we know exactly who is noble, and who is middle-class. We have to, because the impingement of one upon the other is one of the themes of the novel. That certainty eludes us in Chekhov's case. Olga, Masha, and Irena belong to a social class that has no counterpart in America. We see them as a kind of provincial nobility (partly because we have got to them so often through English accents), whereas they represent the lowest rung of a rural aristocracy, a sort of down-at-the-heels upper middle class living in the country: squires going to seed, a gentry saddled with land that no longer interests them, fitful leftovers unable to cope with the unfamiliar and the new. Chekhov's plays suffer from classlessness in translation, and more than classlessness in certain productions: maids become heroines and stable boys stars. The main difficulty is: one can hardly imagine Irena in Kansas, say, stretching her hands toward an imaginary New York. She would have already been there, traveling by jet. And, in *The Seagull*, would anyone have the faintest notion of just what *kind* of bank Madame Arkadina kept her much-discussed securities in?

But power, as a source, is general no matter the specific version, and both Natasha and Soliony are interested in it. Each is allowed to inherit a particular world: domestic tyranny in Natasha's case, the completed fantasy of the romantic egoist in Soliony's: the destruction of the rival lover. The passivity of the others gives them permission, it invites them in.

An embittered fact-monger, Soliony is unable to respond to any shade of irony. And though Irena is too young to know it, to be literal and humorless — qualities equally at home in the romantic and the dullard — can be as poisonous as deception or ingrained meanness. Worldliness is never an issue in *Three Sisters*, though it might well be. Vershinin brings a breath of it in the door with him, but it is the weary urbanity of a disappointed middle-aged man. A lack of worldliness in people forced to live in the world is always a potential source of suffering. Those people doomed to love late and to be ultimately denied love, like Masha and Vershinin, arrive at knowledge by way of lost opportunities and through a web of feeling. In *Three Sisters*, we get two warped versions of worldliness: Natasha's grasping selfishness and the doctor's cynicism. They are the merest echoes of the real thing. What we have in its place is calculation on the one hand and frustration on the other. There is no wise man in the play for the others to turn to; there is no mother and father for children who remain children, though they walk about as if they were adults, to run to for comfort and advice. In Chekhov's view, even worldliness, we suspect, would be another inadequate means of dealing with life, as powerless as innocence to fend off its evils, and, because it comes in the guise of wisdom, perhaps the most deceptive of all.

It is not always clear in various editions of the play that these revelations occur over a period of five years. We watch Irena, in fact, change from a young girl into a woman. The time scheme is relatively long, the roles are enigmatically written and need to be played with the finest gradations in order to develop their true flavors and poisons. If Natasha is immediately recognizable as evil, or Soliony as the threat of the play, a great deal is lost in characterization and suspense. Irena's cry of "Moscow! . . . Moscow!" at the end of the second act should be a note in a scale, not a final sounding. She has not realized, she is *beginning* to realize that what she hopes for will remain a dream.

Compared to *The Seagull* and *Uncle Vanya*, a technical advance occurs in *Three Sisters* that may account for a greater sounding of the depths. Chekhov's mastery of the techniques of playwriting may be measured by his use of the gun; it is farther offstage here than before — not in the next room but at the edge of town, which suggests that it might, finally, be dispensed with, as it is in *The Cherry Orchard*, where the only sound we hear, ultimately, is an ax cutting down trees. As he went on, Chekhov let go of the trigger, his one concession to the merciless demands of the stage. The gunshot in *Three Sisters*, unlike the shot in *Vanya*, is terminal. But Tuzenbach's death has further implications; it is partly the result of, and the price paid for, Irena's lack of love. Something suicidal colors Tuzenbach's death, and we pick it up in his last big speech:

TUZENBACH: . . . Really, I feel quite elated. I feel as if I were seeing those fir-trees and maples and birches for the first time in my life. They all seem to be looking at me with a sort of inquisitive look and waiting for something. What beautiful trees — and how beautiful, when you think of it, life ought to be with trees like these!
(Shouts of 'Ah-oo! Heigh–ho!' are heard.)
I must go, it's time . . . Look at that dead tree, it's all dried-up, but it's still swaying in the wind along with the others. And in the same way, it seems to me that, if I die, I shall still have a share in life somehow or other. Goodbye, my dear . . . (*Kisses her hands.*) Your papers, the ones you gave me, are on my desk, under the calendar.

Tuzenbach never had much of "a share in life"; he has always been a "dried-up [tree] . . . swaying in the wind." If Irena had been able to love him, would he have tried to talk to Soliony or to Dr. Chebutykin and in some way mediated the pointlessness of this ending? A pointlessness equally vivid, one suspects, whether he had married Irena or not.

The key to Irena's heart, that locked piano, is lost. Neither Tuzenbach nor Soliony ever had it. So their duel, though in deadly earnest, turns out to be an ironic, even a ludicrous footnote. Who holds the key to Irena's heart? Someone offstage — like the gun — whom she hopes to meet in Moscow. "The right one" is how she describes him, the unmeetable ideal who dominates the fantasies of schoolgirls. The doctor may comfort himself with bogus philosophy and claim that nothing matters, but the others tend to confirm not his thesis but its perverse corollary. By the indecisiveness of their actions, by their inability to deal head-on with what is central to their lives, they make, in the end, what matters futile. They unwittingly prove Dr. Chebutykin's false notion: what *does* Tuzenbach's death matter? Would Irena be any more lonely with him than without him? Would he have been content living with someone who doesn't love him, he who needs love to make himself feel lovable? Would Irena have joined him in "work" — her idealized version of it — and now be working alone? At what? Reality intrudes upon a pipe dream, but even the reality is dreamlike. The Baron's sacrifice does little for the cause of either work or love.

Of the three sisters, Olga is the least interesting: nothing romantic attaches to her. She is neither unhappily married nor unhappily *un*married. A person of feeling who has suppressed or never felt the pull of the irrational, she is the substitute mother or the spinster-mother — a recognizable type for whom the traditional role is the aunt, boringly earnest but secretly admirable. She represents a standard of behavior unwillingly, almost painfully, for her nerves are not equal to the moral battles in which she must take part, yet those very nerves are the barometric instruments that register ethical weather. Two sets of values are in conflict in *Three Sisters* as well as two social classes, and nothing makes those values clearer than Olga's and Natasha's confrontation over Anfisa, the eighty-year-old nurse. To Olga, Anfisa deserves the respect accorded the old and the faithful. Natasha uses Anfisa as another means of enforcing a pecking order whose main function is to make her status visible. She demands that Anfisa stand up in her presence like a soldier at attention. In this clash of feelings and wills, Olga doesn't defend Anfisa as she should: in true opposition, in attack. She is too stunned, too hurt. She says, ". . . everything went black." Natasha, out to win, wins in spite of what would ordinarily be a great drawback — her affair with Protopopov. Even her open-faced adultery, commented upon by the doctor in the third act, doesn't undercut her position. People prefer to ignore her rather than precipitate a series of crises whose logical end could only be an attack on Andrei. And Andrei cannot be attacked. Affection, pity, and, most of all, necessity are his three shields. Natasha has found the perfect nest to despoil. Andrei was always too weak, too self-centered, in spite of his shyness, to guard his sisters' interests. Now he is not only weak; he is torn.

But Olga is too morally good to let Natasha's rudeness to Anfisa pass without protest — as so many other instances have passed: Natasha's request for Irena's room, made both to Irena and Andrei, for instance, which is met with a kind of cowed acquiescence. It is a demand so basically impossible that no immediate way of dealing with it comes to hand. Natasha apologizes to Olga, but it is an apology without understanding, without heart. Actually, it is motivated by Natasha's fear that she has revealed too much, gone too far. Finally, Olga removes Anfisa from the household. There is a tiny suite for her at the school where Olga becomes headmistress, a place where Anfisa may stay for the rest of her life. It is easier — and wiser, too — to get out than to go on fighting a battle already lost. But whether the existence of that suite sways Olga in her decision to *become* a headmistress is left hanging.

Though Natasha and Soliony are the movers and shakers of the play, another neurotic character, invisible throughout, is a spur to its conflicts: Vershinin's suicidal fishwife of a mate, whom he fears, comes to detest, and yet who controls his life. He is weak, too, unable to make a clean break with his own misery. Chekhov points up one of the strangest true facts of emotional life; nothing binds people closer together than mutual unhappiness. And that is why Chekhov is sometimes so funny. The very horrors of people's lives — short of poverty and disease — are also the most ludicrous things about them. Vanya with a gun! How sad! Yet everyone laughs. The absurd and the tragic are uncomfortably close. Like the figure of the clown, and the wit in black humor, Chekhov teeters on a seesaw. Even a suggestion of the excessive would be ruinous. One gunshot too many, one sob prolonged a second longer than necessary and we have crossed over to the other side. Chekhov, to be played properly, has to be played on a hairline.

Vershinin's mirror-image is Masha, the most interesting of the three sisters, an interest dramatically mysterious because we know so little about her. But we know she is a woman of temperament, a woman capable of passion — and that in itself distinguishes her from Olga, to whom something of the old maid clings, just as something of the ingenue mars Irena. Masha wears black throughout the play, reminding us of her namesake, Masha Shamrayev, in *The Seagull*, who also always wears black because she is "in mourning for [her] life." (It may be of some interest to note that, in the same play, Madame Arkadina's first name is Irena.)

Masha is the onlooker who comments or withholds comment, often to devastating effect. She is the one free-speaker of the play. She tells us the truth about Natasha from the beginning, if only by implication; as a matter of fact, she tells us the truth about everything, even herself, blurting out the facts to her unwilling listeners, Olga and Irena, who don't want to hear of her love for Vershinin, don't want to be involved in a family betrayal. If adultery is a black mark against the detested Natasha, what must one make of it with the beloved Masha? The categories begin to blur, the certainties become uncertain. Like a lot of truth-tellers, Masha is morally impeccable in regard to honesty but something of a menace; she puts people in impossible positions. She is the romantic heart of the play just as Irena is the romantic lead. Unlike Irena, Masha is a lover disillusioned by life, not deluded by it. She married her schoolmaster when she was a young student and bitterly learns that the man who struck her as superior is at heart a fool. The reigning intelligence of the play is Masha's. It might have been the doctor's if intelligence were not so dangerous a gift for a man who has taught himself to be disingenuous.

Masha is still something of an impulsive child, a far different thing from being an adolescent like Irena, or living a self-imposed second childhood like the doctor, whose drunken dream is to make second childhood permanent. Masha isn't interested in intelligence *per se* and the doctor can't afford to be. If he ever let himself know what he knows, it would destroy him. And so he protects himself by a kind of slow-motion destruction, infinitely easier to handle. He keeps telling us how impossible it is to bear reality in a play in which everyone else keeps saying how impossible it is to know what reality is.

In spite of a loveless marriage (from *her* point of view),

Masha has Kulighin who, for all his absurdity, has something everyone else lacks: a true position. Too emasculated to oppose Masha's affair with Vershinin, he nevertheless loves her, sticks by her, and would be desperate without her. A stuffed shirt, a mollycoddle, a bower and a scraper, his ridiculousness masks the genuine feelings of a boy — he loves out of dependency, but who else is able to love in *Three Sisters?* Masha, yes, but her love is romantic; Irena, no, *because* her love is romantic. Kulighin ends up with something: he may wander about the stage calling for Masha, who never seems to be there, but he has the *right* to call her and knows she will go home with him in the end. She has nowhere else to go.

The three marriages in the play — Masha-Kulighin, Vershinin and his offstage wife, and Natasha-Andrei — are all unhappy. Strangely, Masha and Kulighin do not have children, and no mention is ever made of their childlessness. A matter of no significance, it seems, yet it becomes important in regard to Natasha, for it is through the cardinal bourgeois virtue of motherhood that she manipulates the household. Masha provides no counterweight. A subterranean notion percolates at the lowest level of *Three Sisters* — moral righteousness as the chief disguise of self-interest. Power is consolidated under the smoke screen of moral urgency. The Dreyfus Affair, the Reichstag fire, and Watergate are extensions of the same basic principle. Natasha's emotions are as false as her values. Under the camouflage of maternal love, she gains possession of Irena's room and has the maskers dismissed. Whatever *she* may think, it is clear to us that what motivates her action is not her love for her children but her love for herself.

And something similar may be said of Soliony. The duel, though illegal, was a process by which men of Soliony's day still settled matters of honor too refined or too personal for the courts. But it was also a vehicle for macho pride hidden in the trappings of a gentleman's code. Emotional illness has never found a better front than ethical smugness.

In contrast to the Prozorovs as we first see them, and in spite of her malevolence, Natasha is creating a true family, one with a real mother, father, and children, where only a semblance of family life had existed before. The ghosts of family attachments haunt the wanderers crossing the thresholds of rooms, as if they were searching for a phrase impossible to recall, or had fixed their eyes on an invisible figure. The word "orphan" rings its bell. And Natasha, carrying the energetic serum of the new, has only one goal: to possess a material world. Starting out as a girl who doesn't even know how to dress, she ends up as an unwitting domestic servant of change, dusting a corner here, tearing down a cobweb there. Not one of these acts has a generous motive. She is only a force for progress by being lower class and on the move. She thinks of herself as the mistress of a house that had for too long been in disorder without her. And in a certain sense, that view is not irrational. Two questions that can never be answered are asked *sotto voce* in the play: What would have happened to everyone if Andrei hadn't married Natasha? and, What will Andrei's and Natasha's children be like?

But even Natasha is up against something too subtle to control. Conquerors have their opposites — losers. But Natasha is working not in a house of losers but of survivors. Something too lively makes Chekhov's characters, even the desperate ones, convincing candidates for yet another day of hopes and dreams. One feels their mortality less than their indestructability. Everyone casts the shadow of age ahead; it is hard to think of anyone dying in a Chekhov play who isn't actually killed during the action. Some predisposition to live, some strain of the *type* transfixes the individual into permanent amber, so that, unheroic as they may be, we think of them somewhat in the way we think of Shakespearean heroes. They may languish in life but they refuse to die in art, and with a peculiar insistence — an irony only good plays manage to achieve because it is only on the stage that the human figure is always wholly represented and representative. When we speak of "Masha" or "Vanya," we are already talking about the future. One of the side effects of masterpieces is to make their characters as immortal as the works in which they appear. And so Natasha is stuck among her gallery-mates forever, always *about* to take over the house.

And she is about to do so by exploiting bourgeois morality for ugly ends — an old story. But the subject is the key to Chekhov's method here: the business of unmasking. The soldiers' uniforms hide the same boring civilians underneath. It is important for Tuzenbach literally to take off his clothes and become a civilian "so plain" that Olga cries when she first sees him. Natasha's sash is a tiny repetition of this motif when she reverses roles and comments on Irena's belt in the last act, a bit of signaling uncharacteristic of Chekhov, who rarely stoops to a device so crude. It is already clear that the outsider of Act I has become the dominating power of the household.

Unfulfilled wishes allow for seemingly random duets that enrich the texture of the play by showing us major characters in minor relationships — psychological side pockets of a sort that cast desperate or ironic lights. Olga and Kulighin, for instance, in their discussion of marriage, defend it as an institution and as a source of happiness. Yet Olga is a spinster and Kulighin a cuckold. Both schoolteachers, they are drawn together by their profession and by a kind of innocent idealism that overrides fact and disappointment. Theirs might have been the only happy marriage in the play, and Kulighin says he often thinks if he hadn't married Masha, he would have married Olga. In the face of adultery, alcoholism, compulsive gambling, irrational rage, and attempted suicide, Olga still believes in the "finer things," in the vision of human goodness.

Similarly, Irena and Dr. Chebutykin are connected by a thread of sympathy and habit — the oldest and the youngest in one another's arms, each equally deluded, alcohol fuzzing the facts for the doctor, and the determined unawareness of youth providing Irena with a temporary protective barrier. These uneasy alliances are touching because they rise out of needs that bear little relation to their satisfactions. It is precisely Kulighin's marriage to Masha that makes Olga more deeply aware she is a spinster; it is Chebutykin's drinking and his smashing of her mother's clock that will finally curdle Irena's affection for him. And this kind of delicate interplay between the loving and the hateful aspects of relationships is reinforced often by the action of the play itself. It is Chebutykin, for example, who is the Baron's second at the duel in which Irena is deprived of her husband-to-be, her one chance of making a bid for another life. Trusted by the Baron, Chebutykin has some reason for hoping the Baron is killed — namely, to protect the continuation of his relationship to

Irena. If that is true, there is a further irony: the doctor doesn't realize that he has already put that relationship in serious jeopardy. And then there are relationships by omission: Andrei's outpourings to the deaf servant Ferapont, Masha never addressing a single word to Natasha throughout the entire course of the play. Masha — like her creator — makes the inarticulate eloquent.

The random duets are complemented by a series of trios. Two are obvious: Masha-Kulighin-Vershinin and Irena-Tuzenbach-Soliony. But a third is not: Chebutykin's ambiguous relationship to Irena provides her with an underground suitor; his is one of those fatherly-grandfatherly roles whose sexual, affectionate, and narcissistic aspects are impossible to unravel, and he places himself in position as a member of a male trio: Tuzenbach-Soliony-Chebutykin. The doctor has a claim on Irena; he was her protector in the past; she is his lifeline now. It is through the subtle shifts of Irena's relationship to Chebutykin that we watch Irena grow from an unknowing girl into a woman who is beginning to see the truth. Chebutykin is onstage, but by being a kind of subliminal lover, he brings to mind, or to the back of the mind, three *off*stage characters essential to the conflicts of the play: Vershinin's wife; Natasha's lover, Protopopov; and the sisters' mother, each an invisible figure in a triangle. If Chebutykin was once in love with the Prozorovs' mother, he was part of an unacknowledged trio: the mother of the sisters, their father, and himself. The mother's image is kept alive in Irena, who resembles her. These offstage-onstage love affairs — one of which we see, one of which we watch being covered up, and one of which we merely hear about — complicate the action and reinforce the play's design of interlocking triangles.

Irena is part of two other triangles, one onstage, one off. A study in ingenuousness, an ingenuousness that will become educated before our eyes, she is joined to Second Lieutenant Fedotik and Rode by the enthusiasms and innocence of youth. If the play were a ballet, at some point they would have a divertissement to themselves. They isolate Chebutykin in a particular way: the contrast between their trio and the doctor makes time physically visible. And then Irena might be considered part of yet another triangle; her dreamed-of "someone" whom she hopes to meet in Moscow is as much of a threat to her happiness with Tuzenbach as Soliony is. It is he, in her mind, who holds the key to the locked piano. Overall, we have our fixed image of a trio, our superimposed stereotype: the three sisters themselves.

The themes of *Three Sisters*, the gulf between dream and action, between hope and disappointment, have finer variations. Even accepting the "real" is thwarted. Irena's compromise in marrying the Baron proves to be impossible. Having given up Moscow, Irena is not even allowed, so to speak, its drearier suburbs. She has met the fate that awaited her all along. Her cry of "work, work," echoed by Tuzenbach, is a hopeless cry. The issue is real, the solution false: What could a dreamy schoolgirl and a philosophical Baron contribute to a brickworks?

But something more than simple evasiveness frustrates the actors in *Three Sisters*. There is a grand plan working out its design, moving the players beyond their ability to act. And the military here perform a special function. When the battery is moved to Poland — its rumored destination was Siberia — the soldiers and officers reverse positions with the sisters, who can never get to Moscow, the dreamland of easy solutions. The sisters are psychologically "stationed" in the house by a force as ineluctable as that which sends the soldiers on their way. The dispatchment of soldiers is an event inevitable in time. And illusion gathers strength in ratio to time: the longer an idea is believed the more powerful it becomes. "If we only knew," the sisters say at the end. "If we could only know. . . ." Know what? Something already known — time moves people without their moving: the soldiers are forced to go, the sisters to stay. The object the doctor breaks in his drunkenness is a clock, and for good reason. Time's pervasiveness — its importance — is stressed many times in the play: the announcement of what time the maskers are to arrive; the hour set for the duel (at one point, the doctor takes out his hunting watch to verify it); the fifteen minutes Natasha allows herself on the sleigh ride with her lover; the no longer avoidable date on which Andrei's papers have to be signed; the very first scene, in fact, which is both an anniversary and a name day. As the minutes tick themselves off, action is always being performed, even by omission. Deluded into thinking time is eternal, events infinitely postponable, the sisters keep hoping problems will solve themselves, somehow, in time. They do, but not as a requital to hope. Birth and death, introduced in the anniversary–name day occasion of the first scene, are more sharply contrasted and connected in the last. Natasha's newest baby is wheeled back and forth in a carriage, a bit of counterpoint to Tuzenbach's death. In between, we have, simply, age — the eighty years of Anfisa's life.

Time sounds a recurrent note in *Three Sisters*; place is more subtly emphasized. The idea of a journey hovers in the air and charges the atmosphere — the journey never taken, the journey never to *be* taken. The repeated sounding of "Moscow!" is more than the never-to-be-reached Eldorado of the work or its lost Eden; it is a symbol of distance itself, that past or future in space from which the characters are forever barred. On this score, the play peculiarly divides itself on sexual grounds: the men want to stay, the women to go. Memory lures them in opposite directions, and Masha's halting bit of verse clues us in. What cannot be remembered takes on importance; it begins to have the force of a prediction in the same way that the unconscious, unable to bring significant material to the surface, determines future behavior. What does her verse mean? Where has she heard it? She says nothing for the first fifteen minutes of the play, she hums a little tune, remembers a line of verse she can't quite place. She has given up the piano. Enraged beyond speech, she feels — when we first see her — that any communication would be a betrayal. What Masha remembers most vividly, and whose betrayal she cannot forgive, is herself. Even music and poetry, because they evoke memory, are forms of conspiracy: they reveal the sensibility she has forfeited for the stupidity of the world she lives in.

The women want to go; more than that, they want to go *back*. Back to a life they once lived (they think), certainly not the one they are living. As for a brave new world, there are no explorers in *Three Sisters*, no wanderers ready to set forth for the unknown. The word "Siberia" runs its little chill through the kitchen. The play is nostalgic, for one set of people would do anything *not* to be removed from where they are (a form of self-miring in the present as if it *were* the past), and one set would do anything, short of what is necessary, to *be* removed. The setting is . . . where? A country town. But it is the least realistic of Chekhov's plays, or at least what is realistic about it always suggests the allusive, one image connecting with or piling up on a similar one. Masha gives up the piano; Irena is a locked piano; Andrei plays the violin. Vershinin receives letters; Kulighin has his notebooks; Andrei is translating an English novel. A whistled phrase is a signal from Vershinin to Masha or vice versa; the doctor bangs on the floor — his little Morse code. Irena gives up her room for a baby; Olga gives up hers for an old woman, Anfisa. These networks are fine meshes thrown over the realistic surface of the play. The webs of character obscure — and enrich — the scaffold of action. And what is allusive about the play suggests the thematically symbolic. Where do people move? From room to room? (Is that why the first thing we see is a room within a room?) But two crucial moves, Irena and Olga doubling up in one bedroom and Anfisa moving out, are overshadowed by the movement, the literal displacement, of the soldiers going to two possible destinations: Poland (where we are still within the limits of the civilized and the credible) and Siberia (where we move into the realm of fear and fantasy).

The sense of danger, a hairsbreadth away from the cozy, becomes actual in the fire of Act III. People can really be forced out of their houses, they can be *made to move* by events beyond their power to predict or control. The fire presents us with a true Apocalypse, its victims huddled downstairs, lost souls wandering about, crying, the rescuers, inside and out, trying to keep the contagion from spreading. Blankets, beds, food are commandeered. Still the shadow of the flames races up the walls. We are in a disaster area, a battlefield. We are also in Olga's and Irena's bedroom. The disaster outside is the general counterpart of the specific horrors within. They have one thing in common: dislocation. For the burning houses are no longer truly houses, any more than the room is now either Olga's *or* Irena's. Natasha has invaded the place of privacy, the source of identity, and we get to know that because it is *after* this scene that Olga moves out to become headmistress and *during* it that Irena decides to marry the Baron and Masha to sleep with Vershinin. And these three decisions prepare us for a fourth: the removal of Anfisa from the household. That is not as simple a decision as it first appears, for Anfisa is the basic — and the last — link with whatever living tradition ties the sisters to their childhoods. The issue of Anfisa is the scale that balances the strengths and weaknesses of Olga and Natasha, the turning point of the act and the breaking point of the play. In a psychological terror scene, the fate of the Prozorovs is decided. Natasha's taking over of the house is played against the bigger landscape of the fire destroying the adjacent houses. But the small wreck and the large are equally devastating.

Each sister is given an opportunity for moral or emotional expansion and is finally enclosed in the limited world of the possible. Each outlasts a wish and is forced to go on living a life without any particular pleasure or savor. The sway of compulsion is important to the play because compulsion suggests what must be limited: to be compelled is the opposite of being able to make a free choice. And there are enough examples of the irrational in the air to make the fearful and the uncontrollable real: Vershinin's wife's suicide attempts, Andrei's gambling, the doctor's alcoholism, Natasha's temper, and Soliony, our capital case, because he brings about what we are most afraid of: death. The departed, the unloved, the disappointed — all these are pale imitations of true oblivion. Soliony is the darkest cloud of all.

Three Sisters is enigmatic — it would be hard to say just

how the last speeches should be played: sadly, bitterly, as a kind of cosmic, ridiculous joke? or realistically, as if in the face of hopelessness it were possible to conceive a Utopia? Only *Hamlet* offers so many unresolved possibilities. Could the doctor have saved Tuzenbach in the last act? Does he let him die to ensure his own continuing relationship to Irena? Is there a homosexual undercurrent in the relationship between Soliony and Tuzenbach? It was suggested in the Olivier–Bates version of the play. Are the trio of Irena's suitors — the doctor, Soliony, and Tuzenbach — an ironic or merely an instrumental little mirror-play of the sisters themselves, trio for trio? Is Vershinin's vision of the world to come just another more cosmic version of the never-to-be-attained Moscow of Irena's dreams? There are overtones and undertows. More clearly than in any of Chekhov's other plays, fantasy imbues consciousness with a strength similar to the power of dreams in the unconscious. The play teeters on an ambiguity: if coming to terms with reality is a sign of psychological maturity, philosophy offers a contrary alternative: in letting go of an ideal, the sisters may be depriving themselves — or being deprived — of the one thing that makes life worth living.

These positive-negative aspects of the play are not easily resolved. Ambivalence enriches the action but fogs the ending. The problems *Three Sisters* raises have been presented to us with a complexity that allows for no easy solutions. Yet the curtain has to come down, the audience depart. And Chekhov, almost up to the last moment, keeps adding complications. In spite of its faultless construction, or because of it, the play is full of surprises. Andrei's moving and unexpected speech about Natasha's vulgarity, for instance. He knows how awful she is, and yet he loves her, and can't understand why — an unusual, and far from simpleminded, admission.

The sisters long to accomplish the opposite of what they achieve, to become the contrary of what they are. Masha is most honest about this and most hopeless; she cannot console herself with the optimistic platitudes of Irena or shore herself up with the resigned puritanism of Olga. Irena is about to rush off to her brick factory and Olga to her schoolroom. Masha lives with and within herself — a black person in a black dress, beautiful, loving, without joy. *Three Sisters*, in spite of its ambiguously worded life-may-be-better-in-the-future ending, might properly be subtitled, "Three Ways of Learning to Live without Hope." It is a drama of induced stupors and wounds and its tagged-on hopefulness is the one thing about it that doesn't ring true. People use each other in the play sentimentally, desperately, and, finally, fatally; there is no reason to assume that, given the choice, they will ever do anything else.

What we hear in *Three Sisters* are the twin peals of longing and departure. They are amplified by human ineptitude, human error, human weakness. And behind them we hear the clangings of the extreme: the childish, the monstrous, the insane. The Brahmsian overcast of sadness that darkens the action — little outbursts of joy and gaiety always too soon stifled or abandoned — help to make what is essentially a terrible indictment of life bearable. Sadness is at least not hopelessness. A play of girlhood, it is a play of loss, but not only feminine loss, though that strikes the deepest note. The drums and fifes offstage, the batteries that occasionally go off, the gambling house and the office — male institutions and trimmings — are shadowy and have nothing of the power and the immediacy of preparations for a meal, the giving of gifts, the temperature of a nursery — the force of the domestic, whether frustrated and virginal, or fulfilled and turning sour. A play about women — men are strangely absent even in the moment of their presence — its author clearly saw what lay at its most profound level: helplessness — a real, social, or contrived trait associated with, and sometimes promulgated by, women. Social class and the accident of sex work hand in hand to defeat desire and ambition. Watchers watching life go by, a stately frieze longing for the activity of movement, that is the central image of *Three Sisters*. Not so much "If we had only known . . ." as "If we could only *move*. . . ." Temperament, breeding, upbringing fix the sisters to separate stakes. They go on, hoping for the best, getting the worst, which is, in their case, to stay exactly as they were.

After *Madame Bovary*

Flaubert is 36 at the beginning of this second volume of his letters. The scandal, trial, and triumph of *Madame Bovary*, his eight-year affair with the blue-stocking siren Louise Colet (whom he called his "Muse"), and the 1849–1851 trip to Egypt and the Near East with Maxime DuCamp are behind him. The major events of a lifetime are over. But because the letters of a great writer are the communicated record of his inner life and a diary of ideas sent through the mails as well as a chronicle of day-to-day events, these new letters have the same fascination and compelling narrative drive as those in the first volume. That is a tribute not only to Gustave Flaubert but to Francis Steegmuller, who has translated and edited the letters with exemplary care and cast so wide and knowledgeable a net around them that they generate the excitement of a suspense story.

Flaubert is, throughout, mainly at Croisset, a southern

outpost of Rouen, in Normandy, living alone with his mother in the house in which he was born and in which he was to die. It faced the Seine and the exhilarations of the Atlantic, and sometimes merely its fogs. Paris was the other end of the Flaubertian line, with its Sunday literary salons (Zola, the Goncourt brothers, Turgenev, Huysmans, de Maupassant, Daudet, and Henry James were frequent visitors), its court life, and its theater. A genius commuter, Flaubert was drawn to the rails in despair at the boredom of a backwater only to hurry home in stupefaction at the brainlessness of a city. For the most part, he preferred to stay put. Croisset was the center of his work and the touchstone of his emotional life.

The Flaubertian compass was seemingly small, but the storms that raged outside and within were equally violent. If the absence of the steamy letters of the first volume to Louise Colet makes itself felt, we miss them for another reason: they were the emotional blueprints to the inception, composition, and inner processes of *Madame Bovary*. No unquestionable masterpiece, with the exception of *Three Tales* (1877), was to follow. Luckily for us, as well as for Flaubert, the "Muse" has a Platonic successor in George Sand, who, without being able to elicit mash notes of supreme literary importance, was more intriguing in every way. George Sand is the heroine — or, as she would probably preferred to have been called — the hero of these letters.

And how she will surprise most readers who know only the stereotyped version of her as the cigar-smoking lover of de Musset and Chopin! She and Flaubert could not have been more different. She was fluent, expansive, with a gift for narrative and romance as natural as it was copious. She produced over a hundred books in her lifetime and was the temporary adherent of various forms of feminism and socialism. Flaubert's detachment, his perfectionism, his struggle with page after page of prose were as foreign to her as her fluency was to him. Yet they came to adore each other in a relationship of natural sympathy — a relationship conducted at long distance between two literary intelligences who could never be reconciled to each other's point of view. The portrait of George Sand is completely sympathetic and, for the most part, self-drawn, for her letters are included along with those of Flaubert.

Charmed by the woman, and an admirer of her work on a necessarily selective basis, Flaubert was less taken with the doctrinaire side of George Sand, who took up and abandoned so many causes. She had been a pamphleteer in the revolution of 1848; he was a misogynist who went so far as to write, "As far as literature is concerned, women are capable only of a certain delicacy and sensitivity. Everything that is truly sublime, truly great, escapes them." Yet George Sand's intelligence was a match for Flaubert's, and, in one splendid rebuttal she felt important enough to publish rather than send, she outdoes him. It appeared under the title of "Reply to a Friend" in *Le Temps* and is translated in full by Steegmuller and printed as an appendix. It is a marvelous letter both as an essay of pure style and for what it says — a defense of commitment against detachment and of human possibilities against disillusionment. Overall, however, Sand's communications get a bit sticky with their upbeat humanism, genuine but tiresome, just as Flaubert's endless complaints about the impossibility of the task before him (chosen, always, by himself) become habitual and occasionally tedious. Flaubert, agonizing over every word, referred to *Salammbô* as "an erection . . . by dint of self-flagellation and masturbation" — a sexual image he used more than once to describe the progress of his work.

He was a greater writer and a greater thinker than George Sand, a fact she and the world recognized, but she had strings to her bow that were out of Flaubert's ken: she was famous as a lover, was a happy and dutiful mother and grandmother, and her house in Nohant (the great setting and comfort of her life) overflowed with children, lovers, ex-lovers, friends, and dogs. Neither could have lived the other's life for a moment, and it remains a wonderful source of human mystery to think they were so mutually drawn to each other. If Louise Colet had been sensuous to that perfect degree where manipulative pornography and an affair of the heart are difficult to distinguish, George Sand equally eludes being pigeonholed. She may have been the purveyor of some of the more fashionable ideas of the 19th century, but she was also as good-hearted and generous a comforter to the forlorn as one can imagine. From the evidence of these letters, she is a writer in need of rediscovery.

That George Sand is able to dominate a book that has for its background the Franco-Prussian War is a tribute to her power. Both writers suffered the imbecilities and cruelties of that misbegotten conflict. During the horrors of the Commune that followed, when French fought French, Flaubert's house was occupied by German soldiers, and the world we see of France at the time has something of the crisscrossed purposes of present-day Lebanon. Flaubert became more embittered. George Sand went on being hopeful — an odd composite of Clara Schumann, George Eliot, and Golda Meir.

Flaubert emerges from the letters as a salty mandarin who

felt betrayed as well as shocked by the vulgarity of his times. One sentence sums it up: "The entire dream of democracy is to raise the proletariat to the level of bourgeois stupidity." For democracy, however, Flaubert had no clear antidote. A cast of natural aristocrats somehow beautifully qualified to rule the world (and especially France) is what he would have preferred — a notion as unreal then as it is now.

Flaubert's deepest feelings were reserved for a friend of his youth, Alfred LePoittevin. Because of LePoittevin's early death, their friendship was one of those adolescent crushes that remain fixed in amber. And it was LePoittevin's love of the East that Flaubert shared as a boyish enthusiasm. (This was after the years of being a child voyeur in the dissecting room of his father's hospital, in Rouen, and after the epileptoid seizures, now more properly seen as hysterical episodes, that kept him safely at home, interrupting his law studies, which he detested. A writer is all he ever wanted to be.) Enthusiasm for the East persisted in the adult, led to the trip to Egypt with DuCamp, to the travel journal (as edited by Steegmuller, *Flaubert in Egypt*, one of the best travel books ever written), and to the oddly unsympathetic novels *Salammbô* (1862) and *The Temptation of Saint Anthony* (1874). We know only the third and last version of the latter; the first was withdrawn after the totally negative reactions of the young LePoittevin and DuCamp. Flaubert never wanted to write the same kind of novel twice and never did. *L'Education Sentimentale* (1879) was the only other "modern" novel he ever wrote. That Flaubert should be eternally dubbed a "realist" when he was drawn to the epical and the exotic is one of literature's ironies. *Madame Bovary* was an impediment to a more grandiose vision and needed to be got out of his system. It was while he was in the East that his most famous novel became clear to him as an emotional constellation of place and feeling — as distinguished from a "plot" or a "story" — a floating world that needed only to be anchored to a specific incident, which was supplied soon after his return. The Carthage of *Salammbô* and the ancient world of *The Temptation of Saint Anthony* coalesced in his study at Croisset just as *Madame Bovary* had taken hold on the Nile. Distance was a necessary ingredient of his work, and perspective rather than "realism'" is the key to it. Still, the ironies pile up. No one pretends that any of the other novels were masterpieces on the order of *Madame Bovary*, though *L'Education Sentimentale* has partisans as distinguished as its detractors. The letters we deal with, all post-*Bovary*, cannot transfuse life into the novels themselves, each a failure in its own way even to the sympathetic eyes of Sainte-Beuve, the Goncourt brothers, and Turgenev.

Flaubert worked on *Salammbô*, "a richly colored historical and imaginative reconstruction of a vanished civilization," from 1857 through 1862, and made a short visit to Tunisia to renew old impressions of Carthage and to confirm facts. No one was more conscientious in research: Flaubert read 1,500 books as background material for his "Homeric tale," described by Guy de Maupassant as "a kind of opera in prose." Flaubert made one other trip during the period these letters cover, to England, perhaps to renew his long-term but widely spaced liaisons with the Englishwoman who was his niece's former governess.

Salammbô was hardly what the enthusiastic audience of *Madame Bovary* expected. It — along with *The Temptation of Saint Anthony* and even *L'Education Sentimentale*, set in the Paris of the 1840s — required not only prodigious feats of research but of attention. One Flaubert letter, refuting the "facts" in Sainte-Beuve's three-part review of *Salammbô*, is superb, but a second letter to one G. Froehner, an assistant curator in the Department of Antiquities at the Louvre, is a masterpiece of understated wit and malice, refuting point by point the academic objections raised. Flaubert had defended *Madame Bovary* in a court of law; *Salammbô* was defended privately but to no less effect. Sainte-Beuve and Flaubert remained friends — neither was vengeful. Through misplaced arrogance, M. Froehner has achieved immortality.

After *Salammbô*, Flaubert was torn between two conflicting projects, a modern novel, which became *L'Education Sentimentale*, and another about his "two copy clerks" or his "two troglodytes" (ultimately the unfinished *Bouvard and Pécuchet*), an oral history of the inane molded into novel form.

The saddest letters are those to Flaubert's niece Caroline, whom he adored. She was brought up by Flaubert and his mother after his sister died in childbirth. But he gave Caroline some disastrous, middle-class advice: "I'd rather see you marry a philistine millionaire than an indigent genius" — an opinion worthier of Bouvard or Pécuchet than of Gustave Flaubert. She took his injunction literally and, years later, when her husband became virtually bankrupt, he dragged Flaubert to the brink of financial ruin at a time in the writer's life when he had the right to an earned security and at least an outward show of calm. "Respectability" and "honor" were sometimes surprisingly interchangeable concepts to Flaubert, in part a nicety of sentiment, in part ordinary bourgeois shame and pride. His entanglement with Caroline and her husband grew uglier and led to the break with Edmond Laporte, one of his few remaining lifelong friends. Out of loyalty to Caroline, and possibly as a result of inaccurate information, this painful rupture did nothing to sweeten the last years of Flaubert's life, already darkened by accumulated grief at the death of many friends and the ambiguous, sometimes hostile reception of his late work. The whole affair is a sorry one; for once in Flaubert's life he was morally compromised from the beginning in wanting for Caroline a security neither worth having nor possible to have.

Flaubert is still too often referred to as the high priest of art for art's sake, tearing his hair out as he revised yet again a sentence already refurbished a hundred times. Like all celebrated notions of the famous, this single-minded notion is a half-truth. These new letters qualify once more our impressions of Flaubert without diminishing his commitment to the art of the novel. A compulsive worker, Flaubert was also, among other things, a romantic yet hard-headed partisan of "justice," by which he meant something closer to "standards." How one behaved, the quality of one's work, the integrity with which one countered the world's flatteries and seductions were inviolable tests — tests Flaubert often failed himself. This moral starchiness had nothing whatever to do with sexual prudery — as anyone who has read *Flaubert in Egypt* would know. Flaubert's sense of values was based solely on excellence — high levels of achievement, splendor of spirit, and purity of motive and action. In so intellectually sophisticated a man, uniquely combining traits of the peasant and the aristocrat, innocence lurks behind the great pronouncements (as a certain naiveté lies behind the work of any artist), and, along with the innocence, a great deal of confusion. Flaubert's political "ideas" do not inspire confidence; inconsistency is their true hobgoblin. But he is infalliable on literary matters and refreshing and profound when he thinks spontaneously. These letters can be read not only for what they reveal about Flaubert but as a book of wisdom. We have, in the guise of letters, what comes close to being a full-fledged biography and is, unmistakably, an incomparable handbook on writing.

One Hundred Years of Proust

THAT a giant can be done in by flies is an old story, but that he could be mistaken for one is not. Marcel Proust was often just so mistaken in his lifetime, and he often still is. His life — at least a good part of it — lent credence to the error. Though he worked much harder than is generally supposed — the seven-hundred-and-forty-four-page *Jean Santeuil*, an earlier version of *Remembrance of Things Past*, was abandoned as early as 1900 — there is enough firsthand evidence to support the stereotype of the hothouse neurotic, snob, and social climber. But the mistake gets its strongest support from another source. Blurring the distinction between reality and fiction, Proust named the narrator and hero of *Remembrance of Things Past* Marcel, and from that moment on the confusion between his life and his work was fixed. The choice of name was deliberate — Proust had thirteen years in which to change his mind — but he might just as well have hung a sign saying "Reflections Inside" in front of a house of mirrors.

He once could have been considered a snob (though he dissected snobbery down to its ultimate fishbone) and a social climber (though he wrote the most devastating attack on society in literature), and this, added to the mix-up of the two Marcels, has resulted in a cloudy critical muddle. Over three thousand works in many languages (one of the two or three largest bibliographies of this century) trail after *Remembrance of Things Past* like a gigantic smoke screen, yet it is odd to note the peculiar condescension that often accompanies what appear to be salutes to his genius.

A recent one appeared on the front page of the *New York Times* Book Review, and I quote it because it represents a persistent view of Proust that survives all the adulation. Bearing the marks of time and study devoted to Proust as an act of homage, the article ended with "And perhaps one day soon we shall find ourselves pleasantly immobilized, comfortably hammocked or mildly ill; one day when the guns are gone and the looters are out of the suburbs; when all the threats have been withdrawn, and time lies as empty in our hands as an office present, then perhaps — I won't say we shall read Proust again — but then, perhaps, we may make a start."

This notion of Proust as irrelevant or frivolous, as a kind of dessert, is not supported by *Remembrance of Things Past*. For Proust was a moral and political writer, and the widely held view that he was some sort of society columnist who watched over the disintegration of France's aristocracy as court chronicler is at best simplistic and at worst a distortion. In *Remembrance of Things Past*, the great political and social scandal is the Dreyfus trial, with its stench of anti-Semitism and military duplicity. Because of both, the Dreyfus trial sheds light on every modern political crisis of the Western world, from the burning of the Reichstag to the publication of the Pentagon Papers. Proust examines the Dreyfus case with a thoroughness and an objectivity in regard to the stupidity displayed on both sides that are all the more remarkable in view of his personal commitment to Dreyfus. Proust's ability to examine men and issues with the dispassion of true judgment is not a fashionable ability at *any* time, but he performed a task that time makes necessary in the long run.

Without the benefit of years of hindsight, Proust understood the human and social forces that led to the First World War, and his portrait of the cravenness, vulgarity, and pettiness, the inner corruption of people who held power in their hands is icily cold and crystal clear. His depiction of Norpois, the diplomat, is cruelly instructive. Where else could one turn in fiction to find so damning a picture of self-interest, lack of political principle, and their consequences? Just as it was only one step from Neville Chamberlain and the Munich Pact to the invasion of Poland, it is only one step from Norpois to the aerial bombardment of Paris. It is a step Proust explicitly takes. Proust's skill in dealing with every class and type of character would stamp him as a first-rate social novelist in the old-fashioned nineteenth-century sense even if *Remembrance of Things Past* made none of the other claims it makes — to literary experiment, profundity of thought, psychological originality, and philosophical speculation. And it contains in its first two volumes the most accurate and evocative re-creations of childhood and adolescence I know. If one substituted Mann or Joyce in the sentence I quote from the *Times*, there would be letters of outrage. In short, though Proust is rarely under direct attack, he always needs to be defended.

And not only from the charge of preciousness. Another view flourishes right alongside the first: that of the task to be got through, the labor constantly postponed because its demands are too formidable. These twin, conflicting misconceptions — that Proust is not worth reading because he is effete, that it is one's duty to read him because he is major — have kept more than one reader from picking up *Swann's Way*. Every other important writer of this century is read for pleasure or has been made into a movie; there are even those once so unimaginable screenwriters Lawrence, Mann, and Joyce. Only Proust still bears the stigma of the unapproachable, even though *Swann's Way* is read in modern-novel courses as if it *were Remembrance of Things Past*.

Proust presents a unique problem. The original French edition was not published in its entirety until 1927, five years after the author's death. Many readers who enjoyed *Swann's Way* in 1913 weren't around to attend the terrifying party the Princesse de Guermantes throws in *The Past Recaptured*. How could they have ever dreamed that the Princesse, in this final volume, is none other than hideous Mme. Verdurin, twice remarried? Were those readers interviewed on their deathbeds, their notion of Proust would be similar to that of the many readers who are under the misapprehension that one volume of the novel is the novel itself or who have stopped somewhere along the line. The impossibility of containing what is a single work between the covers of a single book tends to obscure not only the various views of it but even various memories of it.

Only one thing is worse than getting the wrong attention, and that is to be ignored. On the occasion of Proust's centennial, the one book the American publishing community could muster that attempts an overall evaluation is imported from England — *Marcel Proust 1871–1922: A Centennial Volume*, ten essays on facets of Proust, with photographs and reproductions, and an introduction by its editor, Peter Quennell. A strange combination of gift book and serious critical study, it oddly misfires on both counts. Anyone interested in Proust would want it, anyone interested in literary gifts would have to consider it, but there are other gift books, even literary ones, less limited in scope and more lavish. And the essays have a tendency to stop just when they are developing their themes, as if the writers were afraid of going too far or had just become aware of how far there was to go. The result is that they often seem too detailed and specific for the general reader and not thoroughgoing enough for the specialist.

As far as I can make out, there are four kinds of Proust criticism:

(1) *The guessing game:* Questions like "Was the Duchesse de Guermantes really the Comtesse Greffülhe or was she really the Marquise de Chevigné?" are posed and answered, but not definitively, for they are asked over and over again. A good deal of what passes for Proust criticism consists of pretending that *Remembrance of Things Past* is a *roman à clef.*

(2) *The counting house:* (a) How many laundry images did Proust use? (b) How many times does the word "disappear" appear?

(3) *The construction gang:* Though Proust wrote the beginning and the end of his novel first, the ever-expanding accor-

dion of what came between has led to three differing views: (a) *Remembrance of Things Past* is a perfectly formed work, and all the additions Proust made to it serve only to prove how tightly shipshape it was right from the start. (b) It's a mess, but a beautiful one, and its very messiness allows for all those wonderful digressions by which we define the word "Proustian"; that is, when it isn't being confused with the word "reminiscent." (c) It is a compromise. It was superbly conceived, architecturally, as a three-volume novel, but two unforeseen events threw it wildly out of gear: Proust's relationship with his chauffeur, Alfred Agostinelli, and the First World War.

(4) *The real thing: Remembrance of Things Past* is the story of a man in search of a vocation. Primarily concerned with memory, and particularly involuntary memory, it is a book in which the idealizations of youth are destroyed by time, only to be triumphantly resurrected in art. Critics who write about it as a work of art, and of its connection to life, past and present, include Samuel Beckett, Roger Shattuck, Leo Bersani, Germaine Bree, and Georges Prioué. None of them is represented in Mr. Quennell's collection.

It *does* include such first-rate writers as Elizabeth Bowen and Anthony Powell, two very different masters of style. Miss Bowen tackles the character of Bergotte, Proust's novelist — one of the trio of artists who provide continuing motifs in the novel. Her essay is meticulously organized and wonderful to read, but it throws the collection out of kilter because the two other members of the trio — Elstir, the painter, and Vinteuil, the composer — are not treated in separate essays. A general and informative piece by I. H. E. Dunlop, "Proust and Painting," good as it is, doesn't plug up the gaping holes. The lack of a chapter on Proust and music is particularly damaging. Vinteuil — as a character, as the composer of the Sonata, as the father of a lesbian daughter whose friend, the very cause of his early death, pieces together his Septet, assuring his immortality — is so obviously one of the cornerstones of the book that the omission of an essay on him is inexplicable.

In "Proust as a Soldier," Mr. Powell repeats an anecdote. Asked "What event in military history do you most admire?" Proust wrote, "My own enlistment as a volunteer." The idea of Proust as a soldier is as alien to his "legend" as the notion of Ronald Firbank as a Marine sergeant, yet the facts are there, and Mr. Powell traces the effects of Proust's one year in the ranks on the military events, characters, and scenes in *Remembrance of Things Past*. Mr. Powell plays a version of "the guessing game," but he plays it with authority and style, going after facts rather than surmises:

> Captain de Borodino . . . is one of the characters in the novel drawn from life. His prototype was Captain Walewski, a Company Commander in the 76th, a grandson of Bonaparte by a Polish lady, an affair well known to history. As it happened, the Captain's mother, in addition to his grandmother's imperial connections, had been mistress to Napoleon III. That such a figure, with origins, appearance, and behaviour all crying out for chronicling, should turn up in Proust's regiment illustrates one of those peculiar pieces of literary luck which sometimes attend novelists. Borodino represents the most extreme example of "putting in" — that is to say, no doubt whatever exists as to his identity, owing to the exceptional nature of his background.

An essay on the Faubourg Saint-Germain quotes an illuminating remark of Proust to the Duc de Guiche: "The

Duchesse de Guermantes resembles a tough barnyard fowl whom I formerly took to be a bird of paradise — by transforming her into a puissant vulture, I have at least prevented the public assuming that she was just a commonplace old magpie." A valuable study, by Sherban Sidery, of Proust's "Jewishness" brings up a simple point not often made: unlike his creator, the Marcel of the book is neither Jewish nor homosexual, those attributes being assigned to other characters. In a discussion of the influence of other writers on Proust, Baudelaire and Balzac are seen as his opposing magnets, but only brief mention is made of the *Arabian Nights* and none of Saint-Simon, two well-established influences on Proust. After "The World of Fashion," and a note by Francis Steegmuller on "Proust and Cocteau," it is left to Pamela Hansford Johnson to explore the larger themes of the novel: memory as the only preserver of time, art as the only preserver of memory. In ten pages, she does a fine if understandably breathless job, and redresses the notion of Proust as merely the portraitist of a vanished world.

When Illiers — the town Proust transformed into the fictional Combray — was officially renamed Illiers-Combray this past spring, more than the interests of poetic justice were served. In a very particular way, the gesture, blending nature and art, echoed the work in whose honor it was made. In *The Past Recaptured*, passages from the Goncourt brothers (it seems) confront the reader, who at first thinks they're genuine. It takes some time to realize they are a pastiche — as much time, I'd say, as it takes to realize that the final Guermantes party is not a masquerade. Marcel, who has been away from Paris for years, is under the impression that it is. It slowly dawns on the reader, as it does on Marcel, that he is not attending a costume party: the partygoers have simply grown old; they are transformed, all right, but only by time. Just as nothing could be farther from Marcel's mind when he talks about time than the little world of it represented by the French aristocracy, nothing could be less like his idea of literature than the inspired reportage of "The Goncourt Journal" — so like, so *unlike* what he plans to do. That *Remembrance of Things Past* should be judged in the same light is profoundly ironic, for Proust, as a warning against the judgment, included a species of what he was *not* writing in the very book he wrote.

In *Remembrance of Things Past*, characters who actually lived — the Princesse Mathilde, Celeste Albaret — are minor and dwarfed by the reality of the created ones. Though Françoise is primarily based on Celeste Albaret, both are included. In Proust, the reporter and the fabulist are entwined. He was one of the first writers to see the relation between the document and fiction, and the psychological truth implicit in the relation. Most people's lives are questionable documents in which illusion and fact are interchangeable, in which love and status, say, as in the case of Swann, may be real personal and social powers but — from a viewpoint only one turn of the screw away — also ridiculous shams and pretension.

And Proust had something else in mind. One of the profundities of art is the form working itself out, in the same way a musical theme is sounded, developed, and concluded. In Proust, it is not the content of the motif but its function that is the point. He explicitly makes a distinction between Swann's experience of Vinteuil's Sonata as remembered emotion and Marcel's experience of Vinteuil's Septet as form itself. That distinction ultimately separates the nonartist from the artist. Human interest and philosophical drama aside, *Remembrance of Things Past* can be conceived as an aesthetic object, in which certain colors, tones, notions are planted, allowed to grow, expand, alter, and resound. It uniquely combines some of the characteristics of painting and music, and propounds — and is an example of — the notion that the function of the artist is to add forms to nature as well as to hold a mirror up to it. It is the peculiar quality (and difficulty) of *Remembrance of Things Past* to have met the conditions of the novel in the way, say, a masterpiece like *War and Peace* meets them, and yet to be something else again, more like a gigantic poem or a cabalistic exercise whose characters become phantoms of ideality. Because they do, they must at some point appear solidly real. Proust is a realistic writer, but for a purpose that has little to do with realism. He is like a magician who makes a live rabbit disappear. It is all too easy to forget that the reason the rabbit is there in the first place is to prove not that rabbits are real but that magic is powerful.

Since viewpoint is of the essence in Proust, a viewer — Marcel — is included along with the view. And Proust had a good reason for naming his viewer Marcel. As the fictional Marcel discovers his vocation and becomes a writer — a discovery that, after thousands of pages, takes place at the last minute — we realize we have just read the work he is about to undertake. At that point, Marcel becomes Marcel Proust.

Happy Families Are All Alike

Two stories are told in *Anna Karenina* — Anna's and Levin's. Yet the overall design of the novel does not require the two major characters to confront one another dramatically. Anna and Levin meet only once, and they meet to no purpose relevant to the destinies of either. We have two parallel plots. What is the point of Levin's story in relation to Anna's?

— In earlier drafts of the novel, Levin did not appear at all; the book was exclusively Anna's. What made Tolstoy add another strand to the rope? To give a fuller picture of Russian life in the 1870's? Enlarging the canvas merely for the sake of enlargement would seem unlikely. Tolstoy had only recently completed *War and Peace*. The exquisite attention Tolstoy pays to working out the parallels of the two stories, the fineness of detail everywhere, suggests some other motive at work. At the end of the novel, we are focused on Levin and find we have been engaged in a spiritual search. The original question changes: What is the point of *Anna*'s story in relation to Levin's?

— The famous first sentence of the novel — "Happy families are all alike; every unhappy family is unhappy in its own way" — does not lack for illustration. There are four major examples, each designed to illustrate the point:

The Oblonskys — where the husband, Stepan Arkayevitch, is unfaithful to his wife Dolly.

The Karenins — where the wife, Anna, is unfaithful to her husband Alexey.

The Vronskys — where Anna and Vronsky are unfaithful to the tenets of society and each sacrifices the possibility of an alternate happiness: Anna gives up her husband and child; Vronsky his possible marriage to Kitty and his career.

The Levins — where both partners are faithful.

— Other characters thwart society's conventions but do not threaten its foundations: Count Vronsky's mother, who is notorious for her affairs; Princess Betsy Tverskoy and her illicit attachment to Tushkevich; and so on. Certain relationships are so far beyond the borders of what society thinks possible that they do not constitute a threat either: Nicolai, Levin's brother, and his affair with a prostitute, Masha.

— Out of self-interest, society tolerates a discreet sexual liaison — its members are all in the same boat — but punishes one that openly threatens its pretended standards. Stiva is more upset because his affair with the governess is discovered than because he feels any sense of guilt. Alexey Karenin, in regard to Anna and Vronsky, is more concerned with public appearance than private anguish. Anna is not capable of concealment or discretion; she is destroyed by the forces of society, themselves decadent and corrupt.

— But there is more to be said on the subject. Society's values operate within Anna — she is not an intellectual or a rebel by nature. Primarily, Anna is done in by the single-mindedness of her passion. As it slowly becomes an obsession, she lets go of every other consideration. Since she has chosen (or seems to have chosen) to exist outside the pale of society, what she chooses to exist by must make up for the pleasures and power of society itself. As her relationship with Vronsky fails, there is no one and no place to turn back to; the sheltering trees of family, society, and even God have been uprooted.

— When Vronsky's horse, Frou-Frou, breaks his leg in the race and Vronsky is thrown, Anna — by her display of emotion reacting to Vronsky's danger — is forced to offer some explanation to Alexey about the cause of her agitation, and she tells him the truth about her relationship to Vronsky. The inability to hide emotion is fatal in a society that depends on appearances. What is natural and what is social are opposed. When Anna almost dies giving birth, there is a spiritual enlargement of Vronsky and Alexey in the face of death. They become human beings, not social mannequins; threatened by loss, they give up their rivalry and join forces. Alexey forgives Vronsky. Temporarily. The trouble is, of course, that Anna does not die.

— Though society may depend on appearances, it is because nature overrides society that Anna and Levin are so connected in the reader's mind, even though they meet only once. Levin, naïvely prepared to meet a "bad woman," finds Anna sympathetic in every way. The parallel plots perform a subterranean function: ideally, the two people in the novel most congenial to one another are Anna and Levin. Though they do not know it, the reader senses it. They are the only two people in a cast that comes to include hundreds who are willing to sacrifice their lives to honesty — emotional or spiritual. Neither can exist by a social code; neither is directed in major actions by forces and people from without. They are responsive, think and feel for themselves, have equally delicate sensibilities and minds, and are both in forced states of rebellion. Anna revolts against a sexual code not as a bluestocking but out of necessity; Levin, being aware of larger values, flouts the social conventions because he cannot accept them. Both are obviously "good" characters. We believe in the purity of their motives at every point in the novel.

— In some ways, Levin comes off better as a character. He is "scenic" before he is dramatic; he is glimpsed, caught at the odd moment (his remark about turbot), perceived in small actions, developed gradually and leisurely, whereas Anna appears in the midst of a crisis that almost immediately becomes her own. Before Levin gets involved in any crucial action, we know a great deal about him. And though we never question Anna's charm, beauty, or intelligence, these qualities are not to be the source of her agony — which is the result of a special capacity for love. She is plunged headlong into her affair with Vronsky before we can fully understand why that passion engulfs her to a degree that will ultimately prove fatal. This is partly the result of a certain "lightness" in Vronsky himself. But it is primarily the result of a foreshortening of perspective at the beginning of the novel, where one must take on faith who Anna is. Why is she so susceptible to Vronsky, and why is her relationship to him the all-or-nothing involvement it becomes? We know the answer by the time the novel ends; what I am suggesting is that we do not know it in time, and this leads to certain difficulties later. There is, for instance, a certain lack of credibility in Anna's willingness to give up Seryozha, the son she adores. And the precipitousness of her affair lacks credibility, too, at the time it occurs in relation to the total time-scheme of the novel. Why did not Anna allow herself a lighthearted version of this kind of release before, considering the stultifying pompousness of her husband? The answer might be: that is not the kind of woman Anna is. And the rebuttal to the answer might be: Why do we not know what kind of woman Anna is?

— On the other hand, we see Levin disappointed and badly hurt by Kitty's rejection, and we know something of his impulsiveness, his integrity, and his shyness by the time he is involved in a spiritual crisis. And that crisis can be isolated without further exposition. We know Levin before he is in the drama; we get to know Anna through her involvement in the drama. The canon of the novel would suggest the latter to be a superior method. But that is not so in this case. For *Anna Karenina* is not a Jamesian novel of moral subtlety in which the threads of the drama are pulled tight and a mystery finally unraveled, where sensibility and tension tremble upon a question mark. It is a novel built event upon event and scene by scene, in which the very lack of conflict between the two major characters prevents a certain kind of drama from operating. Levin remains in proportion to the episodic and cumulative effect of Tolstoy's style. Anna does not. Anna's drama within Levin's epic is diminished by it and the very breadth of portraiture that extends to character and action in the novel is absent from Tolstoy's treatment of Anna *up to the point* of her sleeping with Vronsky. That major dramatic action lacks force at the time it occurs. Levin comes to us slowly, Anna quickly, and we understand him better because of it. If one could conceive of the novel being placed on the stage, there would be something slightly false or difficult to explain in Anna's succumbing to Vronsky so quickly.

Levin's story would present no such dramatic difficulty. — But Levin's story would present us with a difficulty of another kind. If Anna is foreshortened at the beginning, the complexity of Levin's thought is rather flatly resolved at the end. There are two weaknesses in *Anna Karenina:* one dramatic — a character is brought to crisis too quickly; and one thematic — a crisis is too easily resolved.

— But these two weaknesses are the defects of an amazing success. It is impossible to think of another writer who, in doggedly piling up chronological events, in running in and out of his characters' minds with the same felicity with which he describes a horse race, a tree, a dress, and so on, could so definitively avoid the problem of viewpoint by ignoring it. There is the confidence of genius overriding all difficulties in *Anna Karenina* and the reader knows it — knows he is in the hands of a master. There is nothing the author is incapable of putting down. One of the strange effects of this genius is to make "psychology" and "nature" inseparable. The transition between a description of a leaf and somebody's thoughts is unnoticeable. The physical energy, the power of the style suggests, finally, that all phenomena are made of the same texture. Some kind of mental unity binds all things together. We are overwhelmed by the truth everywhere of what Tolstoy sees and says. In that sense, *Anna Karenina* resists criticism to the same degree that life resists theory. If what Henry James called "felt experience" did not saturate the pages of *Anna Karenina* with an absolute fidelity to life, the beginning with its cramped exposition, and the ending, with its dubious moral resolution, would mar the total picture.

— Small parallels of action are important in the overall design:

76

— The deaths, for instance. The guard who is killed at the train station when Anna and Vronsky meet for the first time obviously prefigures the death of Anna herself.

— As Kitty falls, Anna rises. As Anna falls, Kitty rises.

— As Anna comes to help reconcile Dolly and Stiva, so Stiva comes to help reconcile Anna and Alexey.

— It is Mme. Vronsky who is proud that Vronsky associates himself with a woman of Anna's class and type. And it is she who comes to loathe Anna and to see her as a degrading and destructive influence on her son. It is Kitty's mother, the Princess, who dislikes Levin for Kitty and then comes to want Kitty to marry Levin.

— These ambiguities, which are a process of life and take time to reveal themselves, are fixed in a quicker breeding ground in the character and temperament of Nicolai, Levin's brother, where the changes of mood and feeling occur minute by minute.

— *Anna Karenina* is full of examples of spiritual humbug, and various religious revelations and conversions take place that turn out to be false. Alexey in the scene where Anna almost dies; Kitty and Mme. Stahl. Alexey's spiritual dilemma is the opposite of Kitty's. Alexey, who lives by the world alone, comes to a spiritual condition of goodness only to have the world wrest it from him by its demands. Kitty, trying to give the world up, finds it mirrored in Mme. Stahl.

— The importance of Tolstoy's fairness to Alexander Karenin. We dislike him; we are never able to hate him.

— The good nurses never change: Dolly's nurse, who fixes the summer house; Levin's nurse, who cares for him at his estate.

— It would be almost impossible to separate the Anna from

the Levin story. If we could, we would have something like an untidy *Madame Bovary*.

— Tolstoy sees humiliation as the most disintegrating factor of identity throughout. For Proust, that factor is obsession. Tolstoy is not concerned with art. Oddly, there are no artists in *Anna Karenina*.

— *Anna Karenina* begins with a common garden variety of adultery and goes on to an adultery that transforms several lives and leads to a tragic death. The minor announcement of the major subject lures us on with a secret hope. We keep wishing that Anna would or could get out of her situation as easily as Stiva got out of his.

— The peculiar fact of Anna and Vronsky having the same dream: the peasant who bends down and speaks French.

— The extraordinary nature scenes — snipe shooting, the mowing (the scene about the water cup), Laska, the horses, the race — all provide an undercurrent to the action. They remind us of the biological underpinnings of life, which no amount of civilization can destroy. Our last glimpse of Vronsky as a soldier going off to the war makes another point: civilization can destroy itself. Though Anna and society are at odds, they are both at the mercy of a similar force: self-destruction.

MARCEL PROUST

ANTON CHEKHOV

HENRY JAMES

THOMAS MANN

Notes on Fiction

IN Chekhov's plays and stories, we have a sense of not being led anywhere, of things just happening. Their naturalness and casualness suggest, when they end, that it is time for the storyteller to go to bed. This effect comes from Chekhov's lack of interest in luring us on to a dramatic conclusion and his detestation of moral preaching. In Chekhov's writing, a moral compass points the way; its true north is "No Lying."

Chekhov externalized the interior of his characters without relinquishing the surface aspects of realism. In his plays, people act out their dreams, yet what they say and do, from moment to moment, seems perfectly ordinary. The monologue was oddly useful in this respect: the governess's speech that opens the second act of *The Cherry Orchard*, or Astrov's long dissertation on trees in *Uncle Vanya*. Chekhov is able to treat psychological nuances as material facts, to make it seem just as real for a character to say, "I am in mourning for my life," as it is for another to say, "They'll be starting the show soon." Chekhov's characters emit words like bird cries, as if they were spontaneously forced out of themselves by internal pressure.

Chekhov has a quality to be found equally in good journalism and good fiction, and for opposite reasons. In the first, the quality of tone never sabotages the verity of fact. In the second, the verity of fact never menaces the quality of tone. A journalist doesn't need a theme since he already has a subject. A fiction writer has a theme and is looking for a subject. (Reason why detective stories can never become literature: no matter how ingeniously devised, how brilliantly written, they are not thematic. They depend on two things, suspense and local color. A good detective story presents the reader with an exotic world; the unknown is made credible. The accuracy of details, or their seeming accuracy, is of tremendous importance, more so than in an ordinary novel because the nature of the fiction — the story — is less plausible. Place and geography are major sources of fascination. But the world is getting smaller. The final detective story will be set in a suburb in Iceland.)

There's a certain point in every novel where one wants to know what everyone had for dinner. Tolstoy is very good on this score, James very bad. There are no bathrooms or kitchens in *The Wings of the Dove* or *The Golden Bowl* (though there is a famous omelette in *The Ambassadors*). Proust offers us a kitchen, a latrine, and a brothel.

Realism supplies us with the number of manhole covers on a particular street. Naturalism splashes around in the sewer.

Chekhov's great victory: the greatest style is to have none. The impenetrable barrier of perfection. Not that he is a greater writer than Tolstoy or Proust. He is more critically inaccessible by seeming so *simple.* Advocates of the New Criticism would go mad if they had nothing to work on but Chekhov. Unlike Joyce, Kafka, and Proust, after a certain point, quickly reached, there is practically nothing to say.

Chekhov: Suicide or murder by gun. Vanya tries to kill the Professor in *Uncle Vanya* and fires two shots, and misses. Treplev shoots himself at the end of *The Seagull.* Ivanov shoots himself at the end of *Ivanov.* At Babkino, in 1885, before he had ever seriously thought of himself as a playwright, Chekhov dressed up as a Bedouin and acted out a mock play with Levitan, the painter. Chekhov shot blank cartridges at Levitan from behind the bushes.

The peculiar correspondences in the lives of Chekhov and Keats. Both studied to be doctors; suffered from tuberculosis; died young — Keats at 26, Chekhov at 44 — and in a foreign country. Chekhov died in Germany, Keats in Italy. Keats feared he could not write an epic poem. Chekhov feared he could not write a novel.

In James, homosexuality is a secret theme. *The Sacred Fount* is the most puzzling of his novels, I think, because James got closest to the subject and, because of a lack of adequate transformation, found himself creating more and more mystification to throw the reader — or perhaps himself? — off the scent. It is a novel about the artist, finally, but if he could have been more explicit, as Mann was in *Death in Venice*, he could have had his symbolic "reverberation" twice over. Voyeurism is essential to both James and Proust but not to Mann. James, attempting to deal with it by implication in *The Sacred Fount*, obscures what he's after. Proust succeeds because the scenes that involve homosexuality and voyeurism are explicit and direct: at Montjouvain, in the Duchesse's courtyard, in the peephole scene in the male brothel.

The voyeur is connected with the writer for an obvious reason: the problem of viewpoint. At what point does the observer close in on the peeping Tom? Proust and James deal with viewpoint as an essential part of the work itself. There is no reality without a viewer. How far should one go in including him? Proust went as far as it is possible to go.

The parody as an unconscious compliment: To have read someone closely enough to produce an acceptable imitation, to have become obsessed to the necessary degree requires an attention and concentration the works of most authors never receive. Beerbohm's *The Mote in the Middle Distance*, which James might have considered cruel, says more about James's style than most critics.

If one were to think of a movie about the invention of the camera photographed by the very camera that was being invented one would have the clue to the technical device Proust employs in *Remembrance of Things Past*.

Metaphor is the key to an understanding of Proust. *Remembrance of Things Past* is a book conceived as a poem and written as a novel, a far different thing from a novel written in "poetic prose." The poetry lies in the conception as well as the execution. Feeling and thought are so finely molded to metaphor that the sensibility by which things are apprehended is indistinguishable from the intelligence that later analyzes the nature of sensibility itself. Proust is a great writer and a great thinker; the fact that no serious division can be made between them is an enormous triumph.

We get to know the canvas of *Remembrance of Things Past* in the same way we get to know our own lives. We do not re-member consecutively and we do not remember at will. It is these two strange and overriding facts of human memory that Proust exploits. It is re-experience rather than experience that is valuable. Experience occurs in time but re-experience *may* occur outside it.

We know every sensation, thought, and connection of Marcel's life more thoroughly than we do the people we think we know best in our own lives. One of the secrets of art is that it takes over the function we mistakenly assume belongs to love. Do we ever truly enter into the personality of an-other being? In Proust, love sets up a barrier of necessity and compulsion that art is free of.

There are two major original ideas in *Remembrance of Things Past:* the true nature of reality exists within ourselves, not outside us; the clue to human salvation lies in the past, not the future.

Chekhov said, "If in the first act you hang a pistol on the wall, then in the last act it must be shot off." Proust might have said, "If in the first act you hang a pistol on the wall, and in the last act it is shot off, then you must build the wall."

Chekhov: "to reveal [people] as they really exist and not as they appear in real life . . ." Very close to Proust, except that after Proust got through with appearances, the matter of existences became questionable.

Chekhov's wit (from a letter): "Now I have four places to live, and I ought to have a wife in each, so that after my death all of them could assemble on the shore of Yalta and tear each other's hair out."

Proust's wit: ". . . there are almost as many deaths as there are people. . . ."

Both Chekhov and Proust had a firm grip on reality and both were absolutely truthful. Proust analyzes and concludes. Chekhov presents and reveals.

"The Black Monk" is not characteristic of Chekhov's other stories, but of Chekhov as a writer. A certain withheld mysticism one senses behind many of the other stories is allowed to occupy the foreground.

I can see no reading of "The Black Monk" other than as a fable of the artist. As such, it is similar in theme to Mann's *Death in Venice* and James's *The Aspern Papers*. The experience of the narrator in the first two stories is extreme — in Chekhov, madness; in Mann, disease; but in the James, where the narrator does not represent the artist, it is reduced to a petty crime, thievery. The point in James is that the narrator is

trying to get the experience secondhand, trying to get the papers without experiencing what made them possible. He wants
to possess the secrets of art without paying for them morally.
That is why he fails; he must relinquish the papers or marry
Tina in order to get them, must go through some version of
the original relationship between Aspern and Juliana that led
to the creation of the poems. (This idea is later elaborated in
The Golden Bowl, where, to possess the artifacts of a civilization, the characters are forced to experience the moral crises
of civilization.) What are fables of the artist in Chekhov, Mann,
and James become myth in Proust. Marcel is his Aschenbach, Swann the anonymous narrator of *The Aspern Papers*,
and Charlus his Black Monk.

Chekhov disliked Ibsen's plays and admired Maeterlinck's.
Peculiarly understandable even if an error in judgment. Chekhov was closer to the Symbolists than any other major Russian writer of his day. Chekhov's sea gull is not merely a bird,
his cherry orchard a grove of trees, though the gull is visibly
brought on stage dead, and the trees are audibly cut down.
Both tenaciously cling, as Maeterlinck's symbols do not, to
the real and supersede it. The great deficiency in Maeterlinck
is that there is nothing to supersede, that his symbols are not
anchored in reality.

Chekhov is not a realist: narrative and fact are not of supreme interest to him. He is not a formalist: he is not interested in methods meant to provide aesthetic pleasure. Character is his obsession, but what he means by character is
different from what other writers mean. Psychology, yes; but
he also sees characters as motifs, as repeated soundings of the
same melody, as if they were subjects in a musical composi-

tion. *Remembrance of Things Past* and Chekhov's plays have this one thing in common: though conflicts of interest exist, it is the motif rather than dramatic tension that is the clue to structure.

Chekhov and James were the last great dramatizers of the unconscious. In Joyce and Proust, the unconscious comes into play on its own: in the interior monologue (Joyce) and the author's digressions on the action (Proust). Only Mann was interested in demonstrating abstract ideas in fiction. That is why the characters in *The Magic Mountain* suffer, why Peeperkorn and Settembrini end up being merely mouthpieces. *The Magic Mountain* stands between two major styles, the realism of *Buddenbrooks* and the symbolism of *Death in Venice*, and lacks the perfection of both.

In *Death in Venice*, there are two characters who are essentially one — Aschenbach and Tadzio — and four minor characters who are also essentially one: the stranger in the cemetery; the old man on the boat; the gondolier; the singer in front of the hotel who smells of carbolic. They all have red hair, they all wear straw hats, and they all move in the same way.

A truly moral man, Chekhov detested morals.

What seems trivial at first in Chekhov's plays always turns out in the end to be the heart of the matter.

The mistake of people who still refer to Proust as a snob. Snobbery was a disease he cured himself of, but he described the symptoms so accurately that it was hard for certain readers to distinguish between the analysis of a former obsession and the obsession itself.

Scientist and writer both, Chekhov was unable to treat human life either clinically or sentimentally. Drawing on the two disciplines of his life, he became a kind of neurologist of fiction and the theater, who, in accurately describing the brain, in the name of truth included its dreams.

In a novel that turns on a moral crisis, the consciousness of the novelist should rarely be felt or not at all. James the great master. But in a novel whose very subject is consciousness, as in Proust, it should be felt everywhere.

Chekhov's symbols are either merely characteristic — Epihodov's billiards, Masha's snuff — or are at first characteristic and then become thematic — Nina's gull, Astrov's trees. Same thing happens in Faulkner's "That Evening Sun." The darkness refers both to the night and to the Negro. Nancy's fear of the dark, which is characteristic, will become the children's fear of Nancy's darkness, which is thematic.

Chapter headings for another book on Proust:
1 The Nature of Consciousness
2 The Screen of Habit
3 The Solution of Memory
4 The Illusion of Love
5 The Mask of Character
6 The Damnation of Time
7 The Triumph of Art

Remembrance of Things Past may be read as a philosophical drama in which no action occurs because the existence of character is finally disproved and the ideality of character made the only measure of reality.

The churches in Proust are important: *Remembrance of Things Past* can also be read as a religious book without a God.

The pleasures of Proust: When Odette walks in the Bois de Boulogne, the women's clothes and parasols turn into flowers.

In the scene at the opera, the theater is seen as society's ritual. The images are aquatic, marine, undersea. The passions, pretensions, and obsessions of the audience are mirrored back and forth between the beholder and the performer.

The aquarium image supersedes the garden image in Proust; Balbec, an aquarium, displaces Combray, a garden. Like the windows in Proust, the walls of the aquarium are both transparent and opaque. The narrator observes his own reflection as well as what his reflection is observing.

Leonie is a potentate and Françoise is her slave. In Leonie's bedroom, the court of Louis XIV is domesticated and narrowed down to two characters who perform its rituals.

The importance of the Jew and the homosexual in Proust: neither has a country of his own. Would *Remembrance of Things*

Past be different if Proust had known of the coming existence of Israel or had read the Wolfenden Report?

The fine connections in Proust: The letter he waits for from Gilberte in *Within a Budding Grove* prepares for the scene in *Time Remembered* when he thinks he has received a telegram from Albertine long after her death. It is really from Gilberte. The irony of the scene is: the letter from Gilberte finally comes when he no longer cares. And the subtlety of it! It is because of an eccentricity in Gilberte's handwriting in the first volume of *Within a Budding Grove* — she makes her *G*'s like *A*'s — that this psychological error becomes plausible in *Time Remembered*, six volumes later.

Proust, the most tonal of all fiction writers, is also one of the most accurate. Imitations of Proust always go wrong in the same respect; they ape the tone but cannot duplicate the accuracy. There is no metaphor in the four thousand pages of Proust that is not precise. Proust's precision allows for any elaboration of style.

Rhetoric is a dirty word only when it is used to mask or ignore the truth. Shakespeare and Proust are rhetorical and truthful. The fear of rhetoric makes most modern writing dull. Reality is reduced to a kind of recipe book of facts in which categorical description becomes a substitute for perception. Novels that begin, "Lorinda hung her red, knitted blouse, which she had purchased at Macy's, on the hook on the green wall next to her unmade daybed, which Percy, her lover, who had gone to Harvard, had just left. . . ." are written by the thousands. Pseudofacts convince the reader, or are meant to, that he is being told the truth. Just as much a way of lying as fake rhetoric of novels that begin, "The evening was hazed over by a mothlike substance; the light, the wool of its temptation, blah blah . . ."

Chekhov's stories tread the finest line between a newspaper account and a fairy tale. Inferior writers step over the line one way or the other.

People Chekhov knew: Tolstoy, Gorki, Bunin, Tchaikowsky, Stanislavsky. Why is Tchaikowsky so surprising?

Proust destroyed the premises of fiction in the creation of a work of fiction. Proust creates identities only to say, "Since I have created these characters, I can definitely prove to you that they do not exist."

Three quotes from Chekhov:

". . . great writers and artists ought to engage in politics only to the extent necessary to defend themselves against politics. . . ."

"Subjectivity is a terrible thing . . . it reveals an author's hands and feet."

"One must not humiliate people — that is the chief thing."

Certain writers inspire affection in their readers that cannot be explained either by their work or by the facts of their lives. It proceeds from some temperamental undercurrent, some invisible connection between the writer and the reader that is more available to the senses and the emotions than to the mind. Bookish affections of this kind are deceptive and irrelevant, yet they truly exist. For me, Colette, Keats, and Chekhov inspire affection. Faulkner, Shelley, and Ibsen do not.

After one has read the work and the biographical studies of certain writers, they come to resemble composite versions of the characters they have invented: Treplev and Trigorin in *The Seagull* seem like Chekhov, and Swann and Charlus like Proust.

Proust is a finer psychologist, Joyce a more daring innovator than Chekhov. It is tone alone that transforms Chekhov's stories into poems, the plays into music, even in translation. Ibsen is a great constructor but deficient in tone. Perhaps a language barrier in translation? Then why does the tone come through so clearly in Chekhov and Proust?

Tone is the most important quality of good writing and the hardest to define. It is not only a matter of relevance and consistency. Tone, a musical word, is essentially a matter of sound, rhythm, cadence, stress, and so on. Because all words are ultimately sounded, tone is that quality of writing which most approaches music and is therefore so difficult to pin down. But definable or not, it is crucial. Something like light in painting or timbre in music. It is that very quality in the use of words which is nonverbal, which does not depend on the *meaning* of the words alone — like the sound of a voice (tone of a voice), or the expression on a face while something is being said. It is what is meant, perhaps, by the phrase "between the lines." Something that is there but which cannot be pointed to specifically. Tone is like the color of water in a sea or a lake. As one takes up a handful to examine it, it disappears in the very process of being isolated and analyzed.

Sometimes there is a complete break in tone between one writer and another — Hopkins and Eliot, say — as there is in music between one composer and another. Debussy is the best example, I think. He must have sounded, originally, as if the history of music had not existed up to the point of his writing. A delusion, of course, but how could one relate him to Bach, Mozart, and Brahms without a great deal of special knowledge? There are, though, connecting links sometimes that are not immediately seen. Such as Turner and the Impressionists.

PART TWO

A Candidate for the Future

CERTAIN writers belong not only to the history of literature but to History itself, and Whitman is one of them. He was crucially positioned: the American colonies had declared their independence exactly forty-three years before his birth in 1819, and the Revolution was still a vivid event in the minds of the adults around him. Psychically, his life stretched from the Revolution through the Civil War to the era of the Robber Barons. Truly an American poet of change, the man and the work tend toward the heroic, the mythological. One of the great virtues of Justin Kaplan's *Walt Whitman — A Life* is his ability to rescue the man from the giant without diminishing his stature. Separating the genius from the diamond in the rough isn't easy, for Whitman was several men in one: Brahman, Bohemian, spokesman for a new democratic society, dandy, creator of an original kind of American poetry — a self-educated and self-intoxicated peasant of the ecstatic. Even the photographs, many never seen before, reinforce the kaleidoscopic sense of an ever-shifting personality. Mr. Kaplan, letting the various Whitmans speak, allowing for ambiguities, comes to no ringing conclusions.

A child of Long Island's "bare unfrequented shore," Whitman became, in time, a printer, newspaperman, teacher, and editor. The son of a dour housebuilder of English stock and a Quaker mother of Dutch descent, his childhood was marred by instability. The record of insanity, intemperance, and failure in the Whitman family makes dismal reading. Living in the country provided no roots; moving from West Hills to Brooklyn and back, the Whitmans occupied a dozen different houses before the poet was eleven. At that age, he stayed behind in Brooklyn, as a printer's apprentice, on his own. There, and in Manhattan, "the blab of the pave" mingled with the "Howler and scooper of storms, capricious and dainty sea" to become strands in an original verbal amalgam that makes "Song of Myself" — the key poem of *Leaves of Grass* — so remarkable.

The first, 1855 edition of that book bore no author's name; an engraved daguerrotype of a gypsylike workman — one of Whitman's guises — adorned the frontispiece. Its poems untitled, the book opened with what is now "Song of Myself." In truth, a song of everyone *but* myself — "of every rank and estate am I / of every hue and religion" — it speaks for a consciousness beyond any individual ego, one made up of many. In taking on its various personas, Whitman's ability to be androgynous and anonymous, his gifts of identification and sympathy are those of a great poet. They developed into an uneasy egotism later in life, as if the many characters of a literary work had filtered into the person who created them. Whitman's notion of himself *as* America, at first the mark of a passive generosity of spirit, grew overbearing, and narrowed into mere ambition. Empathy in the artist was reduced to role-playing in the man; the myth-maker and the self-server became interchangeable.

Whitman's homosexuality complicated his role as an American spokesman, just as his "mysticism" added an eeric note to his social views, those of a freethinker brought up on Quakerism, Carlyle, George Sand, and Margaret Fuller. Divorced from any traditional faith, his spiritual illuminations are closer to the sutras of the Oriental contemplative religions than to the visions of Christian saints. Denial and self-excoriation — the desert and the hair shirt — were alien to him. Divine irrationality, the kind we associate with Blake, Christopher Smart, and Rimbaud, is closer to the mark. Moreover, these illuminations had to be accommodated to the nineteenth-century notion of progress. Queen Victoria and Whitman were born in the same year. "Sex was a major disorder," and Whitman, the only writer of nineteenth-century America completely at odds with Puritanism, was — in his trust in an expansive commercialism, his "pursuit of health as a supreme good" — a true product of the Victorian age. No matter how original his thought, it wove in and out of commonly held beliefs. Phrenology, for instance, was an accepted science in Whitman's time — Horace Mann, Henry Ward Beecher, Ralph Waldo Emerson, Edgar Allan Poe, and Daniel Webster all believed in it — and so was "animal magnetism." "I sing the body electric" was more a literal than a figurative reference. Life was seen as voltage and wattage. People were little wireless posts at the mercy of internal shocks and outgoing currents. Mr. Kaplan sums it up: "Whitman was a sort of storage battery or accumulator for charged particles of the contemporary."

In "Song of Myself" we hear for the first time Whitman's unique blend of biblical cadence (particularly the Psalms), primitive chant, and the ongoing catalogue — devices eventually to be at the service of a cosmic universe made up of American particularities, a secular Bible of sorts, full of contradictions and oddities. No other major poem I know sets itself such contrary tasks: to reveal the oneness of things, to praise the freedom of the individual, to celebrate the multitude in song. The overall title of *Leaves of Grass* is brilliantly fitting: the mass individuated in the unique leaf, the leaf one with the general green. The musical side of the poem sprang from Whitman's love of voices. Aroused as a youth by fiery preachers and professional orators, he savored, as his taste matured, the delights of the theater. Italian opera became a passion. The works — and the singers — opened up, and were exemplars of, a whole hidden emotional life. Sensitive to voices, he was totally responsive to their grandest manifestation. Opera introduced Whitman to the fusion of sound and action, the projection of emotion through virtuosity. Thematic repetition in Whitman is conscious but has a characteristic sounding board. Many of the poems are best approached as long arias, and even the natural music of bird song has the calculated effect of a musical motif entering a score.

In 1848, Whitman, then editor of the *Brooklyn Eagle*, was fired after a political squabble with its owners. Invited to edit the *New Orleans Crescent*, he traveled with his brother Jeff on a two-week journey south and west by train, stagecoach, and steamboat. Whitman's only reference points had been Long Island, Brooklyn, and Manhattan. Words had been his only form of travel. His view of America expanded. A sense of the continent broadened the base and scope of *Leaves of Grass*. And New Orleans, with its French and Spanish heritage, was sensuous and fruitful. "By the time he returned to Brooklyn . . . he had travelled five thousand miles, and seen democratic vistas of city and wilderness, river and lake, mountain and plain." The cosmic intentions of *Leaves of Grass* were accumulating a large continental underpinning.

In his notebook, Whitman kept clarifying his thoughts, perfecting his design: "Make no quotations and no references to other writers. Take no illustration whatsoever from the ancients or classics. . . . Make no mention or allusion to them whatever, except as they relate . . . to American character, or interests." Again, "[to make] the poems of emotions, as they pass or stay, the poems of freedom, and the exposé of personality — singing in high tones democracy and the New World of it through These States." The words after the dash are the kind of sentiments that put many readers off by their air of fake grandiosity. The grandeur was partly temperamental, partly defensive: Mr. Kaplan says, ". . . there were hints that a less robust spirit had once prevailed, a spirit covert, hesitant, perturbed, lonely, and always unrequited. ('It is I you hold and who holds you,' he addressed his reader, becoming his own book, 'I spring from the pages into your arms.')" He was "cautious" and "artful" and told Edward Carpenter, one of his many English admirers, "I think there are truths which it is necessary to envelop or wrap up."

One of them was obvious — but to some not obvious enough. After the publication of the "Calamus" poems,

Whitman found himself in a position for which he had no taste: an international (but unwilling) advocate of homosexual love. John Addington Symonds was relentless in his pursuit of explications. What Symonds really wanted was for Whitman to declare himself. (There was a side to Whitman Symonds could never have imagined. Referring to an essay Symonds had written called "Democratic Art, with Special Reference to Walt Whitman," Whitman said, "I doubt whether he has gripped 'democratic art' by the nuts, or L of G either.") A whole colony of English homosexuals trooped to Whitman's flag. His brother George could never understand why Oscar Wilde would travel all the way to Camden, hardly a pleasure spot, just to see "Walt." It was in a letter replying to Symonds that the six illegitimate children first appear. A "mulatto mistress" was a later embellishment. This story was taken seriously by scholars for years even though no one ever came forward to claim the famous name or the possibly lucrative literary rights.

Whitman was attracted to ferryhands, drivers, and mechanics, enjoying their naturalness, their savvy, their lingo. Peter Doyle, a horse-car conductor he met in his Washington days, was the most satisfactory companion of his life. But even here he pressed too far:

> . . . give up absolutely, & for good, from this present hour, this feverish, fluctuating, useless undignified pursuit of 16.4 — too long (much too long) persevered in — so humiliating.

In Whitman's notebooks, "16" stands for "P" and "4" for "D" — the cryptography of a child. It becomes clear from Mr. Kaplan's book that Whitman's intense emotional affairs were all with men. Ellen O'Connor, the wife of Whitman's friend and critic William O'Connor, fell madly in love with him, and Anne Gilchrist, an English widow, wrote him passionate letters offering her hand in marriage. Whitman tried to put her off to no avail. She came over and lived in America with her children for several years, only to return to England, in the end, disappointed. Not quite able to deny himself any form of idolatry, Whitman welcomed women cautiously, proffering them his person in place of his love. He became a familiar figure in the O'Connor household in Washington and the Gilchrist ménage in Philadelphia. In fact, he liked nothing better than to "join" an already established domestic circle, adopting, and being adopted by, one family after another. In these establishments, he was the overgrown prodigal son come home to roost, or that friendly but remote familiar, the genius-uncle.

Leaves of Grass went through nine editions in Whitman's lifetime, its author striving in each successive recasting for the proper arrangement of the poems, readjusting sections and shifting sequences to accommodate additions to an ever-expanding work, which grew from the twelve poems of the 1855 edition to the three hundred eighty-three of the so-called Deathbed edition that bears Whitman's imprimatur. Lines and phrases were always being revised, stanzas tightened, and, as new poems were added, old ones were jettisoned to make room for them. Juvenile outpourings were discarded. Poems superseded others.

Leaves of Grass was full of prescriptions for the future. Emerson's clever description of it as a "combination of the 'Baghavad-Gita' and 'The New York Herald,' " meant as a putdown, would today be considered a compliment — but only because *Leaves of Grass* is already in place to show the way. (Emerson's comment was a far cry from his first spontaneous reaction to the poem, emblazoned forever in a famous letter: "I am not blind to the worth of the wonderful gift of 'Leaves of Grass.' I find it the most extraordinary piece of wit and wisdom that America has yet contributed. . . . I find incomparable things said incomparably well. . . . I greet you at the beginning of a great career" — the most generous unsolicited response of one writer to another in the history of American letters. Without it, the poetry, which had few takers, might have been lost forever. Whitman sent the letter to the *New York Tribune* and incorporated it into the second edition of *Leaves of Grass* — in both cases without permission from Emerson — two acts of insensitivity in Whitman's long career of self-advertisement. A poet–prophet–public-relations man, he wrote three anonymous reviews of his own book, modestly characterizing it, in one, as "the most glorious of triumphs in the known history of literature. . . .")

The true miracle of *Leaves of Grass* is that, with all its excesses, its extravagant claims, its endless catalogues, it is, at its very best, a poem of pure feeling — feeling that seeps through phrase after phrase, poem after poem. It is so loving that the transformation of its emotions into words on so vast a scale is astonishing. A long love affair with the future, broken in speech sometimes, eloquent beyond anything one remembers, remarkable in the minting of its language, it is a sad poem, a love poem to some "you" never found, some "you" not only personal, intimate, and sexual, but connected with an epic largeness of democratic vistas, as if the poet were in love with future Americans not yet born, or always yet to come. No one has yet explained, including Mr. Kaplan — and certainly not Whitman — where it sprang from. Whitman encouraged the view of the "transformation miracle" — the "journalist-loafer" turned into the great poet and prophet, as if at the touch of a wand. His followers, sodden with worship, helped the idea along. Actually, Whitman worked on it for years. It was *almost* a miracle, but a flawed one, for there is always the problem in Whitman of the false prophecy, the naïve dream, the wished-for fulfillment seen as accomplished fact. Its unevenness is too obvious to be commented on.

Leaves of Grass did more than change opinions; it altered the intellectual climate of the world. (And the moral climate, too. "Free love?" Whitman once asked. "Is there any other kind?") Van Gogh, working on *Starry Night* in Arles, was affected by it; Gerard Manley Hopkins took it to heart; LaForgue translated the "Children of Adam" poems; it was crucial to D. H. Lawrence and Hart Crane. People as wildly different as Thomas Eakins and Tennyson, Gertrude Stein and Henry James felt its impact. In our time, the Black Mountain School, the Beats, and the New York School of Poets emerged from it.

When the Civil War started, *Leaves of Grass* had been through three editions. "Out of the Cradle Endlessly Rocking," the "Children of Adam," and the "Calamus" poems had all been added. Its message of brotherly love became literal. Just as one brother, Jeff, had been party to Whitman's expanding conception of America, it was concern for another, George, that led Whitman to the battlefields of the South. In a garbled casualty report, Whitman learned that George had been wounded. No news followed. Whitman left Washington for Virginia in search of him, found him, and saw at first hand what the war was really like.

He dealt with it the only way he knew — as a healer. He returned to Washington to become a "wound-dresser" at Armory Square Hospital. Seventy thousand sick and wounded crowded every inch of it.

Whitman came into the wards like "a rich old sea captain, he was so red-faced and patriarchal-looking and big." He entertained the wounded, recited Shakespeare and Scott, told stories, wrote letters for the illiterate and the disabled, attended the feverish young, assisted at the grisly amputations, and comforted the dying. The suffering was indescribable: ". . . by the end of the war Whitman figured he had made over six hundred hospital visits and tours, often lasting several days and nights, and in some degree ministered to nearly a hundred thousand of the sick and wounded on both sides. . . ."

Yet there were compensations: the alleviation of pain, the sense of being part of a great design, of contributing. Paternal concern, brotherly companionship, mothering compassion were mixed up with emotions sometimes dangerously close to obsession. In the end, he was undone not only by the physical and mental suffering of the patients, and the fatigue of the work, but by his barely controllable feelings. Here is a letter from Whitman to Thomas P. Sawyer, one of the soldiers:

Dear Comrade, you must not forget me, for I never shall you. My love you have in life or death forever. I don't know how you feel about it, but it is the wish of my heart to have your friendship. . . . If you should come safe out of this war, we should come together again in some place where we could make our living, and be true comrades and never be separated while life lasts. . . . My soul could never be entirely happy, even in the world to come without you, dear comrade. . . . Goodbye, my darling comrade, my dear darling brother, for so I will call you, and wish you would call me the same.

Here is Sawyer's reply:

I fully appreciate your friendship as expressed in your letter and it will afford me great pleasure to meet you after the war will have terminated or sooner if circumstances permit.

The generalized "you," the beloved addressed in Whitman's poems, had, like Plato's universals, an idealized counterpart in President Lincoln. As a poet of the body, Whitman believed "The scent of these armpits is aroma finer than prayer / This head is more than churches or Bibles or creeds"; but as a poet of the soul, having eschewed Christianity, he needed a god of his own. ". . . Lincoln [became] his personal agent of redemption, a symbolic figure who transcended politics, leadership, and victory." His mother was the only other person in Whitman's life who had had this idealized aura. The "Drum-Taps" poems came out of the war and were dutifully added to *Leaves of Grass*. Their price was high: "The perfect health Whitman was so proud of broke in the hospitals along with a delicate structure of denial and sublimation. Love became irreversibly linked with disease, mutilation, death, absence." In 1865, Lincoln was assassinated; in 1873, Whitman's mother died. Long before, he had written a line that now seemed perfectly appropriate: "Agony is one of my changes of garment."

The year Whitman's mother died, he became partially paralyzed. Strokes were to cripple Whitman the rest of his life. After living with the family of his brother George in Camden for several years, he bought a small house of his own. Some of Mr. Kaplan's most charming pages are devoted to Whitman's last years. Confined more or less to an upper-front bedroom-workroom, he recovered only to be laid back again by another bout of illness. "It was not until old age," according to John Burroughs, the naturalist, who knew Whitman for over twenty years, "that Whitman's presence and ambience became fully achieved. . . . He created an overall impression of sunniness, equanimity, and contemplative leisure." Whitman, still fiddling with *Leaves of Grass*, stirred the mass of papers at his feet with his cane. Everything natural, found, or man-made was source material for the mesmeric catalogues of the poem. The house had the air of a ship's cabin, landlocked and foundering in debris, in spite of the sailor's widow who kept house for him. Whitman was a collector of people and things, but, in both cases, the choices had nothing to do with market values or current fashion. Like a bird building a nest, he knew exactly what he needed (not much) for his comfort, and what he had to have (everything) for his poem. Whitman needed help to get around and always found it; he was surrounded by people who revered him to the point of idolatry. In 1893, he was finally laid to rest in the elaborate tomb in Harleigh Cemetery that had cost him more than the Camden house. By the time the reader comes to Whitman's death, he can almost take "My foothold is tenoned and mortised in granite / I laugh at what you call dissolution" as the literal truth.

Whitman's life is enigmatic not only by virtue of genius; it is steeped in the deliberately muddy waters of destroyed evidence and manipulated fact. Putting a coherent Whitman together is an exercise in conjecture; the more insistent the claim the more suspicious its truth. Mr. Kaplan never insists; he merely presents. If he is sometimes long on Freud and short on philosophy, his is still the best all-around portrait we have of a man whose influence can only increase. Whitman bears a relation to Lincoln not unlike Shakespeare's to Elizabeth I and Michelangelo's to the Medici. In each instance, as the years pass, the more obvious it becomes that the representative figure of the age, like a negative gradually developing in time, is not the ruler but the artist.

Great Themes, Grand Connections

No recent visitor has had a good word to say for present-day Alexandria. Caesar and Cleopatra would be offended, it seems, by its crowded streets, and Euclid and Plotinus would wrinkle up their noses at its garbage-strewn alleyways. Alexandria is over two thousand years older than the United States, but hardly a stone is left to remind its Arab citizens of its Ptolemaic splendors. An echo chamber of Greek, Jewish, Roman, and Christian voices — pasts within pasts — its fabled nature remains invisible. Because it does, other cities vibrate inside the real one — cities of the imagination, hidden but waiting to be discovered — and they have excited philosophers and writers through the ages: most recently, Lawrence Durrell, in the *Alexandria Quartet*, and E. M. Forster, who wrote the city's most authoritative guidebook, *Alexandria: A History and a Guide*. In it, Forster says, "Then, as now, [Alexandria] belonged not so much to Egypt as to the Mediterranean, and the Ptolemies realised this. Up in Egypt they played the Pharaoh. . . . Down in Alexandria, they were Hellenistic." And so it is not surprising that the truest Alexandrian voice of all should belong to a native son and a member of the Greek diaspora — Constantine Cavafy, born in 1863. Nondescript except for his extraordinary eyes, vastly intelligent, he worked as a civil servant in Alexandria's Third Circle of Irrigation for over thirty years, lived with his rather silly mother and slew of brothers in genteel poverty, and escaped at night to the seediest part of town to sleep with boys. For all these reasons, or for none, he became one of the most fascinating poets Greece has offered the world — the Greek language, not the state, for Cavafy never set foot in Greece until he was thirty-eight, and then only briefly.

Robert Liddell's biography *Cavafy* begins with a genealogy almost as complex as that of the Ptolemies. Odd facts complicated Cavafy's life. His father, who had worked in England, became a British national, conferring automatic British citizenship upon his son. Cavafy was Greek by inheritance, an Egyptian by residence, and a British citizen. There were nine children in all — two dead in their first year, and one of those the only girl. Constantine, her replacement, was his mother's favorite, and she kept him in frocks and curls as long as she could. Of the others, his next two older brothers were important to the poet: Paul, with whom he lived for many years, and John, the closest to Constantine in temperament and understanding. Paul, debt-ridden, alcoholic, and homosexual, finally ran off to the Riviera to spend his declining years. John wrote poems and translated some of his brother's. Commerce (including embezzlement in one case) was always a stronger thread than artistry in the Cavafy family, but after the father died the Cavafys, once notable and rich, were poor; they lived the sort of life led by "well-bred" people who have lost their money — a fading luxuriance up front, and a tightening of belts behind doors.

At the time of his father's death, Constantine was seven. His mother remained in Alexandria for the next two years. Then the English connection asserted itself, and the family began one of those pilgrimages that must seem biblical to a child, stopping off at Marseilles, Paris, and London, and finally settling in Liverpool. The oldest son engaged in "unhappy speculations," the second lost his shirt in sugar and United Bonds. The tiny Cavafy inheritance dwindled to a pittance. The sense of shadowy cities and of a dynasty ending may have communicated itself to Constantine; he never forgot that he was the son of an extravagant man. The family moved from Liverpool to London, remaining fixed there for a year; reversing course, they returned to Paris and Marseilles. Five years after they started out, they were back in Alexandria. The poet was fourteen, and, except for three forced years of exile in Constantinople (after the Arab "troubles" and the British bombardment) and a trip or two to Europe, he lived in Alexandria for the rest of his life. It was in Constantinople, according to Liddell, that Cavafy had his first homosexual experience.

Liddell follows Cavafy from birth to his death, in 1933, but what there is to follow is meager. Rémy de Gourmont's remark about Flaubert is true of Cavafy: "Apart from his books, he is of very little interest." Sensible and forthright, Liddell's biography does all it can with the available facts, exhausting the Greek sources and providing the necessary checks and balances. It rescues Cavafy from the Freudians, working up from below, and the Marxists, determined to turn everything into a poster.

Before 1911, Cavafy was, by and large, a sentimental poet, writing what he later called "trash." It would have taken a clairvoyant rather than a critic to see the promise of a major poet in the first work. Cavafy was always grateful that he hadn't published early. In fact, he never published at all in any conventional sense: no volume of his poems came out during his lifetime. Poems in manuscript or broadsheet were sent to a select list of people — elected subscribers — and later, Cavafy included reprints and offsets of magazine publications. Two pamphlets appeared, in 1904 and 1910; a bound booklet in 1917. These slowly accreting works filled folder after folder with what Cavafy's translators, Philip Sherrard and Edmund Keeley, refer to as "the canon," a group of a hundred and fifty-three poems. Sherrard and Keeley have added to the original canon twenty-two "unpublished" poems, some among Cavafy's finest, in their edition of the *Collected Poems* — a hundred and seventy-five poems in all, only thirty-five of which come from the period before 1911. The time between a poem's composition and its "publication" could stretch to as long as a quarter of a century. The intervening years left open the possibility of endless revision and the repositioning of poems once Cavafy had come to see his work in terms not of single poems but of a sequential order as complex as the huge territory and time that became his subject.

In a well-known poem, "Days of 1909, '10, and '11" (the

"Days of 19 . . ." poems are part of a series, which has been picked up and revoiced by James Merrill in *his* "Days of 19 . . ." poems), Cavafy sees a boy in an ironmonger's shop, a boy willing to sell his body in order to buy a few cheap pieces of clothing. Under his "cinnamon-brown suit [and] mended underwear," the naked boy is perfection, at one with the beauty of ancient Greek statues, the heads of the favored stamped on precious coins. It was through images such as these that Cavafy began to connect a banal marketplace with a major seam in Greek civilization. What was at first a guilty burden became in the end the means of discovering great themes and grand connections. Cavafy was moved by correspondences, and saw in them the true gestures of history. And thus it was through the erotic that the historical came to life. But though correspondences were moving, they were also ironic, because power — Caesar, Sparta, the Roman Empire — could exist only to be swept away, and had little effect, ultimately, on the repetition of human patterns, the endless tale of construction and pillage. Correspondences were not metaphors to Cavafy — his poems are almost completely free of them in any literal sense — but ongoing dramas, and so the poems are usually monologues, the speaker a fictitious or real person in history, the tone contemporary but the voice timeless.

The historical poems tell their stories in a disinterested way: their savor is the dry accumulated wisdom of someone who has taken the measure of two thousand years of imperial struggle, if not always the measure of himself. They have, as the poet says in "Dareios," "a certain insight into the vanities of greatness . . . [its] arrogance and intoxication." Scene after scene adds up to a play whose dimensions dawn on the reader only slowly. Edmund Keeley, in his completely knowledgeable critical study, *Cavafy's Alexandria*, a model of compression and concentration, lists as an appendix the principal settings of Cavafy's poems in the ancient world of Hellenism: Athens, Eleusis, Argos, Thermopylae, Macedonia, Ithaca, Delphi, Rhodes, Sparta, Rome, Poseidonia, Sicily, Syracuse, and so on. They read like a roll call of what we never knew, or have long forgotten. Sometimes we are in Libya, sometimes in Persia. And, using only Cavafy's titles, I would add a few dates to suggest the grand strategy of the poems: "Of Dimitrios Sotir (162–150 B.C.)," "Of the Jews (A.D. 50)," "Young Men of Sidon (A.D. 400)," "For Ammonis, Who Died at 29, in 610," "Days of 1903." These are poems of statement, forbidding at first in their lack of color, their wide frame of reference, their historical data. The extraordinary thing about them is not Cavafy's ability to see the ancient world alive with character but the accumulated sweep of the whole. Reading them, one feels that history is a vast reality one can dip into at any particular moment. The past being perpetually present, and alive, history becomes permanent. These poems do one of the big things poems should do: they make one aware of time. Cities whose names appear in the newspapers every day make Cavafy's point over again — Beirut, Sidon, Jerusalem, Cairo — and though "historical" suggests the textbook, the opposite effect is at work here: these poems are the products of sensibility, not of scholarship. The method is that of ironic reversal: Claudius justifying his role in *Hamlet*; an invasion of barbarians who are conceived as rescuers rather than destroyers. Young men looking for the main chance — say, in Sidon in 300 B.C. — appear as if they were familiar strangers glimpsed at a bus stop. If one could imagine a contemporary American poet standing on a balcony — as Cavafy stood on his in the Rue Lepsius — resurveying the entire history of the American continent, including its Indian past, one would have some notion of Cavafy's accomplishment.

But that accomplishment seems to me peculiarly patchy, for the great poems stand out — poems like "Waiting for the Barbarians"— and the love poems tend to diminish the cumulative effect of the whole, even though they are the source of its vitality. A worldliness that sometimes brings to mind its supreme example, *Antony and Cleopatra*, alternates with a provincialism that is purely emotional, as if we had in the same person and the same works greatness and a diminishment of it. Most writers of Cavafy's stature save that kind of immaturity for life, but because his life *was* the poems it has entered into the bloodstream of the texts themselves. Impeccable in tone, scrupulous in having rid themselves of every shred of rhetoric, they manage nevertheless to suggest lost opportunities. Cavafy divided his work into three categories: historical, erotic, and philosophical. He is superb in the first, risks sentimentality in the second, and is weakest in the third. Intelligence is not philosophy, any more than insight is psychology. The depth of thought in these poems is not always equal to the genius of the sensibility that created them. When we compare Cavafy with Eliot — a perfectly reasonable comparison, considering the period, the roles they cast themselves in, and their ultimate achievement — we find in Eliot components missing in Cavafy: philosophical reach, an awareness of traditions other than Hellenism, and a feeling for the natural world that provides a balance between personal history and the historical record.

The urban voice is distinguished from the nature poet's by more than consciousness and irony. The nature poet is usually religious and seeks a god, the city poet mythological and seeks a hero. (Certain works — *Moby Dick,* for one — though ostensibly belonging to the first category belong to the second. The crew of the *Pequod* are the inhabitants of a small city at the mercy of an evil essentially man-made, though in the form of a natural monster. The whale is more Ahab's creation than God's.) Nature is conspicuously absent from Cavafy's poems; he is moved less by the pastoral conventions and the cycle of the seasons than "by seeing something of this city I love, a little movement in the streets, in the shops." And he uses the city in unexpected ways. It is not only the past in the present but the tangle of mortal and god that gives these poems their impact. The heroic is humanized but never condescended to. In what is possibly Cavafy's most famous poem, "The God Abandons Antony," a shift in emphasis reveals both his devotion to the city and his mining of a tradition. After the defeat at Actium, Antony is abandoned to his death. In Plutarch it is Dionysus who abandons him, in Shakespeare it is Hercules, but in Cavafy it is Alexandria herself. By association, the city has taken on a triple quality: the god, the hero, and the civilization for whom they exist.

Cavafy was one of the first modern poets openly to acknowledge his homosexuality. He made good use of it, for it connected him with the "Alexandrian mode," which Keeley defines as

first of all to search for the hidden metaphoric possibilities, the mysterious invisible processions, of the reality one sees in the literal city outside one's window. If one is Cavafy, the mode is then to dramatize and expand these discovered possibilities until they carry a broad mythic significance. Cavafy's use of the mode begins with his choosing to move from personal metaphors to communal and historical metaphors, and from there to the projection of a self-contained mythical world that serves to represent both his special view of Greek history and his image of the perennial human predicament.

Homosexuality is invisible, and so is the Alexandrian past. One develops its secret negative in the dark, the other is a library of countless lost photographs. The homosexual has certain built-in advantages as a spokesman for the city. The search for the hero is not merely literary, and if alienation and loneliness are the marks of the city-dweller, the homosexual is set apart simply by being sexually categorized. (One would become more aware of this if the distinguishing characteristic of a person's nature were to be described as being heterosexual.) In most homosexual lives, the search for a partner to go to bed with and/or love cuts across artificial social barriers; the bellboy and the ambassador, the governor and the mechanic may be found in each other's company sub rosa. Exploring byways of the city usually, but not always, outside the bourgeois domestic circle, the homosexual gets to know the city in ways most people don't — strange places at strange hours. Secrets contain within themselves a hidden spring — the compulsion to reveal them — and this compulsion has something in it of the quality of history: the story not yet revealed, the truth under the appearance of it, the onion skin of façade endlessly waiting to be peeled away. It isn't hard to understand why the only occupation imaginable to Cavafy other than the poet's was that of the historian.

In *Cavafy's Alexandria*, Keeley traces the poet's development through various projections of the city itself, and his
chapter headings are a precise guide to his method: "The Literal City," "The Metaphoric City," "The Sensual City,"
"Mythical Alexandria," "The World of Hellenism," "The
Universal Perspective." It is the method of the stone thrown
in the water, making ever-expanding ripples.

To me, there are striking similarities between Cavafy and
Proust, and homosexuality centered in a mother with whom
a relationship lasts intact through middle age is the least of
them. The chief bond is how each of them rescued himself
from frivolity by converting sexuality into an obsession with
the past. The tinkle of salon music is a never-distant menace
in both cases. Each managed ultimately to resist that peculiar
mother-derived nicety of necktie and manner characteristic
of the social lives of "good" families — the whole upper-
bourgeois apparatus of balls and carriages, the meaningless
events to which so many lives are dedicated. Preoccupied
with younger men, Proust and Cavafy both contrived to
emerge from the palm court onto the plains of myth, if myth
is history transformed into a body of work one can permanently refer to, which grows out of and transcends the limits
of its creator and touches perimeters so wide that the generic
begins to take the place of the specific: the Cavafy voice
speaking through many heroes, the Proustian tone and intelligence shedding light on everything. In each case, the history of a people came to the rescue as a force and focusing
agent: it would be utterly impossible to read Cavafy without
Greece and the Hellenic world in view at all times, and completely mistaken to read Proust without knowing that the

Guermantes are — no matter how flawed and stupid in their immediate versions — the means of leading back through the great genealogical family names of France to the roots of a language and a culture.

Yet Proust's and Cavafy's attitudes toward homosexuality couldn't be more different. For Cavafy it was the release and abandonment of the pagan, for Proust the guilty secret of Christian and Jewish morality — though he regretted, if Gide quotes him correctly, having put in only his "bad" homosexual experience and left out all that was charming. For all their resemblances, Proust and Cavafy were on opposite sides of the fence: Proust found in love a form of bondage, and Cavafy in sex a means of connection. There is a moral tone in Cavafy, whereas in Proust there is always a certain Mosaic ring. Cavafy is closer to Whitman, who, by one of those historical coincidences that seem preordained, had just published the "Calamus" poems in 1863, the year of Cavafy's birth.

Cavafy was one of the first "modern" writers in his fidelity to his own experience, his disdain for rhetoric and decoration, his use of demotic Greek as well as the high style, and he belongs to a tradition whose outlines are now clear. By apprehending the present and the past as simultaneous realities, the major figures of twentieth-century literature have worked private worlds into epic proportions, reinventing the image of the self (Proust), a city (Joyce), a country (Yeats), or a tradition (Eliot and Pound) as the reflected image of a civilization. In Cavafy's case, as in Joyce's, the mythological city is forged out of disparate elements: the commonplace life of the streets and the splendor of ancient tales and legends, in which the ordinary man of the first could become the unwitting hero of the second. The process was, we now know, reversible: at the time that Joyce was turning Bloom into Ulysses, Cavafy was, so to speak, turning Ulysses into Bloom.

Goodbye to Wystan

Thank You, Fog contains Auden's last poems. The book is posthumous and, as his literary executor explains in a short preface, half the ghost of what it might have been. Writers, being human, are not in a position to choose their monuments. This one is more Audenesque than Auden, hardly fitting as the final words, the summing up of a man who set his mark on an age. As he developed into a superb writer, he became something more: an intellectual and moral touchstone for three generations of Englishmen and Americans. None of the obvious sources, as a leftist of the thirties, as a High Church Anglican of the sixties — or even the work itself — quite account for it. History and genius worked in magical combination: Auden was in Spain in 1937, in China in 1938, in Germany in 1945. He was, after Pound and Eliot, the only international poet of the English language. (One can write poetry and be an international figure without being an international poet.)

Auden's poetry was a conductor of history — "conductor" in its electrical, its travel-guide, and perhaps even its musical sense. He was our supreme journalist of the imagination, not only the recorder and the interpreter of the event but the conscience that gave it perspective. History is hard on people who feel its impact fully at any particular time, and Auden himself had harsh words to say about poems like "Spain" and "September 1, 1939." The role of the automatic moralizer, the too-easy invoker of love was one he came, naturally, to distrust. And because so many poems sprang from the immediate occasion he may have lost something in depth to what he gained in range. Though I don't think anyone doubts Auden composed masterpieces, it is not so easy to say, as it is in Eliot's or Stevens's case, exactly what — which — they are. First, the number of poems is astounding; they form a kind of cumulative masterpiece. And then, for poets of my generation, those born in the twenties, Auden was so formative, so influential that the early poems seem more like natural objects or remembered childhood landscapes than like works of art. Is "Look, stranger, on this island now" a masterpiece? Is "Doom is dark and deeper than any sea dingle"? I cannot imagine the history of poetry without them. To mention "In Praise of Limestone" or "The Sea and the Mirror" is only to begin the list.

Though an addict of the north, Auden was still southern enough to adore Ischia, to have had a cottage on Fire Island, to admire the Goethe of the "Italian Journey." (How fitting, then, that his farmhouse in Austria should have been bought with the proceeds of an Italian literary prize!) He wrote plays, libretti, the narration for documentary movies; inspired a ballet; devised masques, charades; and turned out cabaret songs, popular lyrics, and even a hymn for the United Nations. He had an ear, as any great poet would have to, as finely tuned (at least in the early poems) as the brain it was tuned for was intelligent. Only painting seemed not to interest him very much, though Breughel inspired one of the anthology pieces of our time, "Musée de Beaux Artes," and Hogarth the libretto for *The Rake's Progress*. The range of interests is large and singular: lead mining, opera, theology, detective stories, food, gossip, science, espionage, psychoanalysis, politics, literary criticism, philosophy, mountain climbing, medicine.

After Marx proved to be an untrustworthy guide, was it Freud or Kierkegaard who dominated his thinking? Different as his positions might be at various times, part of the Auden magic was the ability to synthesize practically everything; in the long run none of his views seemed inconsistent. They had a unifying theme: behind the theoretical façades, he waged a long battle against hokum. And when a view of his own began to take on the stale smell of hot air Auden changed it — not to be fashionable but for the sake of the reasonable. Like all men in his position — men who have become public through the practice of what originally seemed a private art — views were ascribed to him long after he had abandoned them, and notions he never subscribed to were laid at his door. There were paradoxes, shifts, reversals, and sometimes plain shockers — show-off ideas he probably only half-believed himself. Not that he lied. In fact, the steady beam that kept being broadcast for almost half a century proclaimed the opposite: he was, if anyone was, our best antidote to lying. At the end, truth became an obsession and, like most obsessions, was taken too literally and too far (he thought Yeats, for instance, had "lied" in saying that "once out of nature" he would never take his bodily form from any natural thing, "but such a form as Grecian goldsmiths make" — "Nobody wants to be a golden bird," Auden once said to me). There was a feeling when he died quite unlike the feelings occasioned by the deaths of Eliot or Moore, to take obvious examples — a voice one had counted on, a voice oddly personal, was gone forever. It was more than an authoritative voice; it was a voice that had helped establish what was to be taken as authoritative. Eccentric but rational, it spoke up for the Good. And it remained youthful even when it was no longer certain of what it was to be young. The phrase "freaked out," for instance, appears in "Nocturne," the finest poem in *Thank You, Fog*. It is a symptom of the wrong kind of vitality. But it is also a sign of how Auden listened.

In "A Thanksgiving," a rather automatic poem, he names the important influences: Hardy, Thomas (Edward), Frost, Yeats, Graves, Brecht — he even thanks Hitler and Stalin for forcing him to think about God — and then goes on to Kierkegaard, Williams, Lewis (C.S.), Horace, and Goethe. What a crew! Auden, by being his own man, went Hegel one better. He was kind but had an exact sense of who he was. There was something endearing about him, and something forbidding; he had the royal air and the common touch: austere Horatian, camp gossip, English gentleman, messy schoolboy. And there *was* something peculiar about being with him. No matter how many times one might say "Wystan" this or "Wystan" that, still there would be the sudden awareness that one was talking to *Auden*. No other famous writer — at least in my experience — evoked quite the same reaction. It was like having lunch with Byron, or meeting Sir Thomas Wyatt at a party.

Auden innocently gave rise to the ultimate snobbishness. Is there anything more exclusive than immortality? After a certain point — say, the early fifties —hardly anyone could doubt he was in the presence of one of English literature's monuments, someone who had already taken his place in the Pantheon. I don't think Auden had the slightest doubt about it either. That Westminster Abbey hurried to make the endorsement official doesn't mean that Auden's life was any easier. He worked incredibly hard; he was — after Edna St. Vincent Millay — the only self-supporting poet in this country, and it couldn't have been fun to go around wearing clothes, no matter how dirty, stained, or unpressed, or write notes, no matter how short, that were already collector's items. A certain air of unreality clung to Auden's efforts to be earthbound. A sign of how unreal he could be in stating a position is the rather pathetic official notice that appeared in *The New York Times* requesting his correspondents to burn his letters. (The subsequent bonfire has yet to be lighted.) And this is the same Auden who valued Keats's letters over his poems, and reviewed Chekhov's letters in *The New Yorker*!

At any one time, there must be five or six supremely intelligent people on the earth. Auden was one of them. How lucid the introduction to *The Greek Reader* remains. How marvelously original the introduction to *The Oxford Book of Light Verse*. How extraordinary his comments on romantic poetry in *The Enchafèd Flood*. Almost everything he touched — with the exception of his own light verse, and that includes the two unfortunately resurrected lyrics from *The Man of La*

Mancha — was of an excellence few writers ever come close to attaining. The gifts were prodigious, including the energy. But he might have become something else —a geologist like his older brother, or a doctor like his father, or even a clergyman like his two grandfathers. No matter the role, the brain would — and did — inform everything: fascinating, fascinated, unique. He was an impatient man, compulsive about time, and he could on occasion be more dazzle than substance. As he was during his Shakespeare lectures at the New School in the forties, where the commentary was so brilliant that one forgot, half the time, that its relationship to a particular play was quite often tangential. Or at a dinner party when he said, "You can tell a man is going to pieces when he starts being late for appointments, and a woman when she stops caring about her looks" — a perfectly legitimate, even provocative remark — followed by "Time belongs to men and space to women," a dubious one. Auden's high-wire performances wound down in quality, naturally, as he got older, but the voice can still be heard, recorded or in memory, a speech more individually characteristic than almost any I can think of — a kind of speech defect, really — a mumbling, childlike (childish?) kind of tumbling forth of words, a moist kind of gabbling, as if the instrument were not quite quick enough for what it was intended to convey.

But in spite of his brilliance, something always seemed to me to be missing. Though the poems belie it, his presence had no animal force — I don't mean anything to do with physical attractiveness — but as if some gut intuition, some inherent instinctive sense of things, were absent, as if the intelligence took up too much room to allow for something else — a coordination of physical elements, a grace, an ease of manner, an awareness, say, of the pleasures and dangers commonly met at any moment by the least of us. As if he were not, in short, quite comfortable in his own skin. How much of this is simply a wrong impression, how much the result of a studied way of protecting himself I don't know.

The important thing is that he restored to poetry what it had for a long time lacked, a relevant human voice. After the Victorian and the Edwardian poets had had their say, the problem was somehow to construct a style out of the real that was neither banal nor elevated. It became the great task of this century's poetry, a labor that often produced the humdrum at one end of the scale and the rhetorical at the other. It also produced those marvels, William Carlos Williams and Wallace Stevens. It was a style that had to be come at through the back door — is that why two separate versions of it emerged full-blown from a pediatrician (Williams) and the vice-president of an insurance company (Stevens)? Auden arrived at it in some way through the language of science and through the peculiar fact of his being the only important poet writing in English to fall in love with the north and the German rather than the Mediterranean and the French —not the Provençal troubadors of Pound but the Icelandic sagas — not the sensuous or the visionary but the rational and the divine, and particularly that version of it struggling with either the animal or the absurd, a line one can trace through Freud, Lewis Carroll, and the mystics that interested Auden: Simone Weil and Dag Hammarskjöld.

It is also a line one can trace through Auden, for intelligence, no matter how high, is not the hallmark of the poet. The true sounds one hears in Auden's best poems derive from the disappointments of the animal and the landscape of his youth. In what may be the most haunting love poem of this century, the loved one's head is merely *human*, the narrator's arm, enclosing him, is *faithless*, and "Time and fevers burn away / Individual beauty from / Thoughtful children, and the grave / Proves the child ephemeral . . ."

Auden brought a new language into poetry, his own. He was in love with words, all kinds of words, and what he did with language and grammar is too complex and original to be dealt with in a short essay. It was part of his originality to revivify the adjective, that most maligned part of English speech, by projecting psychological states into what had been merely colorful or evocative: "Underneath the abject willow," "Fish in the unruffled lakes," or, from poems in *Thank You, Fog*, "the modest conduct of fogs," and "the vagrant moods of the weather." Sometimes a verb would convey this human characteristic — "May with its light behaving," "Time crumbs all ramparts" — an example, too, of Auden's mating of the imperial and the cozy — sometimes an adverb was refreshed by its context: "The entirely beautiful."

This conspicuous but singular personification animated a world of private myth and public statement. The primitive fairy story and folk tale that form a background for the early poems gave way to the social postures of the thirties, and they, in turn, to orthodoxy. First the hobgoblin and the troll, then exhortation and moral pleading, and finally the worldly saint and the City of God. But just as Auden's Marxism was never thoroughgoing but a more stimulating antidote to bourgeois passivity, so his Protestantism seems less religious piety than a return to a formal tradition. As Auden came to distrust the Big, the social and the evolutionary narrowed down to the domestic. Who could be a spokesman for a world no longer capable of being understood, and no longer even desirable except in its immediate surround: the habitat, the old friend, the familiar? The grand pronouncement and the general gave way to praise for the local and the near. And even they tend to close in further — many of the later poems have as their subject the self or the body.

But strangely, as the world Auden dealt with became more specific, his language became more abstract. The great effectiveness of the early poems comes from many sources, but one of them was the poet's ability to take a familiar noun and qualify it with a reference from an unfamiliar world; the language of one kind of discourse modifies another. Who, before Auden, had ever heard of "uncritical islands," "florid music," "aloof peaks," "whorled, unsubtle ears," or "baroque frontiers"? The early poems — the world of the great evolutionary-revolutionary Uncle, the oppositions of We and They — have an immediacy of diction, a musical attraction, or an absolute originality of phrasing the later poems lack. Distrusting the too-ready attitudinizing of the thirties poems, Auden turned against even the poems that had preceded them, where the musical genius of the language is most apparent. And perhaps as he began seriously to write libretti, he decided to leave the composing to others. Whatever the case, he devised a new prosy kind of meditative poem — as if musical effects, in language at least, were simply another form of lying — sometimes extraordinary in the freshness of its thought, or the quirkiness of its wording, sometimes dull because the language has lost its vividness as well as its relation to song.

Auden was generous, self-involved, petulant, and sometimes peevish. There were oracular moments, and moments of simple boyish sweetness. And, as he grew older, he became, like most people, more eccentric. At the end, he had the look of a man who is always catching trains. It seems (from other sources) that all he really wanted to do was to go home and go to bed.

I saw him last at the big send-off at the Coffeehouse just before his return to Oxford. Looking around the room, one could see the interesting collection of people who had been singled out for this last American shindig. It was typical of Auden that the faces should range from the very famous to the absolutely unknown, should include as many women as men, should scale up (or down?) from the very old to the very young, and include friends he was loyal to whom he might long ago have forgotten. And that, at a table raised a little above the height of the others, there should have been a last-minute difficulty about who was to sit next to him. It was impossible to say whether the position was being shied away from or oversubscribed. He seemed then, as he had so many times before, quite alone.

All Praise

Since the nineteenth century, three versions of the poet as dreamer have become discernible: a person idyllically free of social obligations who takes notes on the beauties of nature; a visionary describing a mythological universe of the past or a Utopian one of the future; and an explorer of the unconscious. This triple notion has advantages: it allows the naturalist to be an innocent in a world of corruption; the mythologist or Utopian to criticize the world by analogy or overtly; and the psychologist to mine the corruption within himself. It has its dangers, too: the note-taker can degenerate into the dilettante; the visionary into the crackpot; and the explorer of the dark into the dark itself — it is only half a step from the dream to the nightmare. What has resulted are three sometimes overlapping traditions: descriptive poetry; poetry of nostalgia or social disaffection (in which either the past or the future becomes preferable to the present); and poetry of personal alienation.

In *Questions of Travel*, Elizabeth Bishop's first book of poems since 1955, we do not find the nostalgic phantasist, the prophetic seer, or the social critic — except by implication. And we aren't being let in on the secrets of her diary, either. We would seem to be dealing with a descriptive poet. It is part of the originality of these poems to elude that category, and, in fact, all others. Though these poems take stock of the beauties of nature, as well as its ugliness, with unique exactitude, that is not their major point or merit. Miss Bishop's precision of image is well known and rightly praised. But it is her viewpoint that is wholly exceptional. Observation and temperament have become inseparable; telling the truth is a form of human sympathy, not a moral imperative or scientific curiosity. Since truth is variable and always suspect, how do we know we're being told it? The credibility of these poems derives from a shocking fact: Miss Bishop is completely sane.

The power of these poems is a result of their clarity. By seeing so clearly, their author achieves effects more exciting often than those the unconscious can drag up by way of association and connection. And we, who have become so used to equating calmness with dullness, are surprised to find in her work a further stretch of the imagination. These poems are far from simple, but they can be easily read; all the preparatory work has been done underground. By not using rose-colored or dark glasses, Miss Bishop has retrieved certain Edens and hells that have been obscured by poets whose vision is distorted or who can hardly see at all. She neither ascends into optimism nor descends into murk. A clearly lighted equanimity allows for every note of the scale, including that intensity from which every blur and distraction have been erased. Disinterestedness has become passionate. She has made sanity interesting without lecturing us about it.

Reading these poems, we have the sensation of seeing what things are *really* like, and we take Miss Bishop's authority for granted. It is an authority that rests on discarded temptations; nothing that has not been isolated to be examined, nothing that has not been delineated sharply has been permitted to be written down. These poems are so pure that sometimes we feel their author has been fed on a secret literature unknown to the rest of the world. Has she read the histories of stones, mountains, and waterfalls in their original languages? If so, she has translated them superbly by passing them through a mind so free to receive them that every object is justly valued, each feeling, each thought allowed its true nature.

If all this suggests that Miss Bishop is naïvely in love with the universe, I hasten to qualify the thought. She is ironic, not sentimental. Anyone who thinks these new poems (and one marvelous story) are love letters to the world or impeccably written picture postcards of Miss Bishop's various stopovers in foreign places would be mistaken. Place is important to her not only because she is a traveler but because the world itself is in exile. She is constantly luring it home by pointing out to it its features. They are not always pretty — an armadillo is not armored against fire, Bedlam is no farther away than St. Elizabeth's in Washington, D.C. — but they are always believably used, not exhibited.

No one could be less precious than Miss Bishop, and no one could be less sociological. Who else could write a poem about a "squatter tenant" — "the world's worst gardener since Cain" — in which the idea of condescension would be merely vulgar? The author doesn't insist on being human, because she is, and what makes her so is unselfconsciousness and accuracy. Each demands a great deal of the other. To lie about the world or to rant about it is not to cherish it. Miss Bishop is civilized in a special way: in being herself and in telling the truth, she supersedes manners by setting superior standards. By choosing so carefully what and whom she sees, she is never forced toward the half-lie. What is here in place of manners is a rare combination of naturalness and elegance — elegance of mind, spirit, taste — the real thing, for it is neither learned nor fashionable, but inherent. Not being rarefied there is no need to be colloquial. Miss Bishop never confuses the natural with the primitive or the elegant with the mannered — their debased counterparts. And what is more to the point, she couldn't.

She is an instinctive storyteller, too faithful to the truth to use what passes for the devices of drama. She has had to create a small theater of her own in which character and setting become dramatic not through oddity or conflict but through the charm, the susceptibility of the perceiver. It is a theater of depths as well as surfaces, and it both suggests and defines where questions of travel are truly answered. The last line of "Arrival at Santos" reads, "we are driving into the interior." Only someone unfamiliar with Miss Bishop's way of doing things would have to be told that what she means by the interior is more than geographical.

Few poets are so clearly in touch with the whole of themselves, so able to move from what they see to what they feel without a shift in emphasis. In each poem, Miss Bishop travels right to the center of the bull's-eye. But her own eye exists in two worlds, somewhat like the hero of an earlier poem, "The Gentleman of Shallot," who is bisected by the edge of a mirror. The mirror points out a biological truth: the body is bilaterally symmetrical. But that body — half in, half out of the mirror — is comparable to the poet's viewpoint: every reflection is used as a comment on human experience; but each reflection, clearly, is not all there is to say about it. These poems are profoundly modest. Objects reveal the subjects of the poems more tellingly than might at first be apparent — the real horse in "In the Village" is a counterweight nature supplies to the mother's scream, which is unnatural; the fake horse in "Twelfth Morning; or What You Will" tells us a great deal about Balthazár's song and his life — but it is never called to our attention that Miss Bishop reveals the object. It is simply handed to us, generously, with no fuss.

Though its contents page divides *Questions of Travel* into two sections, it consists, really, of three: eleven poems set in Brazil, a short story — "In the Village" — and eight poems set elsewhere.

In "Brazil, January 1, 1502," Miss Bishop is free to write of nature as a tapestry because she sees the hand that wove the tapestry as well:

> *Januaries, Nature greets our eyes*
> *exactly as she must have greeted theirs:*
> *every square inch filling in with foliage —*
> *big leaves, little leaves, and giant leaves,*
> *blue, blue-green, and olive,*
> *with occasional lighter veins and edges,*
> *or a satin underleaf turned over;*
> *monster ferns*
> *in silver-gray relief,*
> *and flowers, too, like giant water lilies*

up in the air — up, rather, in the leaves —
purple, yellow, two yellows, pink,
rust red and greenish white;
solid but airy; fresh as if just finished
and taken off the frame.

Who else would have thought of "up, rather, in the leaves"
or "solid but airy," both of which so exactly underscore the
points they are making? And who else could have used the
alliterations of "filling, foliage, underleaf, ferns, relief, flowers, fresh, finished, and frame" so naturally in fifteen lines
that we scarcely notice them?

If we follow what Miss Bishop does with the sound of the
letters *f* and *v*, an intuitive architecture becomes apparent.
There are no *v*'s in the first line and none in the last four. In
between, where the leaves pile up in density — "yellow, two
yellows" — we have the *v*'s of "have, every, leaves, leaves,
leaves, olive, veins, over, silver, and leaves," echoes of the
letter *f*, first found in line 3, this second group of repeated
sounds making a subtle background music for the first.

The mysteries that lie behind the ordinary are revealed in
Questions of Travel, but how Miss Bishop manages to make
proportion and reserve emotional is hard to say. "The Riverman," where the magical can only be described in terms its
native narrator knows, suggests how she sticks to the facts
and transforms them:

and the moon was burning bright
as the gasoline-lamp mantle
with the flame turned up too high,
just before it begins to scorch.

In the first two stanzas of "Twelfth Morning; or What You Will," not an ounce of inflation or a shred of rhetoric compete with what is being said:

> *Like a first coat of whitewash when it's wet,*
> *the thin gray mist lets everything show through:*
> *the black boy Balthazár, a fence, a horse,*
> *   a foundered house,*
>
> *— cement and rafters sticking from a dune.*
> *(The Company passes off these white but shopworn*
> *dunes as lawns.) "Shipwreck," we say; perhaps*
> *   this is a housewreck.*

Miss Bishop is one of the true masters of tone. She has an absolute sense of what the English language can do, of how much to say, how much to leave unsaid. There is no fiddling around with syntax, no *evident* concern with the sounds of words, no special effects of typography. We never have to search for a verb or wonder if a pronoun has an antecedent. What she brings to poetry is a new imagination; because of that, she is revolutionary, not "experimental." And she is revolutionary in being the first poet successfully to use all the resources of prose.

Her poems are so natural to read that they seem to teeter on that edge, where, for a moment, we think, "Why, all this could be changed into prose — fine prose indeed, but prose still." But if one tries, say, to write out a Bishop poem as if it were prose, one soon realizes it is impossible to do so. These poems do not advertise themselves in any "poetic" way. We are constantly under the impression that Miss Bishop is in the room with us, speaking, but not making a speech. The voice is friendly but not cajoling, warm but not insistent. She doesn't pretend that she never heard a word longer than a monosyllable or try to dazzle us with the reaches of her vocabulary. In her use of English grammar, she avoids both distortion and excess baggage. It would take some careful searching to find the words *which* or *that* in these poems. Each is a concentrated action that develops organically; prettiness or bombast do not dilute the concentration, and overreaching never interferes with the development. It is relevance as well as accuracy that makes Miss Bishop the fine poet she is. Nothing is turned aside that sheds light; nothing is included that is superfluous. We are in the presence of someone using the orchestra of human speech who doesn't reach down for the drums or up for the harp. We are enchanted to have escaped, for once, the banal and the purple. The result is more than a formal and aesthetic triumph; it is a moral one. Miss Bishop teaches us something precisely because she would be the last person in the world who would want to.

And what we learn — and only by example — is that objectivity need not be impersonal. Miss Bishop has a clear eye, not a clinical one. A poem like "First Death in Nova Scotia," with its careful understatement, fidelity to detail, and meticulous perception remains completely spontaneous. It is in distancing that its author transcends what in lesser writers is merely verisimilitude. She is a master of perspective as well as tone, for we are in the exact center of what would appear to be conflicting forces: painting and drama, austerity of expression, and a personal letter. The intervening layer of the writer seems to have evaporated; we are directed to the material as if neither time nor a persona separated the reader from what he is reading.

In "First Death in Nova Scotia," Miss Bishop is describing

her small, dead cousin, Arthur, laid out in a coffin "In the cold, cold parlor . . ." On a marble-topped table there is a stuffed loon, shot by Arthur's father, who is also named Arthur. (And what a nicety that turns out to be by the time we have finished the poem.) What Miss Bishop does with this interplay of dead images is remarkable. Though she never says so — she just lets *us* say so — there must have been a strange connection in the child-observer's mind between dead cousin Arthur and the dead loon. Wasn't the loon's death caused by Arthur's chief mourner, his father? *That* fact would have escaped almost anyone but Miss Bishop. But when, in describing the loon, she says:

> *He kept his own counsel*
> *on his white, frozen lake,*
> *the marble-topped table.*
> *His breast was deep and white,*
> *cold and caressable;*
> *his eyes were red glass,*
> *much to be desired.*

more than a single intention becomes clear in the last line. Miss Bishop doesn't say, "which *I* much desired." Much to be desired by whom, then? By Arthur's father? Of course; he shot the loon. But the loon's eyes were not red glass *then*. By the child observer? Of course; red glass in all that white! By the loon itself? Just possibly, for hasn't he achieved a *kind* of immortality — the kind that will never be Arthur's?

In the unexpected and resounding "much to be desired," Miss Bishop shows us who she is. It is in the difference between desiring red glass and desiring to kill the loon and being capable of doing so that the distance between the child and the adult, the unawareness of death and the knowledge of it, is measured. And in the barely perceptible rhyme of "caressable" and "red glass," we see how delicately, how forcefully she can work.

Here is the last stanza:

> *They invited Arthur to be*
> *the smallest page at court.*
> *But how could Arthur go,*
> *clutching his tiny lily,*
> *with his eyes shut up so tight*
> *and the roads deep in snow?*

The sudden release of the last line in a poem so compressed that each word is utterly necessary has the impact of a memory held under pressure which is suddenly allowed not to explode but to expand endlessly. Arthur's eyes are shut tight; outside, all Nova Scotia lies dead in winter. But it is the word *roads* that has such large reverberations. Roads are where one goes; Arthur not only wasn't going; he never would be. What the child-observer could not see then is clear now. Arthur could not have walked the roads whether his eyes were open or shut or whether the roads were cleared or deep in snow. And it has taken all the time between Arthur's death and the writing of this poem to discover that — or at least to say so. To point out what Miss Bishop does with the word *forever* earlier in the poem would only illustrate further how subtle straightforwardness can be.

"In the Village" is a story in which indirection pins down a world that is tangible, crystal-clear, and, I would think, permanent. Without using any of the conventional trappings of narrative — exposition, transition, climax — a childhood day surrounds the dark core of a mother's illness. A scream hangs over an idyll and each underlines and comments on the other. An audacity of imagination and a temperance of spirit shape it, as they do the poems in *Questions of Travel*. This new book can only add substance to Miss Bishop's reputation. And that is a strange one. Her work has hardly been ignored; she has won just about every distinction and prize a poet can. But her poems are oddly unknown to the public, even that part of it that is supposed to be interested in poetry. And if obscurity is a general issue in the public's ignorance of poetry, it is not an issue here. Admired by critics, poets, and anyone genuinely interested in writing, her work is not easily labeled. Having no thesis, standing for no school of writing or thought, she is not the kind of poet who attracts public attention. This is partly due to a reticence in the writer herself, to the fact that she has lived in Brazil for the last decade, but mostly to the independence and quality of the poems themselves. Miss Bishop is not academic, beat, cooked, raw, formal, informal, metrical, syllabic, or what have you. She is a poet pure and simple who has perfect pitch. These new poems should be welcomed not only because they are so absolutely and obviously first rate, but because they are one of the few examples of lucidity left in the world.

The Canada-Brazil Connection

Miss Bishop comes from the north and, like a lot of northern people, she went south; but the title of her first book, *North & South*, tells us only part of the story. Its north is New York City, and its south Key West; yet the limits it suggests have wider boundaries, earlier and later counterparts: a more distant north, Canada, and a farther south, Brazil. And so, in the later poems, the earliest Canadian landscape is revived, and Brazil replaces Florida. That the two connections are similar we have no doubt; that they are different explains why a poem like "The Moose" — a late poem — restates and enriches several Bishop themes: a journey, a rediscovery, the magical appearance of an animal, the sudden awareness of a particular kind of consciousness. Though its setting is New Brunswick, one can cross the border quickly into Nova Scotia, where the poet grew up, an area with pastoral views, snow, and an insistence on *its* Anglo connection. There is in Miss Bishop's Nova Scotia something odd, as if the South Pole had been settled by an English middle class. It is exotic, and, at the same time — to use a word she uses so tellingly in "Filling Station" — "comfy."

One figure, not middle class, appears early, and he focuses a concern of Miss Bishop's throughout: the off-creature, the person not part of the comfortable world she found herself in — a comfortable world that had its attendant horrors. (One doesn't become a poet for nothing.) And that figure is the blacksmith, who plays such an important role in "In the Village." A counter to a world that has suddenly become impossible (the mother's scream, her madness are facts, feelings a child cannot take in, or, if taken in, cannot bear), he is interesting in himself: he makes something, horseshoes, and he works in the natural world, his ultimate clients being horses. A native and a craftsman — two good Bishop things to be — he is also an outsider, in the sense of being exotic to the child's world at the time. His peculiarity is to normalize the situation; that is, through his oddity, he makes things all right. And this sense of normality and oddness in tandem appears many times in the poems, notably in "Faustina, or Rock Roses," in "Anaphora," which ends with a beggar on a bench in a park, and in "Robinson Crusoe," a perfect subject: the homely and the fantastic are inherent in it. And since the poet is concerned with the domestic *in* the exotic (a primitive oil lamp, say, contrived from an old Milk of Magnesia bottle and an oil drum), some distancing is required. It is supplied by an obvious source, travel, but also by a more subtle one, perspective. If one is in Key West, New York takes on special aspects, and the same is true of Nova Scotia and Brazil. The imagination, of course, has its own cameras, and if any example were needed of what Miss Bishop can do without traveling six thousand miles, "The Monument" would be a good one. But her particular imagination is excited by new places, or old ones that become new by the switch in viewpoint great distances provide. "Questions of travel" are never resolved by literal answers, yet distance at least provides optical shifts and refreshments of thought.

The blacksmith is the key to a preoccupation and a method. He is a staple of the town's life; yet he is surrounded by flames and the clanking of iron, and performs miracles of fire and water. His magic derives from his storybook quality rather than his usefulness; yet they cannot quite be separated. Something peculiar — and awful — has just happened: the scream. Something odd — and restorative — is posed against it. Could it be that ordinariness hides within it what is magical and at the same time helpful — the mysterious leaven of a cure? This notion of "something shining through the leaves," this prince inside the frog, crops up often, and even in the choice of subject: it is to be found in the factories of "Varick Street," where there are "on certain floors / certain wonders"; in a hired seamstress who may be one of the Fates; in "Jerónimo's House," which is a "gray wasps' nest / of chewed-up paper / glued with spit," but also a "fairy palace" with "writing-paper / lines of light." "Twelfth Morning; or What You Will" is a particularly fine specimen of this kind of transcendence, neither prettifying nor sentimental. These poems — genuine acts of sympathy — skirt dangerous territory; it's hard to think of another poet who could so consistently use servants as subjects, or a squatter as the hero (or anti-hero) of a big poem, without slipping into snobbishness or whimsy.

Sympathy is a form of empathy, and a way of entering another world by way of transference. Where other poets change coats, Miss Bishop sheds skins. "The Riverman" presents us with a totally formed universe felt from the inside, as if knowledge had been transformed into feeling. And the lures of anthropology are present everywhere, because in primitive cultures phenomena are reduced and made clear; the combination of the practical and the occult, of the humdrum and the godlike, is taken for granted. And the poet searches for that fusion in places where it has never existed before — in subjects not considered to be the stuff of poetry ("Filling Station," "The Gentleman of Shalott," "Trouvée"), or in well-known themes made new ("The Sandpiper," "Florida"). Reading a new Elizabeth Bishop poem always evoked a special kind of anticipation; one was surprised to be led not only to a change of viewpoint but to a widening of perception in general. Who else would have connected a sandpiper and William Blake? Or Baudelaire and marimba music?

In these poems, the world works better through dissimilarity than through conformity. Moreover, the poems prove, in the precision of their descriptive details and the special nature of their perceptions, that the world isn't conforming by nature. If it consists of the odd, the wonderful, and the strange, we get to know them through their opposites: the banal, the commonplace, and the known. "The Bight," for instance, is "littered with old correspondences" — in both senses of the word: One corresponds via letters, and correspondences are metaphors. Thus, the unnoticed is teased into illumination. No better example could be mentioned than "News Story," in which a battlefield emerges from an ashtray. But since ash is a key notion here, there is, in spite of a feat of the imagination, a literal correspondence.

There is another way the common and the extraordinary are put into play: by viewing differences so clearly, the actuality of sameness is brought into doubt. How useful is a word as general as "bird," for instance, if "unseen hysterical" ones "rush up the scale / every time in a tantrum"? Tanagers are flashy, pelicans clown. It's odd how clearly these words bring to mind their creatures almost instantly. And what about a fish whose "eyes . . . were far larger than mine / but shallower"? No one before, I think, has revealed that fact: the largeness of fish eyes compared to human. *Certain* fish eyes, that is. As soon as we think of that image, we search for its accuracy in life, but also for its contradiction. We test an image by its reality, and by its reality we test the truthfulness of the writer. It is by what one chooses to see and *how* one chooses to see it that this underground proving takes place. Not only does the image lead us to comparisons and, therefore, to thought; but those eyes, in a second, put both the viewed and the viewer onto the scale.

By its accuracy, by its choice of what is to be put in and left out, Miss Bishop's world begins to take on moral properties. They involve manners in particular and judiciousness in general: there is no scope in these poems that is not measured by a true balancing of weights. And when enlargement occurs, say, in "Roosters," in the introduction of the figure of Saint Peter, we move from the chicken coop to the Vatican, to "old holy sculpture" where "a little cock is seen / carved on a dim column in the travertine," without jarring the imagination or shifting the tone. We move quickly, but with absolute grace, from nature to art, and from there to perceptions that have ethical force. And we believe the lines that explicitly make their points — "There is inescapable hope, the pivot" or "cock-a-doodles yet might bless / his dreadful rooster come to mean forgiveness" — because we have been led to them by a process as natural as it is artful. It is not difficult to lend one's assent, finally, to the statement "that 'Deny deny deny' / is not all the roosters cry."

The henhouse leads us by steps to the New Testament; the blacksmith is commonplace, but begins to take on mythical proportions. If "mythical" seems too broad a word, then "fictional illumination" might be more accurate. The point is: he is much more than he first appears to be. He is ordinary and mysterious, like a living room in which the furniture is dotted with antimacassars but in which there is also a compass lying on an end table. The living room in "First Death in Nova Scotia" is claustrophobic, but the poem ends with the image of a road. In these poems, we are always going someplace (one of the primary conditions for having a good time), and the images, figures, and characters travel, literally and by analogy. The blacksmith is repeated in other characters of a similar transcendence: in Faustina, in Cootchie, or — to get away from servants — even in the nice policewoman with blue eyes who gets off the tender in "Arrival at Santos." I suppose the apotheosis of all these figures is Manuelzhino, but not far behind him are the native in "The Riverman" and the fugitive in "The Burglar of Babylon."

Miss Bishop's cool eye for detail is also a dramatic lens, and her feeling for character is shaded but pronounced. Her little dramas — even the family that makes its greasy appearance in "Filling Station" — suggest the theater; in fact, they suggest that strange combination of talents I have mentioned elsewhere: those of the painter and of the playwright. I do not disparage Miss Bishop's infallible ear when I say she is closer to the painters than to the composers in most of the poems. Abstraction is not particularly interesting to this poet, and music is not famous for dealing with particulars. What can be handled, looked at, examined, walked around, reperceived, turned in different lights, hung up, or laid down — that is of much more interest.

Character is specific, at least what is interesting about it. General qualities, we have come to believe, obscure what could, under more penetrating examination, be separated out. Miss Bishop, a great disbeliever in the general, comes to character often, and most often through landscape, oddly, for it is moot whether the subject of these poems is places or people. On the face of it, place would seem the greater concern. Even titles as general as North & South and Geography Three are more modest than categorical. The tendency in the poems is not to generalize but to point to and specify. Character either possesses landscape or is possessed by it; the binoculars trained on "The Burglar of Babylon" reveal an entire slum. The traditional "character study" is absent. The attendant world, falling into place before and behind, gives the poems their interest, their power, and their wit. The personal has little to do with it. The subtitle of "The Bight," not the text of the poem itself, tells us it is the poet's birthday. As for wit, in "Filling Station," after saying "somebody waters the plant," Miss Bishop slyly adds, "Or oils it maybe." That's funny, but it also makes its own crazy, revealing comment about a world in which oilcan after oilcan spells out "Esso -so -so -so." (And isn't there a possible play here on "so-so"?) Once more we are in a double world, with a taboret, oilcans, wicker, doilies, and a rubber plant — a bourgeois nest in a gas station — a world tailor-made for the Bishop eye. And only the Bishop eye would have seen it.

In a line in "Manuelzhino" — "The world's worst gardener since Cain" — we have a small biblical echo reminiscent of the larger one in "Roosters." Part of Manuelzhino's charm is his inability to handle specifics — not a problem for his creator. Yet they have something in common. Account books turn out to be dream books, numbers wander slantwise across the page, impossible to add or subtract. And slantwise is the way this poet looks at character: from a side, obliquely. As if she had caught it in its natural habitat without its being aware. There is an assumption of character in creatures, in her moose, her fish, her roosters, the boy leading the horse in "Twelfth Morning," even the little toy horse of "Cirque d'Hiver." These are characters, at least of a sort, because insight is not this poet's thing; the world revealed is everything — its immediacy, its exactitude; but not necessarily its significance. The historical and the confessional rarely crop up in these poems. And one would have to search hard for psychological interest of the kind we have become used to: the inner life, neurotic conflict, Baudelaire's "wing of madness." Yet, by plainly presenting character, human, animal, or metaphysical (I refer to the sailor asleep on the top of the mast in "The Unbeliever," to the surprising number of poems in which some religious or biblical reference is invoked, the passing metaphor in "Manuelzhino," the extended one in "Roosters," the extraordinary "The Prodigal," and the grand design of "Complete Concordance") — by presenting character and giving it its eccentricities right up front at the footlights, by some miraculous process of foreshortening or enlargement, it makes a permanent imprint. Who would have thought of the Prodigal Son hiding pints of whiskey under the floorboards? But it makes perfect sense; it makes prodigality real. If one could think of a playwright fascinated by drama and incongruity but rather indifferent to personality, one might have something analogous: the whole surround intensely filled with single objects, and directed and lit by an expert.

This gift is partly a matter of clarity, of wakefulness, and it is informative, I think, to go over the poems and note how many of them begin at dawn or at daybreak: "Earliest morning, switching all the tracks"; "At six o'clock we were waiting for coffee"; "Paris, 7 A.M."; "At four o'clock / in the gun-metal blue dark / we hear the first cry of the first cock"; "Each day with so much ceremony / begins"; "Dawn an unsympathetic yellow"; and so on. And, conversely, sleep and dream are mentioned often, as if they were conditions opposed to wakefulness — conditions from which it is necessary to be roused. With the exception of "The Weed," dream in its literal sense is rarely invoked, but it runs a thread through the fabric of the poems — important in itself, but more important, I think, as a contending force: not the place where knowledge is to be found, but that state of being that precludes physical observation.

These characters and animations, joined by new servants and creatures in the later poems — the depressing seamstress in "House Guest," the headless chicken in "Trouvée" (another poem beginning at dawn) — have qualities in common: they are humorous and unappeasable, and, with the exception of the chicken, survivors. Manuelzhino, one feels, will outwit, in the end, the poet's landowner-friend, whose voice we hear throughout — will outwit her by persistence and inscrutability. What more effective armor is there than a shrewd dreaminess? What these portraits suggest is sympathy, kindness, judgment — behind them all, a set of moral standards is shifting gears — but neither intimacy nor love, though one line explicitly says, "I love you, I guess. . . ." That guess is as far as Miss Bishop goes; yet an understated love poem like "The Shampoo" moves one by its restraint, its minimal claims.

Strength and independence under the façade of weakness arouse the poet's interest. It is not a matter of dissimulation but of simultaneous perception of power and vulnerability, a doubleness manifested over and over again, culminating, perhaps, in "The Armadillo," where all the armor the animal possesses is not proof against fire. And also in the choice of servants as subjects, because a second character is always implicit: servants, after all, are hired and, in one way or another, play roles. They present the poet with a person *and* a persona observable at close range without the risk of presumption. Familiar but aloof, being around so often, they allow for the sureness of external fact and a tacit affection. And around each of them, a world, unlike that of the poet's but peculiarly congenial to her talents, materializes. One would not imagine, for instance, a Rio society hostess being the subject of an Elizabeth Bishop poem. Or even a nice middle-class Canadian lawyer.

This duality is also manifested in the canny manipulation of odd couplings of words, particularly adjectives and nouns, where a tension is set up between them that creates a kind of verbal magnetic field: "awful but cheerful," "the uncontrolled, traditional cries," "commerce and contemplation," "a grave green dust," "the blurred redbud," "the somnambulist brook," etc.

In fact, in spite of the clarity of vision, this two-faceted perception may be the key to what makes these poems work so beautifully, enhancing their surfaces with an electric undercurrent. A deep division — reserve at war with the congenial — undercuts the authority of the poems; more telling than geographical polarities is the implied disparity of "master" and "servant," the yoking together of such dissimilar notions as "awful" and "cheerful." A New England iron in the manner — or, I should say, in the *lack* of manner — in conflict with an easygoing willingness to accept life as it is, its perkiness and variety, is everywhere present. Critical judgment in these poems is more likely to suspend itself for what is harmless, or distant, or struggling, or moving in its persistence, than it is for the suffering or conflicts of peers. No drug addicts, drunks, or suicides make an appearance; no poets, academics, or white-collar workers are alluded to. Infused with a compassion that knows by instinct where true feeling ends and false sentiment begins, the poems are remarkably trustworthy on human terms, considering how descriptive they are generally taken to be. It is as if we discovered in a landscape painter not a psychologist but the surprising gift of portraiture. And when social protest becomes explicit, as it does in "Squatter's Children," or in "Going to the Bakery," there is no sudden tearing of fabric or gnashing of teeth. A style has been arrived at that allows for wider circles of emotion and more direct social comment than is at first apparent. This effect depends, partly, on the personification of objects and ideas: Love's a boy; the high-way leading from the country to the city is a clown with "long, long legs"; "The Man-Moth" is a case completely in point; the weed opens its mouth to say, "I grow / but to divide your heart again"; a cloud is equally articulate: "I am founded on marble pillars," it says; in "Quai d'Orléans," "light and nervous water hold / [an] interview"; an insect becomes a gladiator; a lighthouse stands "in black and white clerical dress" and "lives on his nerves"; the moon, in "Insomnia," "if deserted by the universe," would "tell it to go to hell"; in "Going to the Bakery," "the round cakes look about to faint — / each turns up a glazed white eye."

Part of the effect of lower depths and widening circles stems from a sub rosa notion steaming away under a grating: if Miss Bishop wanted to, she could tell us more, because we always feel that more slides have been taken than are going to be projected. It comes, too, from the existence of hardly noticeable actors. I have read "The Monument," for instance, many times; but it takes a close examination, or a very good memory, to realize that a conversation is going on while the poem proceeds, that an artist-prince is a minor character, that, in saying "Watch it closely" — the poem's three last words — movement, the choices of animate life, grow sketchily alive. And sometimes a figure, suddenly lit, will transform what has been, up to that point, merely descriptive. In "Little Exercise," the sleeper at the bottom of the rowboat is that figure. In "Love Lies Sleeping," the generalization of "queer cupids of all persons getting up" zooms in on an individual. He may be "one, or several," but still the effect is cinematic, a narrowing down that paradoxically allows the poem to expand in unexpected directions by a sudden infusion of emotion. Here are the last two stanzas of "Love Lies Sleeping":

> *for always to one, or several, morning comes,*
> *whose head has fallen over the edge of his bed,*
> > *whose face is turned*
> > *so that the image of*
>
> *the city grows down into his open eyes*
> *inverted and distorted. No. I mean*
> > *distorted and revealed,*
> > *if he sees it at all.*

Why is that last line so moving? It is so simple — a series of the most ordinary of monosyllables. It suggests death or sleep, but whatever it suggests separates the subject viewed from the viewer. *She* sees it, but the protagonist doesn't. And that is a true distance, and a lonely one, that the poems present to us without a word of protest — or caution — and without pointing a finger. One is brought up short in feeling more than a description of morning arriving in a city seems to warrant. It is ways such as these that the poems take in more territory than first meets the eye. Even a portrait as negative as the one in "House Guest" has a shimmer of feeling because the heart was wrung, even if the mind was irritated or the social sense outraged. And, again, there is a lifting up, a surprise, at the poem's conclusion — a "bony foot" on the treadle of the sewing machine, and we are in the presence, perhaps, of one of the three Fates, Clotho, that literal and figurative *spin*ster.

In "Under the Window: Ouro Preto," something more dazzling occurs, something new, a finer grasp of local character, of the razor-thin but most effective use of dialogue, the one-line label that brings to mind a person or an entire world. We get it in " 'Women.' *Women!*' " where the italicization speaks for itself; in " 'When my mother combs my hair it hurts' "; in that macho legend painted on the bumper of a new Mercedes truck, "HERE AM I FOR WHOM YOU HAVE BEEN WAITING"; or the line of the "gallant driver" of the wreck of a car with its "syphilitic nose," "NOT MUCH MONEY BUT IT IS AMUSING." That line might stand as a splendid epitaph for the writing of poetry in America. Wryness and true feeling are a lot to achieve when world-weariness and bathos could so easily have been offered in their place. And in a poem so steeped in local color, to rise to the extraordinary ending is a particular Bishop miracle:

> *Oil has seeped into*
> *the margins of the ditch of standing water*
>
> *and flashes or looks upward brokenly,*
> *like bits of mirror — no, more blue than that:*
> *like tatters of the* Morpho *butterfly.*

The poems, then, seem to me to explore emotions more profoundly than is usually acknowledged. They reject many alternatives — one need merely turn a page or two in *The Collected Poems* to come across the Bishop translation of Andrade's "Don't Kill Yourself, Carlos" to be startled. It's a marvelous poem, but the sudden rise in temperature produces a different kind of weather. Having been pigeonholed for so long as a cool customer, Miss Bishop is ladylike but tough; but also much warmer, much more involved in life, than a mere mapmaker or tour guide. If passion is missing from these poems — and I don't think it is — so is self-absorption. Their seeming casualness belies their extraordinary concentration — a concentration reminiscent of Emily Dickinson at her best. The discarded temptations of the printed Bishop canon have made it a small one, and its smallness has given rise too easily to the word "minor." What we find in these poems is elegance and withheld power. What else does "restraint" mean? One has to have something to restrain, and these poems, so easy to read, give up their secrets slowly. Shedding moral light, affection in these works extends itself more easily to the victor who has battled and won than to the loser who merely survives. Admiring action, Bishop's poems may conceal a fear of passivity in itself: the reduction of the status of the observer to that of the excluded. It would be hard to station the writer behind a movie camera in these poems, to say with assurance from just what angle the movie was being shot. The object is everything; the viewer, the viewer's position — except by inference — the merest assumption. Yet how remarkably consistent that lens is, how particularly keen the eye behind it! There is a great deal to be said for scope, but more to be said, I think, for the absolutely achieved. These poems strike me as ageless; there are no false starts, no fake endings. None of the provincial statements of youth, none of the enticements of facility are allowed to enter. Starting with "The Map," we are in the hands of an artist so secure in the knowledge of what makes and doesn't make a poem that a whole generation of poets — and remarkably different ones — has learned to know what a poem is through her practice. She has taught us without a shred of pedagogy to be wary of the hustling of emotions, of the false allurements of the grand. Rereading these poems, how utterly absent the specious is! There is no need to revise them for future editions, the way Auden revised, and Marianne Moore revised, and Robert Lowell revised. Nothing need be added, nothing taken away. They constitute a body of work in which the innovative and the traditional are bound into a single way of looking. From a poet's point of view, these poems are the ones, more than all her contemporaries', that seem to me most to reward rereading.

ELIZABETH BISHOP

The Long Voyage Home

In Elizabeth Bishop's *The Collected Prose*, a companion volume to *The Complete Poems*, of 1983, the contents are divided into two sections — "Memory: Places & People" and "Stories" — but the recalled and the imagined are unevenly represented. Because only four of the seventeen pieces could properly be called fiction, the work, as a whole, has the effect of a withheld autobiography. A "memory" may evoke an instant as low-keyed as the author's first day at school ("Primary Class") or a visit to a grocery store in Ouro Preto, Brazil, where she restored an eighteenth-century house ("To the Botequim & Back"). Yet the very simplicity of the subjects connects them to the poems — the ordinary, not having been noticed by anyone else, becomes exotic. Childhood, rarely referred to in the poems, strikes the deepest note; we are in the Proustian country of recapture. And even when the subject is not herself what fascinated Bishop in her stylish translation of "The Diary of 'Helena Morley,' " a Brazilian girl's journal written at the turn of the century, was the similarity of its experiences to her own. The introduction, reprinted here, is a model of how to relay information without being boring — a small classic, like the book it introduces.

The objects and scenes described in Bishop's work are illuminated by a mind and eye for which the anomalous held the key to normality and beauty, as if the everyday oddity were the key to every day. The lace-draped taboret in the poem "Filling Station" conjures up bourgeois niceties among the gasoline pumps. The delicate connection made between poverty and courtesy in the reminiscence "A Trip to Vigia" hinges on an unexpected anxiety: the exact moment in a Portuguese conversation when one switches from the formal to the familiar "you" — a change signaled by growing cordiality and the possibility of future relations. Intimacy too soon claimed may be rebuffed; warmth not soon enough expressed may lead to the fatally missed opportunity. And one might say that between those two poles of behavior the moral tone of Bishop's work is set. Equable but surprising, the viewpoint sheds light on the well known, even the typical: maps, fish, roosters, radio towers, gardeners — something caught in the corner of the eye and then looked at so directly, and under such bright lights, that, whatever it is, or was, we realize we have not seen it before.

As against romantic notions of poetry, Bishop's was a poetry of the sane imagination, and not easily reduced to a method. The term "magic realism," a phrase applied to the work of a group of painters in the nineteen-forties, might be relevant. Though no one ever knew quite what the phrase meant, everyone recognized the aptness of the designation. It was an attempt to describe that point where the accurate shades off into the mysterious. Bishop drew from primitive painting and from surrealism without actually imitating the loss of perspective typical of the first or the shock effects of the second. A rigorous syntax helped make two impulses — the childlike and the unexpected — one. The contrary had always been a nourishing source in the Protestant hymns she loved; they united the commonplace and the otherworldly, and were the words and music of her childhood. Yet she was an original, and had the air of having been born civilized, as at home at a Parisian dinner table as she was going up the Amazon in a canoe (that her companion was Aldous Huxley helped). A journalist — if one can use the word literally — with nothing, it seems, to confess, she was a master of the monumental closeup. Bishop fixed the look of a dogwood forever in "each petal burned, apparently, by a cigarette-butt"; a Bible illustration in "The branches of the date-palms look like files." That same gift is evident in the prose. Pursuing a motif until it unwinds, she lets go of a subject at precisely the right moment. In "Memories of Uncle Neddy" (an uncle on her mother's side) she describes the interior of a tinsmith's shop:

> There were blowtorches and a sort of miniature forge, little anvils, heavy sheets in all sizes, wooden mallets, boxes of stubby, gray-blue, flat-headed rivets and, best of all, solder. It came in thick silver rods, with a trade name stamped along them. What I liked best was to watch Uncle Neddy heat the end of a rod to the melting point and dribble it quickly to join a wide ribbon of tin and make a mug, sometimes a childsize mug, then solder on a strip already folded under on both sides in the folding machine for the handle. When they were cold, drops of solder that fell to the dirty floor could be picked up, pure silver, cool and heavy, and saved. Under the bench were piles of bright scraps of tin

with sharp edges, curved shapes, triangles, pieces with holes in them, as if they'd been cut from paper, and prettiest of all, thin tin shavings, curled up tight, like springs. Occasionally, Uncle Neddy would let me help him hold a stick of solder and dribble it around the bottom of a pail. This was thrilling, but oh, to be able to write one's name in it, in silver letters! As he worked, bent over, clipping, hammering, soldering, he chewed tobacco and spat long black spits under the bench. He was like a black snail, a rather quick but cautious snail, leaving a silvery, shiny trail of solder.

Uncle Neddy was the weak, sweet, drunken black sheep of the family. And irresistible to a child, especially one interested in the shape and color of objects, in the change effected by applied processes. One could change a rod of silver into one's name. In the end, one could turn landscapes, people, and feelings into words. *The Collected Prose* is the posthumous fulfillment of the childhood wish expressed in that paragraph. At last, the name is written in silver; at last, all the made works are put together, and the prose reminiscences are the closest we will get (short of a collected letters) to the true keepsakes of Bishop's life.

It was an odd life. She was born in Halifax, Nova Scotia, in 1911. Her father died when she was eight months old; her mother, stunned by the tragedy, went through a series of breakdowns and was committed to a mental hospital, where she remained for the rest of her life. Bishop, at five, was first cared for by her Canadian grandparents. Then, in a kindly meant gesture, her richer American grandparents took her in. The change from Nova Scotia to Worcester, Massachusetts, was confusing to the seven-year-old girl, who felt as if she had been "kidnapped." She found the less prosperous coastal farm more congenial than the upper-middle-class New England house. Life with the American Bishops ended in a series of chronic illnesses, one of which, asthma, was to be a lifelong affliction. (Bishop read Proust with a fellow-sufferer's interest.) She was rescued from the Worcester unhappiness by her Boston Aunt Maude (her mother's sister), summered in Nova Scotia until she was thirteen, and went on to Vassar, where she made an impression on her classmates.

Allegiance to the two branches of her family eventually widened into larger conflicts — between cities (Key West and New York, New York and San Francisco), countries (Canada and the United States), and, finally, continents (North and South America). In the prose as well as the poems, the sense of place is strong throughout, and though it is not always the same place, it figures both as a sustaining background and as a hoped-for scene of adventure, as if the prodigal son (the theme of a splendid poem) were to inhabit his two opposing locales at the same time. Most often, one has to go a great distance to discover what was truly close at hand — the theme of displaced experience eventually recovered is shared by works as dissimilar as "Robinson Crusoe" and "King Lear." It was very much a Bishop notion. A prodigal orphan crossing an international border, she could never be sure of the home ground itself. Her feeling for locale was based on a true displacement. It is no wonder that two usually opposed ideas — home and travel — took hold simultaneously, and merged. Where home *was* became not only a psychological matter but a "question of travel." *Questions of Travel* was the title of her second book and of a revealing poem that ends with the lines:

Continent, city, country, society:
the choice is never wide and never free.
And here, or there . . . No. Should we have stayed at home,
wherever that may be?

Her Biblical poem "1000 Illustrations and a Complete Con-cordance," where the yearning for another place becomes the longing for another time, concludes on the same note of pro-found wistfulness:

Open the heavy book. Why couldn't we have seen
this old Nativity while we were at it?
— the dark ajar, the rocks breaking with light,
an undisturbed, unbreathing flame,
colorless, sparkless, freely fed on straw,
and, lulled within, a family of pets
— and looked and looked our infant sight away.

The family she could never take for granted had assumed some of the aspects of mystery. "A family of pets" brings to mind the one moment of pure joy in "A Country Mouse," the story of her transition from Canada to the U.S.A. — the gift of three Golden Bantam hens from her paternal grand-father. Just as servants provided her with opportunities for meditations on character, so animals served to flesh out a catalogue of qualities that ranged from the despairing to the ennobling — from the armadillo fleeing the engulfing flames in "The Armadillo" (he is not armed against fire) to the gran-deur of the startling appearance of the moose in the poem of the same title. In between, we have almost every shade of experience, from the ironic but moving "Roosters" — St. Pe-

ter's appearance in the middle of the poem begins an exquisite counterpoint to the prevailing tone — through those com-
panions in loneliness, the curious seal in "At the Fishhouses"
and the quirky, mechanical horse in "Chemin de Fer" or that
saluted survivor "The Fish."

Because of the traumatic nature of her mother's illness,
sanity must have had a heightened meaning for Bishop, and
she investigates it both in prose ("Mercedes Hospital" and "In
the Village") and in poetry ("Faustina, or Rock Roses" and
"Visit to St. Elizabeth's"). She is drawn to the singular by
temperament, having been an outsider herself — just as she
is drawn to the primitive. Actually, what connects them is
the truth. The primitive is unaware of convention (in at least
our sense of it) and the eccentric has either bypassed or transcended it. With the exception of members of her immediate
family, the middle class makes few appearances in Bishop's
work. The question of where oddness ends and insanity begins has troubled not only Bishop, and her way of dealing
with it is to "visit" it, enhancing the role of the observer by
the expansion of a human connection. The role of the visitor
falls somewhere between the roles of the observer and the
traveler. By definition, a visitor comes to see someone. That
small human demand is important in Bishop, because it saved
her from the abstractions of geography and anthropology; there
is a sense, somewhere below the narrative level of the prose,
of the dispossessed, the loner retrieved. She kept looking for
a place to settle, but whether that was truly a matter of lo-
cation or of self-definition remains ambiguous. She did settle,
but until the last remove to Cambridge never permanently.
She had the glamour of the person familiar with distant places,
and the bravery attached to it. There was a domestic side to

her at the other end of the spectrum. Her true genius lay in the ease with which the humdrum and the fabulous were joined. There was always another country beckoning, another house, something to be seen in the curious, the phenomenal, the not-yet-looked-upon. Traditional enough to restore an architectural treasure, to have a clavichord made by Dolmesch (in Paris, in 1934), to write sestinas and villanelles, she was at the same time translating Jorge Drummond de Andrade and Octavio Paz and was herself considered a touchstone of "the modern" by other writers and critics.

In the nineteen-fifties, Bishop traveled to South America, became violently ill, recovered, and decided to stay. Her friendship with Lota Soares was the anchor of her decision to make Brazil her home for fifteen years. The cross-pollination of Halifax and Rio — or, more truly, their outlying towns, Great Village and Petropolis — proved fertile. Adult life in Brazil released the Canada of childhood because the nineteenth century was alive in both places and because maritime provinces and mountains preserve different but analogous aspects of nature. Privacy — Bishop's need for reticent disappearances, an enclosable world that was congenial but unfamiliar enough to arouse interest — was insured also. Those needs had led her to Key West in the first place. In Brazil, there was just the right blend of the familiar-foreign; the landscape and language were new; the Muse was refreshed. Bishop, never keen on talking about herself, found new subjects and interests. Strongly opposed to confessional poetry as a matter of principle, she found it offensive to her sense of propriety, and possibly threatening in risking disclosure of a personal life that she kept determinedly personal. That habit may have begun early, with her mother's mental illness. Sexual glimpses, intimate attachments of a personal nature — there are none. And I think proof of this discretion can be seen in how little we know of her adolescence from either the poems or the prose.

The heroine of the story "In Prison" describes the longed-for cell of her ultimate confinement with the same hungry, rhapsodic precision a New Yorker might use to decorate in fantasy an unobtainable apartment. There is something in it both of Kafka and of Chirico. The most original of all the stories seems to me "The Sea & Its Shore." Its central figure is a man hired to keep the beach clean, who picks up various papers on his pointed stick, and either burns them or takes them back to his hut at night, trying to piece the torn-up letters, discarded newspapers, thrown-away shopping lists, remnants of books, and personal memos into a coherent whole. A beachcomber and a drunk, he is also a scholar and a collector of sorts, and he could be a stand-in for the author herself, piecing the history of literature into a whole, and creating out of the random fragments of a world words that fit together. The hero of "The Sea & Its Shore" lights huge bonfires at night in the steel trash baskets provided by the municipality — a minimalist version of the burning of the library at Alexandria. It would be tempting to read "In Prison" and "The Sea & Its Shore" as parables of the writer, but something starchily priggish in the tone of the first and the quotes from the beachcomber's reading material in the second suggest an ironic undercurrent — wit rather than comedy. In both, the desirable and the repellent are equally strong. To be imprisoned is an odd ambition until one realizes that the fantasy of confinement masks another: to be acknowledged as the leader of the other prisoners. To withdraw from society is the story's hope, to be recognized within a society of the withdrawn its message. "In Prison" is, like "The Sea

& Its Shore," monastic and claustrophobic; its wished-for cell measures "twelve or fifteen feet by six feet wide"; the beach-comber's hut has neither windows nor doors. The sense of being closed in is menacing, possibly suffocating. Written within a year of each other, in the late thirties, they may have been related to intermittent attacks of asthma, an illness threatening enough at one point to have prompted Bishop to move from New York to San Francisco. Constraint in the stories derives from contrary impulses: the deciphering of words or their destruction in "The Sea & Its Shore," retreating from society and leading it in "In Prison."

Robert Giroux says, in an impeccable introduction to *The Collected Prose*, that "In the Village" has, since it first appeared in the pages of this magazine in 1954, been "generally acknowledged as a masterpiece." Rarely has a work so personal been able to generalize experience with such natural certainty. Both self-pity and irony have been washed from the palette, and what remains has the conviction we associate with reality but also with the folk tale and the fable. Each is believable in its own realm. Delicate but powerful, "In the Village" brings the realms together. Told in the first person, it is a true story of Bishop's childhood. Her mother's scream hangs over the landscape, and yet the story is marvellous in bringing the curative into play at almost the same time the reader is faced with pain. The clang of the blacksmith's hammer rises to drown out the mother's scream. Innocence confronts the nightmarish and the pastoral with the same steady look. The natural world — the child leading the cow to pasture — and the smithy's magic are set against the horrors of the disrupted house, where adults weep and tell lies, and the child is forbidden to know what she already half guesses. One of the hardest stories to write imaginable, its essence is the stuff of pathos, and yet there isn't a shred of sentimentality in it. Like the poems, it is spontaneous and perfect.

Bishop's reputed disinterestedness, by now a cliché, has been celebrated at the expense of the emotional impact of her writing, as if objectivity and feeling were permanently at odds. One of the great attractions of Bishop's work is their reconciliation, and people who do not understand how feeling is enhanced by restraint will never see it. I don't know a love poem more subtly breathtaking than "The Shampoo" or a poem on loss that states its case as quickly and as deeply as "One Art." The prose has the same immediacy as the poems and often their fineness of detail, but it lacks both the native sense of structure and the wideness of the cast net that make, say, the poem "First Death in Nova Scotia" more overwhelming than the story "Gwendolyn," although both are concerned with the same subject — the death of a young child in the poet's earliest years.

Bishop's diffidence is often confused with remoteness, and the implicit social comment of the work is rarely mentioned — poems like "Varick Street," "Squatter's Children," and "Pink Dog." The fanatical and the obsessed — those qualities that produce artists, madmen, and saints — attract her in "Mercedes Hospital," "Gregorio Valdes," and "The U.S.A. School of Writing," in the present volume. If servants are often the subjects of poems, they are never treated with condescension. Rather, Bishop's relation to them imposed more or less the same ratio of distance to intimacy she practiced with everyone — a distance whose farthest remove is the binocular view of the slums in the poem "The Burglar of Babylon."

It is a mark of the crosscurrents — and the difference —

between the prose and the poetry that it is almost impossible to discuss the prose without reference to the poems, whereas the poems stand on their own. But the prose provides hundreds of connecting threads to incidents, characters, and even phrases in the poems. The last sentence of "A Country Mouse," for instance — "Why am I a human being?" — is the very question asked in a major poem, "In the Waiting Room." Sometimes the prose style winds down — that is unfortunately true of a memoir of Marianne Moore — but, in general, Bishop is an instinctive storyteller, intuitively handling character and scene and indifferent to plot and action. Interested in the homely and the fantastic, she sought the attached connection everywhere both metaphorically and personally; that it could be missed — might never be truly found — was the emotional secret lying just below the unruffled surfaces of her poems. But her declared insights were broader. She knew that few people escape the circumscriptions of their personal history, or history itself, and this knowledge has never been more beautifully or forcefully stated than in the first stanza of "Anaphora":

> *Each day with so much ceremony*
> *begins, with birds, with bells,*
> *with whistles from a factory;*
> *such white-gold skies our eyes*
> *first open on, such brilliant walls*
> *that for a moment we wonder*
> *"Where is the music coming from, the energy?*
> *The day was meant for what ineffable creature*
> *we must have missed?" Oh promptly he*
> *appears and takes his earthly nature*
>   *instantly, instantly falls*

victim of long intrigue,
assuming memory and mortal
mortal fatigue.

Genius tries to pass itself off as less than it is — the strain, in ordinary life, is too great. But in Bishop's case it was difficult to disguise, once the work began to accumulate. Emotionally dependent, she was extraordinarily autonomous in her judgments, literary and otherwise. None of these conditions were real choices. They were simply unavoidable fates. Grounded in the basically middle-class values of her Canadian grandparents, Bishop was, as a writer, something startlingly different — a kind of Baudelaire without the bohemian trappings, too original and intelligent not to be slightly scared of herself. Because normality wasn't in the cards, there's a particular emphasis on it in the autobiographical pieces. A great many of the memories stress the little-girl commonplaces she shared with others, in spite of the oddness of her early life. But a certain disparity exists between the beauty of the writing and the service it's put to. It's as if Debussy were to tell us he studied piano just like everybody else, and then launch into a performance of the twenty-four Preludes.

In these final prose pieces, Bishop literally encompasses — a word appropriately geographical for her — everything congenial to her imagination, and leaves out of the circle, as the legs of a compass inscribe only the radius it has been set for, what it naturally cannot contain. What is left is full of curious stirrings and revelations but has one limitation: exactitude is everything, and what cannot be rendered exactly is not rendered at all.

A Thin, Curly Little Person

In an early letter to Pamela Hansford Johnson in *Selected Letters of Dylan Thomas*, Thomas explains his ideas about poetry. It is a letter from one aspiring young poet to another. Miss Johnson and Thomas had not yet met. Thomas was nineteen.

> Nearly all my images [come] from my solid and fluid world of flesh and blood. . . . To contrast a superficial beauty with a superficial ugliness, I do not contrast a tree with a pylon, or a bird with a weazel, but rather the human limbs with the human tripes. . . . Only by association is the refuse of the body more to be abhorred than the body itself. . . . All thoughts and actions emanate from the body. Every idea, intuitive or intellectual, can be imaged and translated in terms of the body, its flesh, skin, blood, sinews, veins, glands, organs, cells, or senses.

Here is Thomas on himself, at the same age, again writing to Miss Johnson:

Don't expect too much of me (it's conceit to suppose that you would); I'm an odd little person. Don't imagine the great jawed writer brooding over his latest masterpiece in the oak study, but a thin, curly little person, smoking too many cigarettes, with a crocked lung, and writing his vague verses in the back room of a provincial villa. . . . I am not a particular nuisance, and I smell quite nice. I look about fourteen, and I have a large, round nose; nature gave it to me, but fate, and a weak banister, broke it; in cold weather, it is sufficiently glossy to light up my room. When I am about on winter nights there is no need for the gas. Cough! cough! cough! my death is marching on. . . .

The difference in tone between Thomas theorizing about poetry and Thomas describing himself is not a difference in theme. A split between his notion of the body as a metaphor and the dim view he took of himself as a person always existed, and, as the years went by, it widened. What started out as a charming diffidence ended up as serious self-accusation. Like his feeling for Wales — often hated when he was there and longed for when he was not — his attitude toward the body pivoted ambiguously. Because he held the body in such awe, his own did not delight him. It was the only one he had. As a poet, Thomas was not interested in the institutions of the world and relied on an organic unity between himself and a landscape conceived in biological terms. More than most poets, he was, therefore, his own universe. What he was most committed to were the poems. He increasingly came to dislike not their subject but their source.

The split wasn't helped by two obvious stumbling blocks: a lack of money and a need for alcohol. Thomas's father was a schoolteacher, and the Welsh town of Swansea, where Thomas spent the first nineteen years of his life, was not opulent. Poverty became a really grim fact when Thomas married, fathered a family, and tried to settle into some sort of permanent home. The move to the Boat House at Laugharne, the place most associated with his life and work, was made in 1949, when he was thirty-four. In between Swansea and Laugharne, he lived in London, Hampshire, Wilshire, Cardiganshire, and Oxford. For a person rooted in a particular place for most of his life, a later lack of stability and need for money can be especially excruciating. Yet it would be impossible to say that Thomas drank because of outside pressure. Here he is at seventeen, a newspaper reporter on the *South Wales Evening Post* and an amateur actor playing in *Hay Fever:*

> Much of my time is taken up with rehearsals. Much is taken up with concerts, deaths, meetings and dinners. It's odd, but between all these I manage to become drunk at least four nights a week. . . . It's a Sunday morning; I've got a head like a windmill.

At eighteen:

> I have a villain of a headache, my eyes are two piss-holes in the sand, my tongue is fish-and-chip paper. . . . It is difficult to write, because the bending of the head hurts like fury. And my hand ain't what she was.

Thomas occasionally escaped from the condition of poverty, but never from the sense of it; alcohol became increasingly inescapable.

But the gulf between Thomas the poet and Thomas everything else — reporter, actor, novelist, film writer, playwright, lecturer, short-story writer — rather than being divisive was one of the signs of his hold on life. He knew from the beginning just what kind of poet he wanted to be and was.

> I have been writing since I was a very little boy, and have always been struggling with the same things, with the idea of poetry as a thing entirely removed from such accomplishments as "word-painting," and the setting down of delicate but usual emotions in a few, well-chosen words. . . . there is always the one right word: use it, despite its foul or merely ludicrous associations. . . . It is part of a poet's job to take a debauched and prostituted word, like the beautiful word, "blond," and to smooth away the lines of its dissipation, and to put it on the market again, fresh and virgin. . . . [The artist] is a law unto himself, and . . . has only one limitation, and that is the widest of all: the limitation of form. Poetry finds its own form; form should never be superimposed; the structure should rise out of the words and the expression of them. I do not want to express what other people have felt; I want to rip something away and show what they have never seen. . . .

Thomas, who could write almost anything, kept the idea and the practice of poetry sacrosanct. A natural light verse writer — the letters are full of enviable examples — he published none, wrote few occasional pieces, and the poems, though they decrease in quantity, show no falling off of pitch or intensity. Thomas remained whole as a poet without compromise, though he may have had to compromise almost everything else to do so. The letters reveal two essential facts: his most productive period as a poet came between the ages of sixteen and twenty; his absolute refusal to allow the journalist, entertainer, and comedian a foothold in the poems. The decision to separate the obvious talent from the chancy genius was made early.

The baneful self-absorption, the adolescent miseries of the early letters are commonplace. Their intelligence and humor are not. What is rare is the quality of the writing — almost everywhere so remarkable, so natural that, in the end, the letters, rather than Thomas's published prose, make his second greatest claim to genius after the poems. No biography can touch them in immediacy, and nowhere else is Thomas so mordantly funny. In the letters, a personality unfamiliar to the poems makes his most spectacular appearance: the childlike but knowledgeable observer-storyteller with an inexhaustible verbal imagination.

But two notes struck early, little chimes we try not to hear, become peals: guilt and self-disgust. The whining after money is real and terrible enough. At one point, Thomas had a wife and three children to support, no means of income, and the worry of a sick mother and a dying father living on a small pension. In spite of the cold fact of poverty, the apologies, the self-torturing explanations of why he did not get to where he was supposed to be, of why he did not do what he was supposed to do finally make a psychological point. Thomas was a dependent person who took on enormous responsibilities he couldn't handle, and there is a kind of childlike insistence on being taken care of which, when thwarted, threatens *him*. Self-defeat stamps the letters like a watermark. It is not finally avoidable as a symptom. Recognition was no problem; it came almost immediately. Money did not come with it. That Thomas should have had to mooch his way through film scripts and BBC broadcasts, to depend on patrons to scrape out a living, is deplorable but not unusual. Other poets were and are in the same boat. What is peculiar is not taking on and relinquishing responsibility, or playing out the role of the roaring boy drunk — two typical versions of how poets behave — but the inability to distinguish between the important claim and the peripheral one in a person who is able to distinguish so much. That may have been one way of safeguarding the poems, the most important claim of all. Often, the confusions of drink seem just as likely an explanation.

Drunkenness kept Thomas endlessly open to further apologies and deeper self-disgust. Extremely aware of sham and pretense, he took a very poor view of his own, and his ability to act was weakened by his insight. Emotionally a provincial, he was in every other sense extraordinarily worldly. In fact, part of the charm of his conversation and of these letters is the odd mixture of the adolescent and the wise man, of someone who seems to know exactly what the world is like, only to fall short of dealing with it, time after time. That defect eventually became a virtue to a large audience, which was awed by his accomplishment and allowed to feel compassionate about his personal life. The "Dylan Thomas legend" was built on that double standard. A spellbinder with a fine comic sense of life's absurdity, the mind and vocabulary of a great poet, and no official armor is a luring combination, especially when it is made so publicly available. Thomas kept literally giving himself away, counting on a reserve that was pure energy sparked by alcohol. Nothing is more attractive than ironic despair to an audience who can enjoy the irony without having to pay for the despair.

Thomas was supremely intelligent but not an intellectual, and abstract concepts get short shrift in the letters. That is not true of ideas, and he is fascinating on everything he touches with the exception of politics, on which he is simple-minded and murky. He is particularly good on the craft of poetry, the dissection of character, the random incident, and landscape. The virtuosity of Thomas's language is hypnotic — an extra dividend whenever he is talking about the arts, because his opinions are so sound. Even when there is a certain brash exaggeration in his judgments, they are never without truth. Here he is, for instance, on Wagner:

Wagner moves me, too, but much in the same way as the final spectacular scene in a pantomime. I won't deny, for a moment, that he's a great composer, but his greatness lies in girth rather than in depth; it lacks humour and subtlety; he creates everything for you in a vast Cecil de Mille way; his orchestration is a perpetual "close-up"; there is altogether too much showmanship and exhibitionism about him. His Valhalla is a very large and a very splendid place, but built in the style of a German baronial castle; the tapestries are too voluminous & highly coloured, there is too great a display of gold; while the gods that hold dominion over it are florid deities, puffed out with self-importance, wearing gaudy garments and angelic watch-chains. . . . he reminds me of a huge and overblown profiteer, wallowing in fineries, overexhibiting his monstrous paunch and purse, and drowning his ten-ton wife in a great orgy of jewels. Compare him to an aristocrat like Bach!

Thomas believed that "a born writer is born scrofulous; his career is an accident dictated by physical or circumstantial disabilities." The least attractive motif in the letters — the begging and wheedling — suggests a disability beyond necessity. Something determined or compulsive seems to have lurked behind his difficulties in handling money, in meeting

commitments, in living up to promises — perhaps some rebellion in which failure was a more viable criticism of the world
he found himself in than success. Thomas saw too much about
which there was nothing to do. Independence and success may
have meant giving up some version of childhood on which
the poems depended, and joining the enemy. Thomas never
did. He remained true to the person he basically was. Or
perhaps it was only by trying to make himself small that he
could fit his odd largeness into a world that had no particular
pigeonhole to accommodate his particular pigeon. Unlike all
poets, he was kind; but like most poets, he was nervous, thin-
skinned, and not adaptable.

Often in Thomas's conversation, one could hear a somewhat different tune than the words implied orchestrating them
somewhere off in the distance. The letters have something of
the same effect. Priceless as a record, wonderful to read, they
are, as a whole, finally chilling. We are enchanted. We are
charmed. It takes some time to realize that what we are being
charmed into is a nightmare — the history of a wildly gifted
and brilliant child, not only stumbling and bumbling his way
to the grave, but digging it for himself in the process.

JOHN BERRYMAN

DELMORE SCHWARTZ

ROBERT LOWELL

Good Poems, Sad Lives

Memoirs that commemorate the dead belong to a genre that requires more trust than any other; self-interested justification, the need for revenge, and the risk of exploitation are real. Worse is the possibility of subtle distortion; memoirs are not objective accounts but the case as presented by so-and-so. Eileen Simpson's *Poets in Their Youth* — which takes its title from Wordsworth's lines, "We poets in our youth begin in gladness; / But thereof comes in the end despondency and madness" — is a record of her life with John Berryman. (Married in 1942, separated in 1953, and divorced in 1956.) We never doubt the truth is being told of those dozen or so years of intimacy, but we never doubt, either, that the truth is partial.

Poets in Their Youth is not meant to be a home companion to the work of the many writers who appear in it: Berryman, Delmore Schwartz, Robert Lowell, Jean Stafford, and R.P.

Blackmur in major roles, and Randall Jarrell, Mark Van Doren, Allen Tate, and Robert Giroux in minor ones. Too for-
giving by far, sometimes naïve (the last word of the title is
meant to be taken seriously), and over-interpretative, it is also
discerning, often probing, and remarkably free of rancor considering what it must have been like to be married to John
Berryman, or the several versions of him that unfold before
us.

The book is loving, at long distance, and from the remove
of forty years, and sometimes uncomfortably so, as if everything had been got just a little too neatly in place in a long
process of understanding from which hostility has been filtered out. Eileen Simpson, who was Berryman's first wife
(there were three in all), is the author of a novel, *The Maze*,
and of *Reversals*, an account of her victorious struggle over
dyslexia. Now a psychiatric therapist as well as a writer, her
interpretations are long on Freud but far from inaccurate-
sounding, and, to get the worst over with first, if an occasional note of smugness creeps into the text, it is rarely more
than that smidgeon the healthy reserve for the sick and the
quick for the dead.

Berryman is given every latitude by Mrs. Simpson, who
understood him very well at close range. The question arises
of how far that understanding extends to others. A pantheon
of the Forties and Fifties is being spread before us and the
figures in it are complex and elusive. In Mrs. Simpson's version of the Berryman story (corroborated by others, and
sometimes by the poet's work as well), the key to the Berryman disaster is an unusually tangled family history. Hardly
news, but, in this case, notes macabre and genteel combine
to make the story eerie.

Martha Little, a schoolteacher, married Allyn Smith, "a Minnesotan from a Roman Catholic family." She was eighteen and he twenty-seven. Allyn Smith was John Berryman's real father. (If Berryman had taken his paternal name, the author of *The Dream Songs* would be known to us as "John Smith," reason enough, perhaps, to welcome any change.) A bank examiner, Smith gave up his job after a quarrel with a colleague and moved his family from Oklahoma to Florida in 1925. Smith, who went broke in the Florida real-estate boom, was as unsuccessful in love as he was in business. His wife fell "madly and irrevocably" in love with Bob Kerr, about to become a senator when she knew him, and later the governor of Oklahoma. The Kerr affair, if it was one, was not quite as irrevocable as Martha Smith believed. The Smiths lived in the same house as one John Angus Berryman and he became Martha Smith's lover at the very time Allyn Smith was financially ruined.

Allyn Smith committed suicide by gun, though his wife claimed he had died accidentally while cleaning it. (John Berryman was twelve at the time.) Her explanation was a denigrating one. "You see, Allyn was a weak man. He wouldn't have had the courage to kill himself." Martha Smith married John Angus Berryman as soon as the funeral baked meats had been whisked off the table, her two sons were adopted, and took their stepfather's name, a source of lifelong guilt for Berryman:

What I should have done, what I cannot forgive myself for not having done, was to take the name John Smith. This act of disloyalty I will never, never be able to repair. To "make a name" for myself. . . . Can you see how ambivalent my feelings are about this ambition?

Mrs. Simpson goes on: "In the years to come, I realized that the circumstances of [Martha's] first husband's death were part of an ever-changing myth she periodically reworked, usually in response to her older son's longing to be convinced that she was not responsible for driving his father to suicide." When disturbed by an emotional crisis he would want the ground gone over anew and "she would oblige, sometimes in person, sometimes in three- and four-page, single-spaced typewritten letters, with fresh inventions and interpretations."

Martha Berryman was not the villainess of some oversimplified Freudian primer. She was an "intelligent, energetic" woman who "introduced [John] to Faulkner and Hemingway" and "shared the same library books" with her older son, for whom she felt a " 'passionate devotion' " (*her* phrase) from which "both Allyn and Bob [John's younger brother] were excluded." She was attractive, coquettish, single-minded, and manipulative.

Along with his father's suicide, there was a second story John could never get straight. Berryman is speaking:

> One day, Daddy, agitated and depressed, took me on his back and swam far out in the Gulf of Clearwater, threatening to drown us both. Or so mother claimed. Another time he took Bob.

But neither John nor Bob could really remember the incident or disentangle — as is often the case with children — the story told from the real happening. Actually, the original story involved Bob only, switched later to John, and stayed permanently John's story from then on, in spite of the events being dubious and the characters confused. The difference between the hazy legend and the true facts remained forever veiled in ambiguity, and there were now two childhood "stories," each implicitly torturing and each impossible to pin down. If guilt was one of the draining forces in Berryman's life, obsessive doubt was another. "By insisting on a divorce when her husband was frantic with worry, had she not pushed him to that last, desperate act?"

All his life, Berryman seesawed between two versions of the truth and two feelings about it: sympathy for his mother — wasn't she entitled to some happiness, too? — and mourning (and shame) for his real father. "How could he sympathize with a mother who might have driven his father to insanity and suicide by her insensitivity?"

When Berryman returned from England, where he had attended Cambridge on a fellowship, his mother was working in an advertising firm. Wanting to appear young, she pretended her sons were her brothers, without realizing how damaging an effect this would have on John. This patent lie increased his doubts about the Clearwater swimming incident and Allyn's suicide.

In the bitter quarrels with his mother he had weapons of defense "more damaging to himself than to her: the threat of suicide, and episodes of fainting." Berryman was diagnosed as an epileptic suffering from attacks of petit mal (an incorrect diagnosis in Mrs. Simpson's opinion), and though he was never convulsive, his seizures sound more like grand mal in their ultimate effect: "he would remain in a semicomatose state for hours." As for suicide, his trick was to walk (particularly when drunk) on terrace walls or high ledges in a balancing act that terrified his mother and, later, his wife. Mrs. Simpson is particularly acute when she changes a first opinion: Berryman wasn't *playing* the suicide; suicide was a premonition and a threat to him from the beginning. His life was a long postponement of his taking it, an act rehearsed, abandoned, and revived, as harrowing in its compulsiveness, duration, and final achievement as the suicides of Sylvia Plath and Anne Sexton.

Because his mother's ambitions for him were special, John Berryman attended South Kent School (which he hated), played the role of the macho-jock, belonged to a fraternity, and excelled at sports. He was a very proper schoolboy wandering around in the American dream. But there was another Berryman slow to emerge and slow to develop. Mother-dominated, Berryman seemed always to need a male figure who would serve both as a friend and as a mentor, someone who could fit into the pattern of an older, wiser guide, an intellectual but also emotional tie that had to have, at its roots, a shared interest in poetry, the one steady reference point in the whirling series of transformations.

He was either lucky in his choices or had a good eye for quality. Bhain Campbell at Wayne was brilliant and handsome — though here there was a romantic overcast to the relationship that distinguished it from those before and after. Campbell's tragic death from cancer affected Berryman deeply. Campbell followed Mark Van Doren at Columbia, and was succeeded by Delmore Schwartz at Harvard and R.P. Blackmur at Princeton.

Berryman pivoted on the roles of student and teacher, and Mrs. Simpson describes the necessary preconditons for being Berryman's wife:

The combination of near-ignorance (no wrong-headed notions to be dislodged), eagerness to learn (from what better teacher?), an exalted view of his craft and the promise of devotion.

A good pair of ankles helped.

A *déjà vu* familiarity attaches to certain portions of Mrs. Simpson's book because her characters have turned the same material into biographical pieces of their own, thinly disguised fiction, or poetry. Does anyone need to be told that the sixth chapter of the book, "Damariscotta Mills: Jean and Cal," uses much of the same material Jean Stafford worked into a lethal group portrait in "An Influx of Poets," a story published in the November 6, 1978, issue of *The New Yorker?* That the setting of Robert Lowell's "The Mills of the Kavanaughs" has the same background? Or that John Berryman's story "The Lovers" is a disguised (but emotionally accurate) description of the situation his father, mother, her lover, and her son found themselves in? More factually described in the present book, it is the same story.

Poets in Their Youth begins with a dramatically telling scene, Mrs. Simpson's first meeting with Delmore Schwartz, the only Cambridge friend Berryman could claim after a year of teaching at Harvard, and it is a good scene because it brings past histories into play, is revealing in the present, and holds the seeds of future catastrophes. The portrait of Schwartz is cleanly sketched:

Seen close to, Delmore had a big head, made bigger by abundant, wavy brown hair. He had high wide Tartar cheekbones and the full, beautifully shaped mouth of a classical Greek statue.

His face was divided into two parts, as if by a carelessly drawn line, beginning with a diagonal scar on his brow, running along the crest of his broad nose and ending in a cleft in his chin. . . . When he smiled, he smiled broadly, exposing a front tooth that looked as if it might have been injured in a child's game.

The place was New York, the time February 1942, the Second World War was in progress. As soon as the trio were seated in a restaurant, Delmore, who had been easy and charming, became suddenly sullen and tense and began looking around nervously. Finally he asked Eileen to change seats with him: wary and distrustful, he had to have his back to the wall.

During the dinner, poetry, as always, was discussed, and Mrs. Simpson makes a cogent observation:

If Eliot was [Delmore's] hero, in much the way Yeats was John's, there was the great difference that Delmore was not reverential the way John was.

The inability to see things except as absolute and sacred disallowed for a certain amount of perspective in Berryman — not humor; he could be very witty indeed — but balance, literal and figurative. When he loved, he loved completely, when he worshiped, his was the only God. This need to be a communicant always at some adored shrine sprang from innocence as well as virtue, in their profoundest senses, and also from a need, most visible in Catholics, to be at the service of some great thing. It was admirable but also juvenile as a day-to-day, workable view of life. There was something perverse about it as well, as if someone who knew the way of the world were to set standards by which it would always fail. Berryman applied these standards even more strictly to himself, so that there was little room for grace, maneuvering, and flexibility.

The high value set on gossip by the Tates, Jean Stafford, and Delmore Schwartz made him uncomfortable, and the lie (shades of his mother's equivocation) was, for him, an ethical horror. There was some reason to remain morally alert; Schwartz, at the same dinner, gave Mrs. Simpson the impression that the editors of *Partisan Review* (Philip Rahv, Dwight Macdonald, and William Phillips) were "a cross between rabbinical scholars and bookies."

A great deal of Berryman's diffidence was nervous fear:

> I realized that the nervousness had a complex source. It was as dangerous to have one's work recognized as it was to have it ignored.

Here, Mrs. Simpson seems to me to be on the edge of a truth while somehow missing it. It wasn't a question of the *work* being recognized — something Berryman *always* wanted — but of the *self*. Recognition of the work makes its creator no longer anonymous. And Berryman was caught between a desire for fame, which brings with it exemptions, and a wish for anonymity, which doesn't require them. Recognition — as Schwartz was the first to find out — increases not only the demands of the audience but the demands on the self.

Delmore Schwartz's career set the tone for the poets of the Forties. When his inaccurate translation of Rimbaud's *Une Saison en enfer* was lambasted by the critics,

The criticisms . . . made him feel as humiliated as a schoolboy. Worse than ridicule, however, was the terrible anxiety that the attacks were a sign that he was falling out of favor: *Was this the first step on the downward slide?*

The italics are Mrs. Simpson's but they could well be mine. An implicit notion crops up in her last two lines: the poet as careerist being almost as important as the poet as writer. "The first step in the downward slide" would be, to a poet, a lessening in the value of his work in his own eyes. The phrase "a sign that he was falling out of favor" could have been written by an Elizabethan poet in regard to his patron, a Renaissance court composer in reference to his king, or by any writer born after 1850 who found himself at the mercy of a reigning literary power-clique.

Schwartz's fears were well founded. He had been the *Wunderkind* ever since the publication of *In Dreams Begin Responsibilities* when he was twenty-five. The prince hoisted to the top of the hill to survey his domain was not allowed to stay there for long. Like Greek kings, poets raised too high are in for a fall, especially if the hoisting up takes place when they are young. And Schwartz's case was further complicated. To be a bookmaker and a thoroughbred at the same time is an impossible task but one Schwartz attempted. He learned what it is to fall out of favor with the ruling party, of which he had once been a charter member. But his self-doubt and increasingly threatening behavior worked hand in hand to make matters worse: it was difficult for him to work and hard for others to sympathize, for long, with his plight.

Schwartz's swift descent set no patterns except that of muddled eccentricity (masking a disease) and increasing es-

187

trangement. Berryman had to wait for years for the recognition Schwartz had acquired early, and Lowell, also hailed early in his career, was hobbled by being a manic-depressive (like Roethke and Jarrell), never knowing when the next attack would strike. What is almost impossible to take in is the extraordinary work produced by Berryman and Lowell in the face of so much personal misfortune. They managed, no matter, to change the face of American poetry as radically as had Williams and Stevens, and though Mrs. Simpson is very good on personal matters, there is, aside from a few anecdotal connections between the life and the work, little sense of the enterprise to which these men were dedicated.

Poetry could, understandably, seem life-threatening to anyone living with somebody obsessed by it, particularly if that person were suicidal to any degree. The ratio of obsession to suicide is high. In this case, the assumption would have been incorrect. It was Berryman's obsessive nature and not what he was obsessed by where the danger lay. Alcohol, compulsive womanizing, and balancing himself on heights — what Mrs. Simpson refers to as "a high-wire act" — turned out to be more dangerous. Poetry could seem like a destructive force if one took the lives of Dylan Thomas, Theodore Roethke, Robert Lowell, John Berryman, Sylvia Plath, Anne Sexton, and Randall Jarrell as categorical examples. Mrs. Simpson doesn't think so. We find, in a passage near the end of her book, what I suspect (aside from setting the record down on paper) is her real point in writing it:

Many — I, too, at moments — blamed the suicide on John's having been a poet. The litany of suicides among poets is long.

After a while I began to feel that I'd missed the obvious. It was the poetry that had kept him alive. His father had committed suicide at forty. With as much reason, and with a similar psychic makeup, John had been tempted more than once to follow his father's example. That he lived seventeen years longer than John Allyn Smith, that he died a "veteran of life," was thanks to his gift. It had not been the hand coaxing him down from the railing that had brought him back each time, . . . but the certainty that there were all those poems still to be written.

It is a point hard to remember because the constant worry about "reputation," the endless concern of where one stood on the scale of "greatness," the scrimmage for renown finally begins to sound as competitive as jockeys talking about horses or movie studios ranking actors. In fact, the star mentality crops up all over the place; the authors talk about each other as if they were baseball players or movie stars forever courting "fame." This quest for rank is devastating, not only because it reverses the values to which each of these men were truly dedicated but because it repeats the wish the parents had for the child. Poetry, after all, was not the primary concern of either Rose Schwartz, Delmore's mother, or Martha Smith Berryman. Moreover, there's something pathetic about so frantic a struggle in so small a pond. Its false values infect even the author of this book, who can say, immediately after the phrase "first-rate poet,"

I was so sure he would one day be famous.

Devoted to the hard work of poetry, obsessive in their dedication, in their personal lives and ambitions Schwartz and Berryman could no more escape the values of their culture than a shopgirl, no matter how much they paid lip service to debunking those values or how much their work was an implicit or explicit attack on the culture's assumptions. The smaller the world the fiercer the competition — for money, praise, fame, repute.

The suffering this caused was obvious — not only was there never enough to go round, but, being extraordinarily intelligent, they kept seeing, avoiding, and falling into the trap. To read of Berryman's dogged efforts to get a job, of his trudging around Connecticut as an encyclopedia salesman, is painful. But the lack of reality in his view of the nature of his dedication and its possible rewards is painful, too. A refusal to be adult on the world's terms may be a necessary link to childhood and the secret spring for whatever work lay underhand, but its cost in sanity and health was terrifying. Mrs. Simpson is protective of her cast, but sometimes one feels one has opened a book of monsters, pigeonholing the competition for their convenience, grading this one and that with little understanding or charity. The thin-skinned, after a few drinks, take out after the thin-skinned. The poets in Mrs. Simpson's book are witty, brilliant, talents or even geniuses, but they are also sick, frightened, unkind, and, sometimes, ugly.

Blackmur was as complicated as Schwartz or Berryman. Born on the wrong side of the tracks, perpetually ashamed of his mother's having run a boarding house for students in Cambridge, Massachusetts, when he was a child (a fate he shared with Jean Stafford, whose Colorado childhood was similarly blighted), his father unmentionable (described here as an "unemployed layabout"), Blackmur played some combination of *le bourgeois gentilhomme* and the English squire at Princeton, savoring his way through the streets, treating the

Berrymans to a display of which butcher and which green-grocer was *the* one to go to, even though Berryman was heavily in debt and had only a four-month appointment. Blackmur's snobbery wasn't mean-spirited — he wanted others to share his vision of the good life, one he'd struggled hard to attain. He had got to Harvard and then to Princeton the hard way: through brilliance, work, and wit.

An unhappy man, with the stiff exterior of a bank executive, he had something of the quality of a Puritan who gets wildly drunk on Saturday night but is found firmly in place in church on Sunday morning. He took a childlike delight in life, loved to dance, and when drunk could easily make one forget that he set the intellectual climate of a generation. His intelligence (like Berryman's) was extraordinary, his self-taught erudition virtually unbelievable, his ability to see the connection between anything and everything wonderfully enriching and imaginative. His marriage was a dreadful black comedy, a manageable bargain, painfully endured, until his wife, a painter, finally walked out on him after twenty years of incompatibility. (There is, among the major characters of *Poets in Their Youth*, no happy marriage.)

The feeling of "something missed" — a sort of "Beast in the Jungle" aura — surrounds Blackmur as well as Berryman the more we see of them in *Poets in Their Youth*. They had many things in common (how many people could they talk to on the level on which they talked to each other? for one) and one special thing: each was engaged in a lifelong project he would never finish: Blackmur's book on Henry Adams and Berryman's work on a definitive text of *King Lear*.

The portraits of Jean Stafford and Robert Lowell are not as successful as those of Schwartz or Blackmur, possibly because they are fixed in a particular place, at a particular time, two weeks in the summer of 1946 in Maine. We never see them again at any length in another setting. Yet Mrs. Simpson's is the only account I've ever read in which Lowell's charm and humor as a young man come through. The Stafford-Lowell marriage was about to break up at the end of the same summer and there is already more than a hint of a growing drinking problem in Stafford, and a strange inner dissatisfaction in Lowell. They appear as two enormously gifted but strange undergraduates with Stafford's "black tongue" her one antidote, other than "booze," for a deepening depression.

The chapter devoted to the Lowells is the most self-contained chapter in the book, and the events in it occur two years after the publication of *Boston Adventure* and just before the appearance of *Lord Weary's Castle*. The bitterness of the Lowell-Stafford divorce, Stafford's subsequent stay at Payne Whitney, and Lowell's mental breakdowns are all in the future.

The lives of poets being, in this century, so dismal has led to the notion, commonly held, that poetry is somehow to blame. Mrs. Simpson, having no axe to grind, merely presents what happened, as she saw it and lived it. But something more needs to be said. The truth is that there are hundreds of thousands of clinically depressed people in the United States, uncountable numbers of manic-depressives, alarming increases in the incidence of paranoia, and thousands and thousands of suicides. They do not leave behind works like *The Dream Songs* or *Losses* or *Life Studies* or *Boston Adventure* or *The Double Agent*.

Whatever Is Moving

Because he has been ill, on and off, for many years, James Schuyler doesn't give poetry readings, attend literary conferences, or direct writers' workshops — and that is why one of the most original poets in America is known, so far, only to a small audience. He is a poet of the immediate: of views out of train and restaurant windows, of lawns and plants, of upstate New York and New York City. He is interested in love and painting, and old buildings and nature, and one can say things that simple about him because he is not a poet of great ideas, of grand gestures, or of psychological insight (except in passing). In *The Morning of the Poem*, he has written a sixty-page poem (the one from which the book takes its title) as if on a dare — a dare because he could be mistaken for a miniaturist embarking on the *Iliad* — and the miracle is that it is rarely boring. Schuyler has no obvious eccentricities of manner and writes in a mode familiar to many poets, yet what would ordinarily be a difference in degree becomes a difference in kind. The narrow-gauge railroad track takes care of the style ("Write skinny poems," he advises Frank in "Dining Out with Doug and Frank"), and his subject matter, ostensible and real, is the flux of everyday life. But what are merely grocery lists in other hands are transformed into sacred objects in his. By writing so well, he justifies a subject and a method — this-is-my-life, and I'm-telling-it-like-it-is. It is no secret by now that, taken in tandem, they can be one of the great gifts to tedium devised by the human mind. Though Schuyler belongs to a convention, he lets us know what it is by transcending it.

His world comes alive through precision of detail, a trait he shares with the late Elizabeth Bishop, and that precision is tutored by, and is at the service of, the immediate surround. Schuyler trusts immediacy itself to bring to light — through memory and association — experiences that warrant an intensity not justified by mere physical surroundings, often the jumping-off place from which a poem begins. A chronicler of the haphazard, Schuyler depends on the literal aspects of the actual for inspiration: what particular birds alight on a weekend in the country, the real buildings along the route on a walk in the city. Faithful to the scene, fidelity takes its cue from whatever is presented. His work is a poetry of chance sparked by the spontaneous encounter and nourished on the luckily given, and it is not a poetry fixed on the individual line. The fleeting moment is arrested in the very process of movement, and the reader's eye follows the thrust of the syntax down the page as it presses forward. The general effect is fluid, even rapid. Schuyler's randomness (and possibly the ongoing speed of his voice) are in conflict

with a love of the stable, the familiar, and the domestic.
When the ordinarily unnoticed gets down on paper, it can be
something as trivial and flat as

> . . . *To get up*
> *to this morning view*
> *and eat poached eggs*
> *and extra toast with*
> *Tiptree Gooseberry Preserve*
> *(green) — and coffee,*
> *milk, no sugar. . . .*

More often, the animate and the inanimate illuminate
each other in a moment of true perception:

> *The Istrian stone with the silver-pink cast to*
> *it of George Arends that*
> *After a rainstorm enflames itself: no: that's*
> *the bricks (Istrian*
> *Stone and bricks contrasted) that become petals*
> *of roses, blossoming*
> *Stone. Black gondolas glide by, the sure-footed*
> *gondoliers bending and*
> *Leaning on their poles, wearing green velvet*
> *slippers. On Diaghilev's*
> *Tomb a French count left his calling*
> *card: more suitable*
> *Than withering flowers. I left only a glance*
> *and a thought.*
> *But Europe — split, twisted, shivering-leaved*
> *olive trees,*

Grapevines strung high in swags between
poplar trees — Europe isn't
Home. . . .

The scrupulous observation of the minute fact can lead to inconsequentiality: a poetry of trade names can always be said to be accurate. Schuyler is not completely out of the woods in this regard: his freshness depends in part on being childlike, and the childlike can quickly descend to childishness and sometimes silliness. To be childlike is engaging, except when it is not appropriate. Certain relationships, for instance, remain superficial: very little of the person Schuyler refers to as "the most important in my life" comes through on paper — an ex-lover, married, who left him and gave no reason for doing so. Of this person, we get something of the body but little of the mind. What is enigmatic to Schuyler is cryptic to the reader. This shadowiness may be a matter of tact or it may spring from a habit of reference: Schuyler deals only with people who are real, people you can look up in a phone book. If John Ashbery is around, or Schuyler is staying with Jane and Joe Hazen in Water Mill, their names appear undisguised. And perhaps this lover, though real, is touched by an ideality that renders him ultimately unnameable (though he appears, to us, as "Bob"). Because of a compulsion to spell out the facts, the literal truth is the ethical touchstone of the poems, which are, by the same token, descriptive rather than metaphorical. This literalness is not an incapacity to dramatize but a singular and childlike trust in truthfulness. What could be taken as a failure of the imagination is, rather, a belief in a kind of magic: if even one fact or name were faked, the apparatus on which the poems depend — the connection between the naming of things and the reality of the world — might be in danger of collapsing.

As a whole, the poems are less contemplative meditations than attempts to snare the source of action — emotion and thought are susceptible to whatever is moving, usually within a small compass. Schuyler's fondness for ferryboats (which move but do not go very far) produces a small elegy for New York City's ferries in the middle of "Dining Out with Doug and Frank," a deceptively simple poem because it is doing many things at once (one of which is to keep going). When Schuyler, a born storyteller, free-associates, what we usually get instead of images or metaphorical connections is a story — a memory relevant in some special way to the matter in hand. In "Dining Out," for instance, Doug and Frank are "young and beautiful"; their relationship is the theme, however submerged, for a set of variations, one being the story of Schuyler and Bill Aalto, his "first lover." And just as sitting at a bar and restaurant on the West Side of New York brings to mind the romantic notion of moonlit rides on Hudson ferryboats, so the same setting makes Schuyler aware of the sado-masochistic bars along the riverfront, which, in turn, activate ideas of violence, sex, and death. And this "liebestod" notion reminds Schuyler of the actual deaths of Peter Kemeny, a friend who committed suicide by throwing himself in front of a subway train, and Aalto, who died of cancer. In between, almost by happenstance, there is the story of Billy Nichols, who went bird-watching in Central Park, and had his head beaten in because someone wanted his binoculars. Covered with blood, Nichols made it to Fifth Avenue. Several taxis refused to pick him up. At Roosevelt Hospital he waited for hours before he received medical attention. We are told these facts and we believe them because their truth depends less on a roman-à-clef knowledge of the figures involved than on Schuyler's veracity of detail elsewhere — his description, for instance, of the salvaged and revitalized interior of McFeely's Bar at the Terminal Hotel, the setting of "Dining Out":

> *. . . The ceiling is*
> *florid glass, like the cabbage-rose*
> *runners in the grand old hotels*
> *at Saratoga: when were they built?*
> *The bar is thick and long and*
> *sinuous, virile. Mirrors: are*
> *the decorations on them cut*
> *or etched? I do remember that*
> *above the men's room door the*
> *word Toilet is etched*
> *on a transom. Beautiful lettering,*
> *but nothing to what lurks*
> *within: the three most*
> *splendid urinals I've ever*
> *seen. Like Roman steles. . . .*

Throughout, a caressing attention to minutiae is coupled with a gift for swift narrative; Schuyler can sketch in a whole story in one quick breath. A panorama of events races by as we take in the complicated ingredients of "Dining Out with Doug and Frank": a tribute to friendship, an elegy for New York (or a time and view of it), the stories of three deaths ("Terminal Hotel" exudes its own punning, mortuary air), and the ongoing tale of the narrator himself, who has moved to 74th and Broadway but has not yet ventured into Central Park (the Billy Nichols episode, the only one of outer-directed violence, acts as a warning). In "Dining Out with Doug and Frank," parentheses perform their usual grammatical function, but they also bear the burden of a unique task: they become enclosures, safety pockets of memory, each of which is a burial ground: there lies Bill Aalto, and there Peter Kemeny, and there Billy Nichols. These memorial parentheses are sad, of course, being the archaeological debris of time and age, but the dig as a whole is successful: the poem itself is buoyant, exuberant, and full of life and charm.

The nostalgic ferry rides reveal something else: though Ischia and Capri and various Italian towns are mentioned, Schuyler's world is one in which intimacy — and safety — are more important than knowledge. The familiar routes of a ferry are now, it seems, the only form of travel he would enjoy. The known and the loved, renewing themselves, are more salutary than the exotic and the new. The swinging alacrity, the no-nonsense yet feeling attributes of "Dining Out with Doug and Frank" make it remarkable — these stories, elegies, relationships simply happen on the page, as if by a turn of conversation. That is Schuyler's gift: a magical fusion of romance and fact, the enchanting, telling, but offhand reference. He is singular in his effervescence, in his verbal excitement, even when he is dealing, as he so often is, with the seemingly small scale, or the potentially tragic. The overall tone can include them both. "The Payne Whitney Poems" — the second section of the book — which deal with Schuyler's stay in a mental hospital, are a triumph of will over circumstance, and if they sometimes have the air of poems one forced oneself to write, still they prove — again —

that Schuyler can be gorgeous without being pretentious, simple without being stupid, and can move from the comic-strip laconic to the grandiloquent with scarcely a tremor.

He shares with Elizabeth Bishop (once more) the knack of making the lyrical dramatic. Schuyler's theatrical effects come from surprise — a form of suspense, however rarefied. We are kept waiting, in these poems, not for the withheld but for the next turn of the screw, one we could not imagine for ourselves. Some slight distortion of vision (affording even greater clarity, the way certain drugs are supposed to make visible the ordinarily invisible) lends a hand to the effect, the distortions being close enough to rational thought to keep the reader engaged. At the heart of this is a peculiar blend of the cosmopolitan and the native, the innocent and the worldly, perfect for poems but uncomfortable, perhaps, in life, where the secret of dealing with feelings so widely spaced apart is to keep them separate. In Schuyler's work, these double feelings sometimes merge into a single focus, or one is used to illustrate the other. The voice one hears is that of an informed innocent. A frame of reference, at odds with innocence but flavoring it, underlies and intensifies perception, giving it an undercurrent and a reality it might not otherwise have — as if a child were to delight us with naïve observations only to reveal a moment later, that he is the author of a comedy of manners. The poems are energized by an alternating current that flows between natural utterance and civilized speech. In the very best ones, what might have been incongruous voices are forged into a single tone.

Incongruity of another kind works for Schuyler in phrases like "Silver day / how shall I polish you?" or "water so cold it's / like plunging into a case of knives," where the natural

and the domestic play into each other's hands. But incongruity isn't necessary when Schuyler hits on a descriptive notion
that is inherently emotional: ". . . I turned / my back and
this small green world went shadowless." Because, one day,
we will cast no shadow? Schuyler doesn't say that; he doesn't
even hint at it. He simply darkens the scene, and drama,
feeling, and prior knowledge come suddenly into being.

Schuyler's command of visual effects, particularly in
poems that rarely resort to metaphor, is evident everywhere.
What might not be noticed so readily is the subtlety of his
ear. Purely a matter of talent, this innate musicality is without strain or pressure. And the sounds are particularly magical when the range is small. His feeling for duration and
stress is instinctive. In "Song," with its exquisite beginning,
he is as delicate as Haydn:

> *The light lies layered in the leaves.*
> *Trees, and trees, more trees.*
> *A cloud boy brings the evening paper:*
> The Evening Sun. *It sets.*

Or, in "Growing Dark":

> *The grass shakes.*
> *Smoke streaks, no,*
> *cloud strokes,*
> *The dogs are fed.*
> *Their licenses*
> *clank on pottery.*

What we are listening to — we think — in most of the
poems is natural speech filtered through an imagination that

allows the canvas and the score equal power. Just as in the theater dialogue is not conversation but must sound like it, so in Schuyler's poems the "poetic" effects seem as natural as breakfast:

> *You know da Vinci's painting of*
> *The Virgin sitting in her mother's lap,*
> *Bending and reaching toward the child:*
> *Mary, Jesus, and St. Anne: beautiful*
> *Names: Anne, from a Latin name from*
> *The Hebrew name Hannah. The sun shines*
> *Here and out the window I see green, green*
> *Cut into myriad shapes, a bare-foot-*
> *Caressing carpet of fresh-grown grass (a*
> *Gift from Persia, courtesy of D. Kermani),*
> *Green chopped into various leaves: walnut, maple,*
> *Privet, Solomon's-seal, needles of spruce:*
> *Green with evening sunlight on it,*
> *Green going deep into penetrable shade: . . .*

Good as the poems in the first two sections of the book are, we do not take Schuyler's measure until we read the title poem. It has a double fascination: the voyeurism elicited by someone else's diary or journal, and the excitement good poetry affords — in this case, enhanced by the spice of a virtuoso performance. Whether sixty pages of life as it occurs, with flashbacks, asides, set pieces, digressions on travel, nature engravings, and so on, would have been more impressive if they had been exploited in the service of a great idea, an overall large conception, is moot. In place of philosophical speculation or historical sweep, we get hard-earned truths: a special mixture of country wisdom and the savvy of the city.

The poem, more than any other Schuyler has written, demonstrates his uncanny control of tone.

The poem's essential device is a doubling of viewpoint: Schuyler is in East Aurora, a small town in western New York State, staying with his mother in a white-clapboard house he knew as a child. At the same time, the poem is addressed to a specific "you" (though many other "you"s appear in it), Darragh Park, the painter, who is at work in his studio on West 22nd Street in Chelsea, in Manhattan. The poem switches back and forth between Schuyler in East Aurora and Park in Chelsea, but on the way we visit Italy, Zurich, Geneva, Great South Bay, Nantucket, Paris, Maine, New Brunswick, Long Island, and Germany. The constantly shifting landscape — always swinging back to East Aurora — allows Schuyler to test to the limit his free-wheeling ability to catch the atmosphere of places, and his genius for run-on improvisation.

A continuing sexual motif weaves in and out — men Schuyler has been attracted to, described lovingly, fleetingly, and, most often, frustratedly: a muscular, handsome man who leans out a window after a snowstorm in New York City; a moving man; a soldier; the lost lover; a man in a grocery store; a gray-haired German the narrator actually went to bed with, who turns out, later, to have been a "bore." The lost lover is a floating "you" in the poem, a parallel to Park, about whom Schuyler says, in an early passage, "How easily I could be in love with you, / who do not like to be touched." So the poem is, sub rosa, a love poem, whose objects of devotion are offshoots of "Bob," the lost and great love. The sexual frankness of the poem is devoid of the musky odors of the confessional — and even the erotic — the context being expansive enough to absorb Schuyler's recurring sexual preoccupations. Schuyler is never "mythological" or "symbolic" — we are being given the straight stuff. But though he is the plainest of poets he is also one of the most mysterious because, though straightforward and realistic, the effects — like those, say, of Magritte — can be hallucinatory and surreal. The language is rarely distinguished if one separates out a phrase or a sentence. But how extraordinary it is in an extended passage or taken as a whole! What we have, really, in "The Morning of the Poem," is a poetry diary on the order of MacNeice's "Autumn Journal," at least in its method. And because the poem is addressed to a specific person, it has something of the flavor of a letter, a letter being written by an emperor or poet in exile who is writing to a confidant back in the capital. Though once in a while Schuyler falters — asking too many naïve questions, for one, questions that could be answered by making a phone call or opening an encyclopedia — the overall performance is amazingly successful.

It is not without interest that both Ashbery in "Self-Portrait in a Convex Mirror" and Schuyler in his title poem chose a painter (one dead, one alive) as the chief figure in the design of a long work that is basically a self-portrait. And painting is crucial in Schuyler's case because it brings with it one of the essential components of his verse — light. It also allows for correspondences of many kinds: Schuyler uses Park as one factor in an opposition that might read art/city versus nature/country, and the exchange between them has something of the quality of an extended metaphor.

We switch between Schuyler and Park through the poet's favorite device, the colon, and the colon also introduces passages at random — memories, related incidents, the appearance of chance characters, checkpoints of nostalgia. The immediate scene — the mother, the TV set, the view out the window and down the road — always swings back into focus. The transitions are generally smooth, though occasionally we get the jerky effect of an old movie projector. Parts of the collage arrive from a great distance, but they are always pasted in and made to fit the grand design, whose center is Schuyler himself in East Aurora.

The best nature poems seem to be written by people who have had a long experience of the city — perhaps they have the largest stake in the natural. Schuyler is as quirky a nature poet as we have produced, and in the accretion of physical data in his long poem, a view of nature creeps into the work, barefoot, on its own. A version of the pastoral is being promulgated: value is essentially native, home-grown, and surprisingly traditional. The weed as well as the flower, the restored interior of McFeely's bar as well as the Italian Monument — these are the permanent properties, values that attest not only to the age-old continuity of man but to the connection between the child and the adult. Currents of feeling, pulsations of nervous response are aroused by talismanic objects, natural, architectural, and sexual. The natural world is comforting, almost maternal, yet its variety is celebrated with romantic intensity. Love, or let's say sex, has an adolescent aura in the poems, and also a certain camp flavor; the sexual impulses are mainly voyeuristic or masturbatory; the true satisfactions of the flesh are all of the past. The homosexual longing is frank, promiscuous, and runs through the poems as a whole. It neither diminishes nor enhances the character of the narrator; everything is seen in the light of a dispassionate compassion, which is useful even to himself.

We credit, we do not discount, we may even regret — having handed ourselves over so completely to the writer — the adolescent sexuality (and, if it needs to be said, not adolescent because it is homosexual), but it has no negative impact. There is nothing exhibitionistic about it; the deeply felt friendships celebrated throughout the book make a far more lasting impression, and the natural world in which everything is steeped acts as a counterbalance. Nature is sensual; the weed accidentally come upon and the studied specimen are equally well observed. In love with gardens, Schuyler is passionate about wildflowers:

> *Canadian columbine, rusty red*
> *(Or rather orange?), spurred,*
> *Hanging down, drying, turning*
> *Brown, turning up, a cup*
> *Full of fine black seeds*
> *That sparkle, wake-robin,*
> *Trillium, a dish of rich*
> *Soft moss stuck with little*
> *Flowers from the woods —*
> *Bloodroot, perhaps*
> *Rose pogonia, sea lavender*
> *And, best of all, bunches*
> *And bunches and bunches of*
> *New England asters, not blue,*
> *Not violet, certainly not*
> *Purple: bright-yellow-*
> *Centered, so many crowded*
> *Into vases and bowls that*
> *The house seems awash*
> *With sea and sun. . . .*

Behind Schuyler's pastoral backdrops, a moral world begins to take shape. That world is not easy to define, but its
outlines may be suggested in Schuyler's portrait of his
mother. A churchgoer and TV watcher, she starts out as a
"parent," a person of false values, conventional, middle class,
the usual white-collar mother. But by the end of the poem,
she has become a character of strength and integrity, assuming a role somewhat akin to Proust's grandmother, the
central moral figure of *A la Recherche du Temps Perdu*, who,
through a simple quality, natural goodness (and its corollary,
uncritical love), develops into an unswerving force. The portrait of Schuyler's mother is marked by clarity and surety;
without slurring her negative qualities (from the son's point
of view), she assumes a positive aspect. (A similar process of
moral illumination occurs in Schuyler's treatment of Lottie,
the alcoholic wife, in that small masterpiece of a novel *What's
for Dinner?*) Though Schuyler's mother sometimes irritates
him, the loving colors in which she is presented, in spite of
all the outward facts being stacked against her, hold the key
to Schuyler's moral view, more apparent in tone than in
stated attitude, in the way a character is handled than in a
character's intrinsic merit. Remaining true to oneself is, for
Schuyler, the greatest of moral virtues. He can be cruel and
childish, but he is in touch with parts of himself not usually
available for examination and not often handled by most
writers. This can become excessive — as if all truths were of
equal importance. A line like "Funny, I haven't beat my
meat in days — why's that?" seems to me a question hardly
worth asking. And his mother's ingrown toenail may help
establish the genre — the no-holds-barred journal entry —
but the fine line between the necessary fact and the pointless
detail is blurred.

These poems, no matter where they range in space or time, are poems of loneliness, and an unwritten irony spells itself out underneath them — though the world is often chastened, it is still viewed with a puzzled affection. The poems hew close to the bone; the ordinary delicacy that divides life and letters seems not only irrelevant but a form of evasion. The title poem, in particular, is the work of a persistent romantic, and as American as apple pie; in fact, it sometimes reads like a perverse underground commentary on *Our Town*. Schuyler's poems lack the historical sweep, the philosophical perspective one finds in the work, say, of Brodsky and Walcott. But they ring true, translating life into the action and imagery of a poetry that is never telegraphic, journalistic, or confessional. How Schuyler manages to be absolutely truthful and an obsessed romantic at the same time is his secret.

PART THREE

A Pinched Existence

A GOOD case could be made for the short story being the most flexible of all forms and, as such, the key to "modernism": it can accommodate everything from the prose poem to the well-made plot; allows for the undercurrents that emanated from Vienna in the 1920s, the seemingly formless but beautifully condensed character studies that began arriving from Russia with the advent of Chekhov. It can be analytic or lyrical, dramatic or rhapsodic. No other English practitioner of the form — English by way of the Commonwealth — was as influential in the decades that spanned the period between World War I and the 1950s than Katherine Mansfield. Her work is temporarily in eclipse in America, but there is hope of a reassessment.

It is clear from reading two new biographies — *The Life of Katherine Mansfield* by Anthony Alpers and *Katherine Mansfield* by Jeffrey Meyers — that their subject would have understood what Proust meant when he wrote that "the true paradises are the paradises we have lost." Being an expatriate, she was divorced from her childhood in a special way: the distance between the realm of the adult and that of the child took on a physical dimension; her lost paradise could be located on a map. It had not always seemed a paradise, and it took her a long time to realize it was lost. By the time she did, the peripatetic wanderings of the outsider had become the enforced regime of the tubercular: Mediterranean winters, English summers. Dislocation had become chronic.

When Mansfield returned to her birthplace, Wellington, New Zealand, in 1906, at the age of eighteen, after four years of schooling at Queen's College in England, she was unhappy, moody, rebellious; London glittered across the ocean, Wellington was a backwater. And she was haunted by a series of strange or tragic incidents. On the day her mother gave a garden party, a poor neighbor died in a traffic accident (the situation of one of her most famous stories). Though a summer cottage was now available for the use of the children — four girls, of which Katherine was the third, and Leslie, her young brother — it became the scene of an unhappy lesbian affair, her second in the three years that marked her return to Wellington. Saddest of all, her beloved grandmother died, the person she was closest to in the family.

Incriminating papers were found, having to do either with the two love affairs or with an obscure incident involving a sailor, and Mansfield was sent to "King County" on a caravan expedition that left on November 15, 1907, and returned the week before Christmas. The country was rough, the party of eight traveled by horse and carriage, pitching tents when they made camp. They ventured into exotic territory: Maori country, thermal regions, pumice hills. It was a country of white dust and velvety mineral-spring baths, and Mansfield's account of it, *The Urewera Notebook*, is interesting as the writing of a gifted adolescent describing a short journey through a strange culture at a remote time. Though the trip provided Mansfield with the background of a famous story, "The Woman at the Store," she remained restless and obviously determined to get back to London; her father finally relented. She was nineteen when she left Wellington for the second and last time, in 1908. Though she couldn't have known it, more than half her life was over.

That the rest of it could have taken place in a mere fifteen years is amazing, so crowded are the canvases of both biographies, so rapid the changes of address and fortune. On the way back to London, she must have felt relieved; she was going back to a world she thought she loved, the world of the theater, of intellectual exchange, of poetry, of music — everything she felt nourishing and vital. Yet, seven years later, in 1915, when her brother, Leslie, was blown to bits in World War I, that world fell apart, and her childhood in New Zealand took on its true value: like Proust's Combray springing out of a cup of tea, it came back freshly revealed. The New Zealand stories — "Prelude," "At the Bay," "The Doll's House," "The Woman at the Store" — were a far cry from the sophisticated tales-with-a-twist she had been turning out for the English magazines, Orage's *New Age* in particular. The New Zealand stories, her finest work, are commemorations, garlands for Leslie, and there is a touching journal entry in regard to them and to him:

Now, as I write these words and talk of getting down to the New Zealand atmosphere, I see you opposite to me. . . . Ah, my darling, how have I kept away from this tremendous joy?

If "Prelude" and "At the Bay" tend to make the London and Mediterranean stories seem thin by comparison, it must be remembered that Mansfield was a stranger among strangers, that she moved in a world of artists, intellectuals, and writers; they were not, in the end, to be her cup of tea. Something of the ventriloquist's effect clings to most of the European stories, as of voices overheard and reprojected; they lack the allure of subterranean interest. She was dealing with people basically alien to her — people who tended to hide behind masks (as she learned to do). Reality and fantasy had been replaced by gossip. A rich stream of family life — natural-animal-physical — was nowhere to be found. Thin soil produced thin work.

The equivocal nature of the world in which she found herself in 1908 can be suggested by two incidents that occurred much later, in 1917. Virginia and Leonard Woolf set the type for *Prelude* at the Hogarth Press — an act of devotion, though endlessly delayed. But here is the entry in Virginia Woolf's diary on the night Mansfield came for dinner to see the pulled proof of the first page:

We could both wish that ones first impression of K.M. was not that she stinks like a — well civet cat that had taken to street walking. In truth, I'm a little shocked by her commonness at first sight; lines so hard & cheap. However, when this diminishes, she is so intelligent & inscrutable that she repays friendship.

The relationship between Virginia and Katherine was a wary one. They teetered always on the edge of something more — both were capable of loving women — but drew back out of uncertainty and mistrust. They shared, too intensely, in Mr. Meyers's words, "a painful creative conjunction of imagination, isolation, and illness."

In both their cases, much of the charm is masked pain; yet they envied different things in each other: Woolf wrote in her diary a few days after Mansfield died, in January 1923:

> When I began to write, it seemed to me there was no point in writing. Katherine won't read it. Katherine's my rival no longer. . . . I was jealous of her writing — the only writing I have ever been jealous of. . . . and I saw in it, perhaps from jealousy, all the qualities I dislike in her.

And again, with greater sympathy and perception:

> I never gave her credit for all the physical suffering and the effect it must have had in embittering her.

What Katherine Mansfield envied in Virginia Woolf was something quite other. Here, in a letter of complaint, she is writing from Italy in 1919:

> You know it's madness to love and live apart. That's what we do. . . . It isn't a married life at all — not what I mean by a married life. How I envy Virginia; no wonder she can write. There is always in her writing a calm freedom of expression as though she were at peace — her roof over her, her possessions round her, and her man somewhere within call.

The person addressed is John Middleton Murry. Katherine and he met in London when she was twenty-three, he twenty-two and the editor of *Rhythm*, a literary magazine of the day. He became her lover and then her husband; thirteen of the thirty-five years she lived were spent in and out of his company. As her literary executor, he carefully selected passages, and censored or deleted others, in the journals, notebooks, letters, and scrapbooks he edited after her death. The process was self-serving on the one hand, and a genuine attempt to create a literary monument on the other. Running a small Mansfield industry, Murry managed to create an image of Katherine as a limp, sentimental person. He described her as "a flower." Worse, in a series of books, lectures, and statements of his own, he distorted her gifts and her person, characterizing her as "the most wonderful writer and the most beautiful spirit of our time."

This kind of thing does not lack long for a backlash. Murry's aggressively projected posthumous image of Mansfield was the largest single reason for the decline of her reputation. It focused attention on the person at the expense of the work; it made unjustifiable claims and was so patently false to anyone who knew her (the very people who would be writing about her) that falseness became associated with the work itself — a delicate business, since some of it *is* marred by girlishness and obviousness. Mr. Meyers sees Murry as an ass and an enemy — someone who made a reputation for himself out of Mansfield's life and work he never could have achieved on his own:

> Murry was a kind of rancid Rousseau: his thought was equivocal and confused, he had an endless capacity for self-deception, he disguised a total egocentricity behind his mock-saintliness and was always eager to display his stigmata before the public. Katherine, who loathed his self-pity, accused him of being "just like a little dog whining outside a door," and impatiently ex-

claimed: "When you know you are a voice crying in the wilderness, *cry*, but don't say 'I am a voice crying in the wilderness.' "

Mr. Alpers is more lenient. Murry, after all, was poor, remarkably passive, and lacked talent. Whatever may be said against him, he was the single most important person in Mansfield's life. In any case, some of the best English short stories of this century got tarred by the same adolescent brush with which Murry had redrawn the life.

The information supplied by Mr. Meyers and (sometimes in too generous detail) by Mr. Alpers redoes that portrait in more realistic colors. Atypical as the life was, it still had archetypal figures in it: if there is a generic artist's-father, Harold Beauchamp might well be he. "A settler type, a self-made tycoon, and a friend of politicians," he was domineering, not unkind, valued money, and had a remarkably close, perhaps obsessive, relationship with his wife, "an aristocratic-looking beauty," who was delicate, brave, and, to her children, seemingly aloof. The parents' closeness tended to shut the children out, especially Katherine, who was the ugly duckling — fat, homely, wearing steel-rimmed spectacles, and hobbled by a stutter — an ugly duckling who later turned into a beauty. Harold Beauchamp eventually became the head of the Bank of New Zealand, and the Beauchamp children, moving from one more expensive house to another, grew up in an atmosphere that was an odd mixture of frontier democracy and unusual affluence. When the family sailed for England in 1903 to install three of the girls at Queen's College, the Beauchamps thought nothing of reserving the entire passenger accommodations of the ship for themselves.

Katherine had a special reason for wanting to get to England. At thirteen, she had fallen violently in love with a young cellist, Arnold Trowell, fifteen. He was to follow shortly to study music on the Continent.

Her letters to Arnold are the first examples of a too easily proffered affection, a tendency exhibited again almost immediately with Ida Baker, whom she met on her first day at Queen's. Ida responded beyond anyone's wildest dreams. Referred to as L.M. in the journals (standing for Lesley Moore, an invented name), she became a slave, on call at all times, dropping everything to join Mansfield whenever she was needed. The case was so odd, so intense, right from the beginning, that it seems, as Mr. Meyers says, more like one of imprinting than of human affection.

On Mansfield's side, there were the increasing demands illness brings, and in the long years of enforced exile abroad, L.M. was her frequent companion. Mansfield felt love and hatred in equal proportion, and contempt, even revulsion; L.M. was indispensable but a surrogate. To be dependent on someone not quite loved but loyal exacerbates the roles of server and served, caretaker and invalid. Mansfield and L.M. acted out this small range of unequal roles time after time. It wasn't a question of being the wrong sex; the person in need was in danger of being suffocated by the comforter. But for all of Mansfield's complaining, L.M. provided for her what Leonard Woolf had supplied for Virginia: a reliable pillar of strength. In fact, in her relationship with L.M., Mansfield had unwittingly handed Murry a sop for his guilt: no matter how distant, lonely, cold, and in debt Katherine might be, she wasn't *really* alone: L.M. was there, taking care of her.

Mansfield's father, the richest man in New Zealand, kept

her on a small allowance that was "worse than nothing," according to one observer, forcing her to lead "a pinched existence." And her first year in London on her own was a disaster. The romance with Arnold cooled; she switched her affection to his twin brother, Garnet; became pregnant; impulsively married George Bowden, a musician she'd known for only three weeks; left *him* on their wedding night; rejoined Garnet, who was playing in the orchestra of an opera company in the provinces (shades of Colette and Jean Rhys!); and ended up bereft, ill, pregnant, with no one at her side but the ever-faithful L.M. Mansfield's mother was coming to England. When she arrived, Mrs. Beauchamp whisked her daughter off to a German pension to have the baby, and departed. When Mrs. Beauchamp returned to Wellington, she cut Katherine out of her will.

In Germany, Katherine had a miscarriage, but managed to produce the sketches that make up *In a German Pension*, her first book. The strokes are broad, the Germans drawn with exaggerated vulgarity. Later on, even though she was very badly off, she refused to allow it to be reprinted. And, back in England, she began that peculiar searching for a place to live that was to characterize the rest of her life. Even after she and Murry had decided to live together, there were frequent moves, endless flats, more little houses. Poverty was the immediate cause, but one suspects the compulsions of dislocation were at work. Mansfield often seems like a soul searching for a place to rest. The trips to Switzerland and France begin with high hopes and end in terror: the cases of medical bungling are hair-raising; the pleas to Murry to join her abroad, increasingly urgent. The one time they were happy — at the Villa Pauline in Bandol from January through April 1916 — ended with their yielding to the blandishments of the Lawrences, who had a place in Cornwall. The Murrys and the Lawrences met when D. H. Lawrence walked into the offices of *The Blue Review*, formerly *Rhythm*, in June 1913. The two couples took to each other at once, and there were visits to the Lawrence place in the country. After an interval in Paris and several tries at Chelsea flats, the Murrys decided to live on the cheap in the country. They moved into a cottage three miles from the Lawrences. Now, four years later, they joined once more in an effort to realize Lawrence's dream of an ideal little community and Katherine Mansfield's fantasy of a permanent abode — a dream house, referred to as The Heron, after Leslie's middle name. But the Lawrences were violent, Lawrence had a crush on Murry, Katherine disliked Frieda — though she wore the wedding ring of Frieda's first marriage to her grave — and, in the end, it was impossible to work, impossible to live. Lawrence was magnetic, but he and Mansfield were too much alike under the skin, their partners too different. They kept meeting and parting, like two pairs of birds going through their ritual dances. But the joinings were more territorial than nuptial, and Lawrence — to whom Mansfield was deeply attached — was, in the end, unspeakably cruel to her at one of the gravest moments of her life. She was at Menton in February 1920, ill almost to the point of death, and could have used whatever warmth a letter from an old friend might bring. Lawrence wrote: "I loathe you. You revolt me stewing in your consumption. You are a loathesome reptile — I hope you will die." The letter, almost ludicrously vile, has never been found; but Mansfield quoted it in one of her letters to Murry, and L.M. remembered it.

What Lawrence hated most in Mansfield, according to Mr. Alpers, was the mirrored fear of the disease of which he was already a victim and of which he would eventually die.

The death of Leslie had been the first great spiritual upheaval in Mansfield's life. When the world seemed worthless, her work had saved her. As she became more ill, the pleasures of life *and* the satisfactions of her work deserted her. This emptiness in the face of death led to her final decision to join Gurdjieff's community of mystics at Fontainebleau, where body and soul were one; if there was to be a cure, it would be, once and for all, out of the hands of doctors. Although the decision was not an easy one and was a long time in coming, it had been in the air. Orage, Gurdjieff's disciple in London, had taken Mansfield to meetings in which Gurdjieff and Ouspensky were discussed, and she was to some extent familiar with their teachings. She had reached a point of illness where nothing seemed worth trying save a miracle. She had been relinquishing a certain kind of reality and fear for a long time. Tragically, just as she achieved a kind of spiritual inner peace, her confidence in her work slipped away. What should have been a great meshing of inner and outer forces eluded her, though it is clear to a reader — it may not have been to her — that the work got better as the life got worse. She wrote to Murry from Menton on October 18, 1920:

> You know, I have felt very often lately as though the silence had some meaning beyond these signs, these intimations. Isn't it possible that if one yielded there is a whole world into which one is received? It is so near and yet I am conscious that I hold back from giving myself up to it. What is this something mysterious that waits — that beckons?

And then suffering, bodily suffering such as I've known for three years. It has changed for ever everything — even the *appearance* of the world is not the same — there is something added. *Everything has its shadow.* Is it right to resist such suffering? Do you know I feel it has been an immense privilege. . . . It has taken me three years to understand this — to come to see this. We resist, we are terribly frightened. The little boat enters the dark fearful gulf and our only cry is to escape —"put me on land again." But it's useless. Nobody listens. The shadowy figure rows on. One ought to sit still and uncover one's eyes.

She arrived at Fontainebleau on October 16, 1922. L.M. had helped her, but left on October 20 to take a job on a farm. Murry appeared, by invitation, on the afternoon of January 9, 1923. That evening Katherine died of a hemorrhage.

Mansfield's reputation remains uncertain; she suffered the fate of the cult figure: the interest in her life has overtaken the work itself. Rereading her, one is struck by the variety of characters; she deals equally well with shopkeepers, prostitutes, neurotic young women, married men, children (remarkably). She was no mere lyrical twang, no fine piece of iridescent shell endlessly turned to the same light. Her reputation for "purity," her forced martyrdom as an exponent of mere sensibility, has obscured her toughness, the ruthlessness of her judgment, her fine eye and ear. The work varies; the ups and downs are inexplicable, cropping up at all stages of her career. A masterpiece like "The Stranger" is followed by something as meretricious as "Taking the Veil"; the glories of "Je Ne Parle Pas Français," with its controlled masculine point of view, its queer but deadly pace, its frissons slowly building into a chilling portrait — the uncanny effect of its drama as a whole — all this is suddenly deflated, it seems to me, by a story such as "The Life of Ma Parker," a rewrite, with a slight twisting of circumstances and character, of Chekhov's "Grief." "Bliss," though detested by Virginia Woolf and found artificial by Elizabeth Bowen, remains a fine story — until the last scene. Facile but not fake, it bobs on a real current. The slick denouement is one of Mansfield's problems — as if O. Henry and Virginia Woolf had somehow been forced to share the same skin. But there are stories that rival Chekhov, as well they might: he was the one writer above all she adored. Mansfield was the only writer of this century who was devoted exclusively to the short story. Her ability to transform herself into someone else on one long, sustained lyrical note — the true mark of the good storywriter — was a matter of impulse as well as skill.

These two new biographies rest much of their authority on the subject as witness. In a sense, they feed on, and compete with, the journals, notebooks, and letters. Though the Meyers volume is two-thirds the size of the Alpers, Mr. Meyers covers the essential ground and is clear-eyed and straightforward. Mr. Alpers, whose book is a revision and expansion of an earlier work, places the writer in a larger picture and provides a valuable chronology; but he can be intrusive and often fails to distinguish the important from the unimportant detail. Both books rescue a complex and heroic woman from the dullness of sanctity.

Interior Children

For a writer, the wrong reputation can be as deadly as none. Elizabeth Bowen was always noted, but not always for the right reasons. Although she died as recently as 1973, her reputation had begun petering out in the sixties, when to mention love seemed frivolous, and the word "civilization" began to give off a slight stench. Elizabeth Bowen was a civilized writer preoccupied with human relationships. Since her death, the social setting against which the novels are played out has vanished more quickly than anyone could have predicted, and the novels have not had time to slip into the permanent shelters of the more constrained worlds of, say, Trollope and Jane Austen. Although she was alive at the beginning of the last decade, Elizabeth Bowen may be an unknown writer to the present generation. With the exception of *Pictures and Conversations*, a collection of autobiographical writings and other fragments, which was published in

1975, and a paperback edition of *The Death of the Heart* (1938), her books have been hard to find for years. In a recent biography, Victoria Glendinning stated the case for her subject in a few sentences: "She is a major writer; her name should appear in any responsible list of the ten most important fiction writers in English on [the British] side of the Atlantic in this century. . . . She is what happened after Bloomsbury . . . the link that connects Virginia Woolf with Iris Murdoch and Muriel Spark." Now, happily, Avon Books is reprinting all the novels, in paperback — starting backward, with *Eva Trout* (1968).

When she hit on the phrase "the death of the heart," Elizabeth Bowen hit on the key to all her fiction. Her characters, cut off from natural growth, either achieve a worldliness that catches them up short or remain interior children — dissemblers to the world. Thwarted feeling runs through the novels, and landscape plays a special role: nature is not only descriptive but thematic, and sets in bold relief the submerged emotions and sexual detours typical of Bowen's characters, who are plunged into atmospheres recognizable but timeless, as if the owner of a travel agency in the thirties (Emmeline in *To the North*, of 1932) or the head of an international conglomerate (Constantine in *Eva Trout*) were to be found in the Forest of Arden. I can think of no other writer capable of creating Arcadias so oddly sulfurous, in which schoolmistresses, shop owners, moonstruck juveniles, and retired army majors wander; yet the backgrounds never seem incongruous. Because Bowen's command of social comedy is authoritative, her dialogue demanding, and the psychological tension subtle, I don't think it has been noticed that the settings, which pass for versions of reality, are heightened — a unique blend of precise description and landscapes that could exist only in the imagination. Natural or urban, they transform themselves quickly into a series of dissolving and reforming paintings. Here is Karen arriving by boat from England at Cork in *The House in Paris* (1935):

> On the left shore, a steeple pricked up out of a knoll of trees, above a snuggle of gothic villas; then there was the sad stare of what looked like an orphanage. A holy bell rang and a girl at a corner mounted her bicycle and rode out of sight. The river kept washing salt off the ship's prow. Then, to the right, the tree-dark hill of Tivoli began to go up, steep, with pallid stucco houses appearing to balance on the tops of trees. Palladian columns, gazebos, glass-houses, terraces showed on the background misted with spring green, at the tops of shafts or on toppling brackets of rock, all stuck to the hill, all slipping past the ship. . . .
>
> The river still narrowing, townish terraces of tall pink houses under a cliff drew in. In one fanlight stood a white plaster horse; clothes were spread out to dry on a briar bush. Someone watching the ship twitched back a curtain; a woman leaned out signalling with a mirror: several travellers must be expected home. A car with handkerchiefs fluttering drove alongside the ship. On the city side, a tree-planted promenade gave place to boxy warehouses; a smoky built-over hill appeared beyond Tivoli. But Cork consumes its own sound: the haze remained quite silent.

Because of the prevailing notion of being cut off from the natural, of being expelled from a garden, an oblique view of the Creation shapes Bowen's fiction. In her version of the Fall, the gifts of sexuality and knowledge provide the temptation to be human, not evil. Compared to being human, being evil is an easy achievement — it lacks shading. The story of the Creation is moral and possibly funny — never have two people been given such lavish gifts and made to pay for them so quickly and so drastically. To be moral and to be funny are qualities inimical to our age when taken together, but they are the very stuff and weather of Austen and Wilde. All the essential stories (with the exception of the miraculous conjuring of Eve out of a rib) are embedded in the original triangle of man, woman, and tempter. What Bowen saw was how the qualities that save us in one way destroy us in another, and she dealt always in doubles, not only in having major characters underlined by minor counterparts — Lois and Livvy in *The Last September* (1929), Portia and Lilian in *The Death of the Heart* — but in the very depiction of character itself. Portia, the center of the reader's compassion, is at the same time a terrible bore. Stella, in *The Heat of the Day* (1949), is intelligent and yet a pawn. Karen, in *The House in Paris*, is sensitive in regard to her aunt's doom yet evasive and cowardly when it comes to Leopold, her illegitimate child. Leopold is rescued, but not by her, and, as always in a Bowen novel, a larger problem looms: without her, can it be considered a rescue? The heart died hard and is capable of a unique extinction: it tends to expire over and over.

After *The Death of the Heart*, Elizabeth Bowen was tagged as a writer for whom adolescence provides special insights, but her true subject is manipulation — emotional, social, sexual — and particularly the compelling power of the past to direct, compromise, and destroy the living. The late-blooming passion of Irene and Mr. Quayne provides *The Death of the Heart* with the heart in question, but it also adds just the right historical flavor of disheveled romance to the foreground. The letters that Jane finds in the attic in *A World of Love* (1955) — letters written to her mother by a soldier killed in the First World War — become a source of fantasy more meaningful than any reality she has yet known. And Mme. Fisher, an ancient witch, flat on her sickbed in an upstairs room in *The House in Paris*, having destroyed one generation with her neurotic need to dominate, is still busily maneuvering for the control of a second. Throughout Bowen's fiction, convention and habit are not as lethal an enemy of feeling as is doubt. Ambiguity is most brutal to the young, who fight for a single-edged interpretation of the world, only to come up against larger and more baffling uncertainties. The battleground is usually a house, itself double-edged — its architecture and history suggesting the solidity of structure, but a structure whose walls are always shaken by the pressure of the lives lived within them, leading either to decompression or to explosion. In Bowen novels, the two sides of the coin clash, and nowhere more sharply than in the unfinished "The Move-In," the last fiction of hers that we have, in *Pictures and Conversations*, where a carful of young people arrive at night demanding to be let into an establishment (a house) that refuses to admit them.

The battlers are mainly women. The enigmatic men — Markie (*To the North*), Eddie (*The Death of the Heart*), even Henry (*Eva Trout*) — are charming, demanding, and undependable: quicksand into which the female characters stumble. Deeply uneasy, hopeless when not provided with roles, the men often bring an irrelevant and unwanted integrity to bear on situations no longer responsive to it — Edward in *Friends and Relations* (1931), Major Brutt in *The Death of the*

Heart. And there are the malevolent males, each with a beneficent side — Julian in *To the North*, and St. Quentin in *The Death of the Heart*. Compassionate irony is reserved for young males, a touch of gleeful malice for divorcées and obstreperous adolescent girls. The social comedy, even in *Friends and Relations*, is never pure — the psychological insights are too penetrating. *A World of Love* is something else again: pastoral romance edging a ghost story out of the way. Underground eroticism and erratic insecurity leading to violence count for more and more over the years. Three suicides, two murders, one plane crash, and one car crash are strewn among four novels.

Upper-crust middle-class life is the usual milieu, but the family is more crucial than has been acknowledged — and particularly the missing mother in *The House in Paris*, *The Death of the Heart*, *To the North*, and *Eva Trout*. That is where the Bowen preoccupation (but not obsession) with love begins. It is seen as the one important choice people not very free still think they are free to make, and they make it, usually, under a disastrous cloud: they have never known or have lost their mothers.

The disasters continue and proliferate. Overall, the novels are pessimistic and present the reader with an insoluble dilemma: innocence (or the lasting memory of it) and civilization are equally unavoidable. We bring the first condition with us into the world, which provides us, mercilessly, with the second. Between the two, some rite of passage must take place. The Garden of Eden can become rustic, suburban, a jungle, or otherwise hellish — the desert is no more than a stone's throw away. As the story of the Creation makes quite clear, you cannot have it both ways. But there is in the story a dissembler, and it is he — inexplicable, perhaps even help-lessly acting out injunctions he would prefer to avoid — on whom the Bowen instinct for drama focuses. In her version, he assumes his usual role of the manipulator, but he has an unusual aspect. He is doomed throughout eternity not for being evil but for being ambiguous: from one point of view unleashing demonic appetites and murderous intelligence, and from another providing the sources of the greatest hu-man achievements — love and knowledge. In the Bowen canon, the snakes — if you can label them at all — are not only equivocal but reluctant.

Yet to pretend that the snake and tree do not exist is to be a simpleton. Whichever way Portia turns in *The Death of the Heart* is the wrong turn. The world has no use for innocence, and with good reason: everyone has once been some version of Portia, and no one wants to be reminded again of that large, uncurable wound. The innocent are not quite the un-equal contestants one might imagine. They go through their paces in the novels giving tit for tat:

Innocence so constantly finds itself in a false position that in-wardly innocent people learn to be disingenuous. Finding no language in which to speak in their own terms, they resign themselves to being translated imperfectly. They exist alone; when they try to enter into relations they compromise falsify-ingly — through anxiety, through desire to impart and to feel warmth. The system of our affections is too corrupt for them. They are bound to blunder, then to be told they cheat. In love, the sweetness and violence they have to offer involves a thou-sand betrayals for the less innocent. Incurable strangers to the world, they never cease to exact a heroic happiness. Their sin-gleness, their ruthlessness, their one continuous wish makes them bound to be cruel, and to suffer cruelty. The innocent are so few that two of them seldom meet — when they do meet, their victims lie strewn all round.

The profundity of this and the cleverness are inextricably mixed. Its author was herself aware that "cleverness" could be damaging. A certain aphoristic tendency (especially in the early novels) to "smartness" is delightful in itself but suspicious in its virtuosity. This is from *To the North*:

Lady Waters was quick to detect situations that did not exist. Living comfortably in Rutland Gate with her second husband, Sir Robert, she enlarged her own life into ripples of apprehension on everybody's behalf. Upon meeting, her very remarkable eyes sought one's own for those first intimations of crisis she was all tuned up to receive; she entered one's house on a current that set the furniture bobbing; at Rutland Gate destiny shadowed her tea-table. Her smallest clock struck portentously, her telephone trilled from the heart, her dinner-gong boomed a warning. When she performed introductions, drama's whole precedent made the encounter momentous.

But Miss Bowen was so much more than a merely clever writer that the charge deserves merely passing notice. More to the point, she seems to have been born with a genius command of English prose style, and the problem of her kind of gift was what to do with it. Words are the drunken part of her otherwise sober books, and there is a question whether any subject, theme, character, or scene ever became important enough — ever held a match to the style per se. Still, she was able to feel what she had originally felt before the world became transparent, and her ability to recover the past, both in her intellectual grasp of the locally historic — *Bowen's Court* (1942), *The Shelbourne Hotel* (1951), *A Time in Rome* (1960), all works of nonfiction — and in her magic transformation of landscape into its verbal equivalents, is reflected in the mature style. Here are the opening paragraphs of her unfinished autobiography in *Pictures and Conversations*:

The day this book was begun I went for a walk. The part of Kent I am living in has wide views, though also mysterious interstices. It can be considered to have two coastlines: a past, a present — the former looks from below like a ridge of hills, but in fact is the edge of an upland plateau: originally the sea reached to the foot of this. Afterwards, the withdrawal of the sea laid bare salty stretches, formerly its bed; two of the Cinque Ports, Hythe, New Romney, consequently found themselves high-and-dry, as did what was left of the Roman harbour under the heights of Lympne. . . . The existing coast-line, a long shallow inward curve westward from Folkestone to the far-out shingly projection of Dungeness, is fortified for the greater part of its way by a massive wall, lest the sea change its mind again. Inside the sea-wall, the protected lands keep an illusory look of marine emptiness — widening, west of Hythe, into the spaces of Romney Marsh, known for its sheep, its dykes, its sunsets and its solitary churches. On a clear day, the whole of this area meets the eye: there are no secrets.

Not so uphill, inland. The plateau, exposed to gales on its Channel front, has a clement hinterland, undulating and wooded. It is cleft by valleys, down which streams make their way to the sea; and there are also hollows, creases and dips, which, sunk between open-airy pastures and cornfields, are not to be guessed at till you stumble upon them: then, they are enticing, breathless and lush, with their wandering dogpaths and choked thickets.

A true wit, in the Restoration sense, Elizabeth Bowen had a flair for comedy that eluded Virginia Woolf. Bowen suffered the madness of her father, Woolf her own madness; each was in touch with secret springs of irrationality. But Elizabeth Bowen was born in Dublin, not London, and Irishness is not Englishness. She belongs to an Anglo-Irish tradition that includes Sheridan, Goldsmith, and Shaw. Comedy was not only in the genes but in the air. The odd mixture of the truly felt and the devastating is her forte. The view is bifocal. Sentiment and irony, operating in tandem, make one more set of contradictions added to others, beginning with the doubleness that the hyphen between "Anglo" and "Irish" implies: to be extraordinarily verbal and yet to stammer; to inherit a great house and yet to have a strong emotional sense of dispossession; to have a temperamental affinity with the bohemian while being basically conservative; to savor solitude and social life with equal relish. An accident of birth was compounded by circumstance: when Elizabeth Bowen was seven, her father had the first of several mental breakdowns and she and her mother were forced to leave Ireland for England. The scenery of Kent was forever after associated with her mother, while there could hardly be any mistaking the paternal associations attached to Dublin and Bowen's Court. Her mother died when Elizabeth was thirteen, and so, in a sense, she was doubly abandoned. The Gates of the Garden closed behind her twice.

The strategies of Bowen plots re-create analogies of the Garden's story, the action often centering on a triangle, because there one party, at least, is temporarily without knowledge. As the light dawns, the wrecking crew arrives. In the attempt to protect, to save face, to inflict damage — or all three at once — further harm is perpetrated, and the by-stander (a character or society at large) is always happy to rub salt into the wounds. Two of the members of the triangle are often rationally solicitous of one another, like Karen and Naomi in *The House in Paris*, and two hopelessly caught in a magnetic field of attraction, the sensuality of which they never allow themselves particularly to enjoy, like Karen and Max in the same novel. Impulse is converted not into guilt but into something worse: a philosophical awareness of plea-sure. In Bowen novels, the cells of the flesh know one thing, the mind another. Equally powerful, they undermine each other's ability to focus a clear-cut view of reality, just as a highly developed sense of the absurd interferes with passion and commitment. Emmeline's nearsighted unworldliness, Dicey's attempts to dig up the past in *The Little Girls* (1964), and even Eva Trout's blundering stabs at becoming real are all credible pieces of worlds, but the view is always partial, because some key factor is unavailable to the viewer.

The most complex example may be Harrison in *The Heat of the Day*. One of those unsuccessful hangers-on in peacetime who find their true vocation in the confusion of a war, he works for a counterintelligence outfit. Spying upon Stella, whose lover, Robert, turns out to be a genuine spy infiltrat-ing British Intelligence at its highest levels, Harrison hopes to extort Stella's compliance, even her gratitude and love, through blackmail by keeping his knowledge of Robert's trea-son from the authorities. At the beginning, Stella doesn't know Robert is a spy; she becomes aware of it through Har-rison's spying on her. Robert doesn't know about Harrison, and the last thing Stella can do is to let him know. Harrison is a menace but pathetic — he has learned that without power he is unlovable; he's bargaining for *his* life, it becomes clear, as well as Robert's. And certainly Stella is gambling for hers, caught between betrayal on the one side and threat on the other. Whether the bargain will be kept, whether it should be kept, whether it even exists forms the equivocal matter of the novel. Set against the background of wartime London, the novel's moral implications are more than emotional. Like *The Last September*, *The Heat of the Day* reflects a world of national turmoil, in which human relationships become another form of intelligence, of espionage. If there is a death of the heart, there is a little secret service, too.

The strange obscuring of Bowen's achievement stems in part from a misunderstanding: her novels are testaments not to romantic love but to its power, and no two things could be more different. But it also comes in part from life. Because she was Anglo-Irish (the last of the breed, according to Mrs. Glendinning's book), Bowen's views of England and of Ireland were the exact opposite of those of most Americans and Englishmen. For her, Ireland, with its "repetitive eighteenth-century interiors [and] their rational proportions and faultless mouldings . . . without shadow, curiousness, or cranny," was civilized and sane, and England insubstantial and stormy: "Everything, including the geological formation, struck me as having been recently put together. . . . *Would* it last? The edifices lining the tilted streets . . . seemed engaged in just not sliding about. . . . My thoughts dallied with landslides, subsidences and tidal waves." Bowen is essentially the product of a divided culture, a divided family, and a divided nation, and no one is better on the demon relationships of opposing — but mutual — interests that tie servants and masters, the innocent and the worldly, the loving and the unlovable together. Irish in England and English in Ireland, she grasped early the colonial mentality from both sides, and saw how, in the end, it was a mirror image of the most exploitative relationship of all: that of the adult and the child.

Going to Pieces

In the current Jean Rhys revival, the last of her novels to be reprinted (though not to be written), *Voyage in the Dark* (1934), shares a theme with her other novels of the twenties and thirties — *Quartet* (1928), *After Leaving Mr. Mackenzie* (1930), and *Good Morning, Midnight* (1939) — and even with *Wide Sargasso Sea* (1966), a rather different affair from its predecessors. For most people, love and the act of love are the greatest accusations they ever make against the falsehoods of society; we are one thing as lovers and something totally different as working, social, and political creatures. The disparity is as old as Adam and Eve, but the truly innocent (as distinct from the merely chaste) cannot bear it, and that notion is either central or implicit in all the novels. Sins of the flesh, therefore, are often not sins at all but their opposite: innocence, unbelieving, trying to restore itself. What the world makes of this kind of virtue is something else again, and there is not one Rhys heroine (each a species of a generic one) who does not innocently, and somewhat lazily, come up against the Philistines. The latter are sometimes masked as bohemians but are not to be distinguished from the chief enemies — the bourgeoisie and the authorities. Respectability is the great antagonist. It is also the despised haven.

The pattern of the Rhys heroine is set by Marya Zelli in *Quartet* — an unsuccessful actress–chorus girl turned artist's model or mannequin, who slowly drifts toward the vaguer forms of prostitution and is picked up variously by younger men equally wounded — middle-class Englishmen trying to revive themselves — or aging gentlemen fending off, or cynically making the most of, their last illusions — all unable to say what they feel, all afraid of being used, of giving in to emotions damaging to self-esteem. And the truth of the matter is that the men are spoilers, searching out the weak case, just as the women — most superbly realized in *After Leaving Mr. Mackenzie* — can be formidable. One grows formidable by having nothing to lose, by being free of hope. This involuntary process doesn't necessarily work to one's advantage. Meanness here derives from the need to defend that scrap of self-respect each person carries inside him like a furled flag. Even Mr. Mackenzie, even Heidler, a monster of selfishness in *Quartet* — modeled after Ford Madox Ford, an early sponsor of Miss Rhys's work — have a certain pathos, a kind of sinking familiarity, as if the women they help do in were also a denied part of themselves. The awful thing is to come up against someone who won't play by the rules, someone who knows and is willing to say the rules are lies. But one can stay innocent too long. Truthsayers are also threats — to themselves as well as the men they involve. Stupidity and cruelty are parceled out on both sides. Relationships are barters and chillingly ambivalent — the trading of a moment of affection or sex for a dinner or two, a hotel room, some ready cash.

The connection between love and money may be Miss Rhys's most original contribution to the history of emotional exploitation. For everything in society is geared to revealing power as masculine and to hiding the thousand subtle ways by which power uses money to enslave. And hers are novels of subjugation: the fat cat and the underdog tied together by invisible threads; subjugation either by addiction — sex or drink — or by the manipulation of passivity. Sensuality is at war with will and can be worked on, from varying distances, to escape the worst of human conditions — isolation. The aging gamine whom Miss Rhys pursues through these books with a relentlessness as cool as it is remarkable, considering the unmistakable autobiographical flavor, slowly goes to pieces. Living day to day, mostly in Paris, at one hotel a little seedier than the one before, she is a girl (later a woman) to whom an encounter, a drink, a sunset, a bar of music have the enchantments they have in life, but who comes to see them, finally, as ends in themselves. Sensuousness in these books is comforting — perhaps their only comfort. And their chief psychological state is uneasiness. Miss Rhys writes of this with an acuteness other writers reserve for madness, and she sees the strong connection between these states of mind. To hate the respectable world and to be dependent on it, to be rebellious and helpless at the same time, produces resignation and rage; there are no more uncomfortable bedfellows. This psychological state is mirrored in a social one: if Marya Zelli, Anna Morgan, Julia Martin, and Sasha Jansen are on the market, ready to be martyred, the male middle class knows a victim when it sees one, being so easily victimized itself. In this case, the predators and the prey are warily conscious of how quickly one step down leads to humiliation and one step up to anonymity and safety. Julia, in *After Leaving Mr. Mackenzie*, and Sasha, in *Good Morning, Midnight*, are on to the game, but they have no more idea of how to change the rules than they have the power to do so. To be a sort of aristocrat of the emotions and a penniless pretty girl, unable to *do* anything, is to be vulnerable. Money is never there when it is needed, affection is elusive when it might be most healing. The girls are too bright and, most of the time, too feeling to use weapons in return. They are slowly driven out of their wits by the harshness and unnaturalness of the world, by its lack of affection and warmth. They come into the world unarmed, and the world smashes them —"smash" is a particularly meaningful word for Miss Rhys — in an unequal war. The battles take place at a restaurant table, a hotel desk, a bar, or an interview — any of the small vectors of power where the victim and the victimizer juggle the balances.

But mainly these beauties are victims of themselves and of time, which has its own sliding scale — the necessary, the bearable, the desperate. They have the blindfold quality of stutterers walking in darkness, unable to speak when speech is required, unable to move, except from room to room, from hotel to hotel, from lover to lover. And when the lovers run out, the one-night stand takes their place. To get to the *tabac*, the beauty parlor, sometimes even downstairs is to walk the prison round. These are novels of dispossession written by someone with a strong sense of place. If all this sounds like "privileged despair" (to use Kenneth Tynan's phrase), it doesn't read like it. Every centimeter of torture is carefully measured out, and with an exactness and a lack of sentimentality all the more painful for being temperamentally unavoidable. To be wretched to the very roots of existence yet to be coolheaded, watching the wretchedness, is the fate of these women, and particularly of Sasha, in *Good Morning, Midnight*, for that book is the culmination of the story, the last sounding of the theme, and the most abstract of the novels, ending with Sasha's ghostly seduction by a man in a white dressing gown who, like a fateful moth, has flittered, seemingly unimportant, through the corridors of her hotel. When he moves from the corridor into the bedroom, he sums up Sasha's fate as he sums up all the strangers, charming and dreadful, who wander in and out of the first four novels. A dead child haunts two of them, the husbands and lovers have different names, but it is the same story we are reading, over and over, in various degrees of intensity, at different stages of the same career — the story of an exile from life, sometimes dressed in an expensive fur coat, a relic of former affluence, who is broke, aging, and alone.

Voyage in the Dark is the most harrowing of the novels because it is the most realistic, a love story that takes place in the present, where no marriage, no broken framework is to be taken for granted from the start. The girl is Anna Morgan, and to counteract the gray drabness of the London skies she keeps remembering scenes from her childhood on the island of Dominica — Miss Rhys's birthplace, where she spent her first sixteen years. But it is only in *Wide Sargasso Sea* that she is able to put together her two landscapes — the West Indies and England. Its ending leads us to the attic in *Jane*

Eyre where the first Mrs. Rochester is confined. In capitaliz-
ing on the fact that the first Mrs. Rochester was born in the
West Indies, and by working backward, Miss Rhys has
opened up a seam in the Brontë novel and then resewn it
with her own peculiar needle. It is a spellbinding book, labeled in its present hideous paperback edition a "Gothic,"
but it bears about as much resemblance to the genre as *The
Turn of the Screw* does to the ordinary ghost story. Good as it
is, something too theatrical attaches to it. For the first time,
Miss Rhys uses the landscape of her childhood as more than
a contrasting backdrop; its tropical color and languor are released as if they had been held under pressure for a long
time. But she has fused it with something bookish, and what
might have been the most personal of the novels is the most
literary. In spite of its staginess, it is marvelously adroit tech-
nically — each of its three sections is told from a different
viewpoint — but, more important, a world is at last revealed
to us that we can transpose backward, with some hesitation,
but with some meaning, to the books as a whole.

And that is the world of magic — the West Indian staples
of voodoo, witchcraft, and possession. It throws a shadow
rather than a glimmer on the psychology of the earlier novels, for the idea that one is being forced to behave rather than
willing one's behavior is a notion as common to the mentally
disturbed as to those who believe in magical forces. One's
fate is held in someone else's hands; and, as we watch An-
toinette turn into the crazed Mrs. Rochester, the passivity
of the earlier heroines takes on a different cast. Not only is
there an exaggerated notion of the male's powers to complete, but magic accrues to certain acts that will soothe and
heal. Clothes are very important in this respect, and so are

makeup and mirrors — strange little throwbacks, once they
are looked at this way, to a world far more primitive than
Paris or London. It makes us realize, perhaps for the first
time, how dominant the idea of fear is in Miss Rhys's work.
It is as if behind the scenes in the first four books a world
had been withheld that doesn't explain action or motivation
but colors them in a new and revealing way. To be down on
one's luck is to overvalue the chance rescue, to give it a significance it doesn't quite have. Once that significance is
granted, the way is clear for seeing significance in everything. And that, in turn, opens the door for the arrival of the
gods.

Though *Wide Sargasso Sea* is the most dramatic of the novels, it is the least telling in the Rhys canon precisely because
the heroine *does* go mad, and because she commits a final
demonic *act* — the burning of Thornfield Hall. Miss Rhys's
specialty is neither action nor madness but the precipitants
that precede them. The suicide at the coastline, not the floating corpse, is her real subject. *Wide Sargasso Sea* is an ingenious tour de force, but it is not the genuine Rhys article.
For the earlier novels — and particularly *After Leaving Mr.
Mackenzie* and *Good Morning, Midnight* — are unlike anything
else in English. They bear a close allegiance to the tight
French short novel expanded to its limits, rather than the
cumulative drama of build-up and crisis. Colette comes to
mind, but briefly. The music-hall flavor suggests a connection, but there is a finer sense of social institutions in the
English writer and a far less developed concern for the natural and the familial. The relationship between Colette and
Sido would, I think, have been outside Miss Rhys's range
(one never thinks of her as having parents), though the rela-

tionships between Hester and her stepdaughter, Anna, in *Voyage in the Dark*, and between the two sisters, Julia and Norah, in *After Leaving Mr. Mackenzie*, are poisonous and true but somehow exceptions, and rather surprising in the work as a whole. Yet Miss Rhys knows something about bureaucratic humiliation, the cold machinery of prisons and hotels, which either escaped Colette or escaped her interest, for Colette is basically a joyous writer and Miss Rhys a despairing one.

The difficulty of saying how or why her books seem so original may be a sign of their authenticity. They seem peculiarly timeless for works focused on such particular times and places as the twenties and thirties in London and Paris. A casualness of style, a natural sense of form suggest either the consummate letter writer or an arduousness belied by their surfaces. They are novels of streets and rooms as unforgettable as maps if one had to navigate by them, yet they manage inside their small frames to be significant. They have the quality of the best books by seeming to have written themselves, and, reading them, one flinches at truth after truth. *Tigers Are Better-Looking* (1974), a collection of short stories, has been brought out by Harper & Row. Miss Rhys is being resurrected in bits. The best story is the first one, "Till September Petronella," in which the now-familiar central figure goes off to join an artist and a music critic, and the girl friend of one of them, in the country. It is a perfect Rhys novel in miniature, a bonsai of compression. It, and a story about a West Indian woman in London, "Let them Call it Jazz," funny and pathetic by turns, are the high points. Selections from her very first book, *The Left Bank* (1927), are included, with its original introduction by Ford Madox Ford.

The right word for these is "sketches," and most of them *are* dated and trifling. They have some historical interest, they fill in a gap. The story is not as congenial to Miss Rhys as — I was about to say the novel. But it is her *version* of the novel I mean — which reads as if a piece of French literature had happened to be written in English — and it is hers alone.

PART FOUR

Reversing the Binoculars

Praised so often as a "craftsman," a "stylist," and a "master of prose," Katherine Anne Porter must occasionally long to be admired for what she is — a writer. Through an inability to compromise and sheer endurance, Miss Porter, who is an artist, has come to represent Art, and though the role has never obscured the quality of her work, it has shifted attention away from the content of the work itself. The first concern of these stories is not aesthetic. Extraordinarily well-formed, often brilliantly written, they are firmly grounded in life, and the accuracy and precision of their surfaces, so disarmingly easy to read, hold in tension the confused human tangles below. Experience is the reason for their having been written, yet experience does not exist in them for its own sake; it has been formulated, but not simplified.

These stories turn on crises as stories should, but two special gifts are evident: depth of characterization, which is more usually the province of the novelist, and a style that encompasses the symbolic without sacrificing naturalness. Miss Porter is a "realist," but one who knows the connotations as well as the meaning of words. Understatement and inflation are foreign to her; she is never flat and she is never fancy. In the best of her work, the factual and the lyrical are kept in perfect balance. She values the symbol, but she is not, strictly speaking, a symbolic writer. Observed life is the generating factor, and though it may connect with a larger metaphor, it is rooted in the everyday realities of people, situations, and places. The names of the three books collected here supply us with a clue to their author's method: though the stories from which they are drawn have, of course, their singular characters and actions, the title of each suggests a wider meaning. Betrayal in "Flowering Judas," death in "Pale Horse, Pale Rider," and precarious balance in "The Leaning Tower" are both specific and general. Their titles do not belie their particular natures; yet, being themselves, they are more than themselves. They have subjects, but they also have themes.

The clarity of the prose in which these stories are written allows for subtle undercurrents. The qualities of poems — compression, spontaneity, the ability to make connections, and the exploitation of the resources of language — are present, but nothing could be more inimical to Miss Porter's way of doing things than the self-consciousness of "poetic prose." Incident and character are her means; syntax is her instrument; and revelation is her goal. Cocteau once made a distinction between poetry *in* the theater and the poetry *of* the theater. Miss Porter is a poet *of* the short story and she never confuses the issue.

Because the ambiguity of good and evil is the major theme, betrayal is a frequent subject of these stories — betrayal of the self as well as of others. Certain preoccupations reoccur: the hollowness of faith, both religious and political; the mask of charitableness used by the uncommitted and the unloving to disguise their lack of involvement; the eroding effects of dependency; the power of delusion. Many of the characters have something in common: their actions being hopelessly at war with their motives, with the best of intentions, they are lured toward an ironic terror.

Representatives of one of Miss Porter's major notions — since we cannot leave each other alone, it is not always as easy as it looks to tell the victim from the victimizer — they struggle to escape the necessity of confronting themselves, and vaguely hoping to do the right thing, they are hurled into the maelstrom of conflict by forces as mercurial and cunning as those used by the Greek gods. Fate is not, however, an abstraction in these stories; it is more the consequence of character — of weakness, dependence, or the inability to let go of illusion — than it is the drawing out of cosmic plots. Only in "Pale Horse, Pale Rider" do forces outside the self, war and disease, become irrational adversaries.

Evil, to Miss Porter, is a form of moral hypocrisy. In the person of Homer T. Hatch, the malevolent, Lucifer-like catalyst of "Noon Wine," who roams the country collecting rewards on escaped prisoners and mental patients, it operates under the banner of social justice in the cause of profiteering. In Braggioni, the successful revolutionary of "Flowering Judas," it is seen as the degraded daydream of the ideal, which has not only been corrupted by power and sentimentality, but has transformed itself into a complacent form of intimidation. In the two Liberty Bond salesmen who menace Miranda in "Pale Horse, Pale Rider," it takes on the totalitarian cloak of enforced "patriotism."

Moral hypocrisy can disguise itself as anything from a worldwide political movement to self-delusion. But the self-deluded are not necessarily evil. In fact, they can evoke our sympathy — perhaps treacherously — but are distinguished from the evildoer by two important facts: evil is single-minded — a rough definition of it in the canon of Miss Porter's fiction might simply be that view of life that cannot see that everything is at least two-sided — and it lies in a special way by producing terror in the *name* of good. By having the power — or worse, by being given it — to impose its vision of the world on other people, it destroys.

The nature of how and why power is given, where the distinction between the victim and the victimizer gets blurred, is the subject of "Theft." More than a purse is stolen; identity and self-respect are lost by a middle-aged woman who allows herself to be victimized. The innocent can be made to feel guilty. But Miss Porter brings up an unpleasant question: By *allowing* themselves to be *made* to feel guilty, are they *not* guilty? The problem becomes more profound as the field widens or deepens. In "The Leaning Tower," the identity and self-respect of a whole nation is at stake. In "Noon Wine," the very nature of what guilt, identity, and self-respect really are is brought under scrutiny.

Miss Porter can reverse the binoculars either way; she is after the small despot as well as the large one. No one knows better than she that tyranny begins at home. The egotism, pride, and self-pity of the Germans in "The Leaning Tower" have their domestic counterparts in an American family in "The Downward Path to Wisdom." It ends with a little boy singing a song to himself that goes "I hate Papa, I hate Mama, I hate Uncle David, I hate Old Janet, I hate Marjory, I hate

Papa, I hate Mama . . ." The little boy, unlike some of the characters in "The Leaning Tower," has not yet learned to hate whole races and nations, but since his song is an early composition, the chances that he will are good.

The closest thing to a spokesman the author allows herself is called "Miranda," but the one truly innocent world that emerges from these stories can be found in the eight reminiscences of the South that were originally published in "The Leaning Tower." Officially "fiction," they seem to be creations of pure memory and are filled with the sights and sounds of childhood recollection. Beyond this limited nostalgia, innocent but often painful, only the natural and the primitive remain undamaged by the counterclaims of the world.

That may be why Miss Porter's two favorite settings are Texas and Mexico. In both, a primitive view of life does not exclude what is morally decent and necessary. The Indian peasants in the Mexican stories, the farmers and Negroes in the Southern ones are neither good nor bad in any conventionally moral sense. They may be violent, but they act from an implicit set of values in which instinct and feeling have not yet been corroded. The heroine of "Maria Concepcion" kills her rival but is protected from the police by her friends — and even her enemies — in a pact as ancient as jealousy and murder. Morality is pragmatic and involves the living; the mere fact of being alive is more important than justice for the dead.

A different but analogous situation confronts Miranda in "Old Mortality." Nurtured on a romantic version of the past, she learns others; having come to doubt them all, she believes that in *her* life, at least, she will be able to separate legend from falsehood — "in her hopefulness, her ignorance," Miss Porter adds. But the code of the Indian peasant is centered on the continuation of life; it is less concerned with truth as a specific fact, and least of all with truth as an abstract generalization. Maria Concepcion is separated from Miranda by a wide gulf. Maria has faith in life, whereas Miranda puts her trust in the truth. Over and over in these stories, they turn out not to be the same thing. Maria (like Mr. Thompson in "Noon Wine") commits an act of murder that is, paradoxically, an act of faith in life. Miranda (like Laura in "Flowering Judas" and Charles in "The Leaning Tower") has no faith in the name of which an act can be committed.

Miss Porter has added to this collection of her three books of stories a magnificent new long one, "Holiday," three shorter ones, and a modest preface. Good as most of these stories are, they are overshadowed by one work. If it is the function of the artist to produce a masterpiece, Miss Porter may rest easy. In "Noon Wine" she has written a short novel whose largeness of theme, tragic inevitability, and steadiness of focus put it into that small category of superb short fiction that includes Joyce, Mann, Chekhov, James, and Conrad. A study of the effects of evil, it is a story one can turn around in the palm of one's hand forever, for so many meanings radiate from it that each reading gives it a new shade and a further dimension. Without once raising its voice, it asks questions that have alarmed the ages, including our own: When a good man kills an evil man does he become evil himself? If the answer is yes, then how are we to protect ourselves against evil? If the answer is no, then how are we to define what evil is? It is one of the nicer ambiguities of "Noon Wine" that the two "good" men in it commit murder while the one character who is "evil" does not.

In the fateful meeting of the farmer, Mr. Thompson, the deranged Swedish harmonica player, Mr. Helton, and the devil's salesman, Mr. Hatch, Miss Porter has constructed one of those dramas that seem not so much to have been written as discovered intact, like a form in nature. In the perfection of "Noon Wine," Miss Porter has achieved what she has worked for — the artist in total command, totally invisible.

No Safe Harbor

KATHERINE Anne Porter's *Ship of Fools* is the story of a voyage — a voyage that seems to take place in many dimensions. A novel of character rather than of action, it has as its main purpose a study of the German ethos shortly before Hitler's coming to power in Germany. That political fact hangs as a threat over the entire work, and the novel does not end so much as succumb to a historical truth. But it is more than a political novel. *Ship of Fools* is also a human comedy and a moral allegory. Since its author commits herself to nothing but its top layer and yet allows for plunges into all sorts of undercurrents, it is disingenuous to read on its surface alone and dangerous to read for its depths.

Except for the embarkation at Veracruz and a few stopovers at ports, all the events occur aboard the *Vera*, a German passenger freighter, on its twenty-seven-day journey from Mexico to Germany in the summer of 1931. There is no lack

of passengers; the cast is so immense that we are provided
with not one but two keys at the beginning, so that we can
keep the characters clearly in mind. The passenger list includes many Germans; a remarkable company of Spanish
zarzuela singers and dancers — four men and four women —
equally adept at performing, thieving, pimping, and whor-
ing; the satanic six-year-old twins of two of the dancers; and
four Americans — William Denny, a know-nothing chemical
engineer from Texas; Mrs. Treadwell, a divorcée in her forties, who is constantly thwarted in her attempts to disengage
herself from the rest of the human race; and David Scott and
Jenny Brown, two young painters who have been having an
unhappy love affair for years, have never married, and quarrel endlessly. There are also a Swede, some Mexicans, a Swiss
innkeeper and his family, and some Cubans. The Germans
are almost uniformly disagreeable — an arrogant widow, a
windbag of a professor named Hutten, a violently anti-Semitic publisher named Reiber, a drunken lawyer, an Ortho-
dox Jew who loathes Gentiles, a dying religious healer, and
a hunchback, to name just a few. Each suffers from a mortal
form of despair — spiritual, emotional, or religious. At Ha-
vana, La Condesa, a Spanish noblewoman who is being de-
ported by the Cuban government, embarks, and so do eight
hundred and seventy-six migrant workers, in steerage. They
are being sent back to Spain because of the collapse of the
Cuban sugar market.

In the little world of the *Vera*, plying across the ocean, the
passengers become involved with one another not from choice
but by proximity. Because of this, not very much happens,
from the viewpoint of conventional drama. Miss Porter is interested in the interplay of character and not in the strategy

of plotting. Her method is panoramic — cabin to cabin, deck to writing room, bridge to bar. She has helped herself to a device useful to a natural short-story writer: she manipulates one microcosm after another of her huge cast in short, swift scenes. Observed from the outside, analyzed from within, her characters are handled episodically. Place is her organizing element, time the propelling agent of her action. The *Vera* is a Hotel Universe always in motion.

As it proceeds, small crises blossom into odious flowers and expire. There are three major events. An oilman, Herr Freytag, a stainless Aryan, is refused the captain's table once it is learned that the wife he is going back to fetch from Germany is Jewish. A wood-carver in steerage jumps overboard to save a dog thrown into the sea by the twins and is drowned. And the zarzuela company arranges a costume party "gala" whose expressed purpose is to honor the captain but whose real motive is the fleecing of the other passengers. The characters, seeking release or support in one another, merely deepen each other's frustrations. Often these random associations end in violence — a violence always out of character and always revealing. Hansen, the Swede, who talks about a society in which the masses are not exploited, clubs the publisher with a beer bottle. The source of his immediate anger is his disappointed passion for one of the Spanish dancers. The funeral of the wood-carver, the gentlest of men, becomes the occasion for a religious riot. Mrs. Treadwell, a carefully contained woman, well aware of the pointlessness and danger of meddling in other people's business, emerges from behind her bastion and beats up Denny in a drunken frenzy with the heel of a golden evening slipper.

If the relationships are not violent, they are damaging.

Schumann, the ship's doctor, falling suddenly in love with the drug-addicted and possibly mad Condesa, risks his professional, spiritual, and emotional identity. The American painters hopelessly batter themselves in an affair they cannot resolve or leave alone. And the most solid of Hausfraus, Professor Hutten's wife, speaks up suddenly, as if against her will, to contradict her husband at the captain's table, an act doubly shameful for being public. Unable momentarily to put up with her husband's platitudes, to support a view of marriage she knows to be false, Frau Hutten, in her one moment of insight, undermines the only security she has. As character after character gives way to a compulsion he has been unaware of, it becomes evident why Miss Porter's novel is open to many interpretations. Through sheer accuracy of observation rather than the desire to demonstrate abstract ideas, she has hit upon a major theme: order versus need, a theme observable in the interchange of everyday life and susceptible of any number of readings — political, social, religious, and psychological. Every major character is magnetized in time by the opposing forces of need and order. Mexico is the incarnation of need, Germany the representative of an order based on need. At the beginning, in Veracruz, there is a hideously crippled Mexican beggar, "dumb, half blind," who walks like an animal "following the trail of a smell." And the very last character in the book is a German boy in the ship's band, "who looked as if he had never had enough to eat in his life, nor a kind word from anybody," who "did not know what he was going to do next" and who "stared with blinded eyes." As the *Vera* puts in to Bremerhaven, he stands, "his mouth quivering while he shook the spit out of his trumpet, repeating to himself just above a whisper, 'Grüss Gott, Grüss

Gott,' as if the town were a human being, a good and dear trusted friend who had come a long way to welcome him." Aboard the *Vera*, there is, on the one hand, the captain's psychotic authoritarianism, with its absolute and rigid standards of behavior, menaced always by human complexity and squalor; on the other, the Condesa's drug addiction and compulsion to seduce young men. Both are terrifying forms of fanaticism, and they complement each other in their implicit violence.

Dr. Schumann is the mediating agent between these two kinds of fanaticism. Suffering from a weak heart, he is going back to Germany — a Germany that no longer exists — to die. He is the product of a noble Teutonic strain, the Germany of intellectual freedom, scientific dispassion, and religious piety. He is a healer equally at home in the chaos of the steerage and in the captain's stateroom. But the Condesa shatters his philosophic detachment. He goes to her cabin at night and kisses her while she is asleep; he orders six young Cuban medical students to stay away from her cabin because he is jealous. Both acts are symptoms of a progressive desperation. First he refuses to express his need openly, out of fear; then he masks it by a display of authority. He becomes, finally, a conspirator in the Condesa's addiction. Since he is not able to separate the woman from the patient, in Dr. Schumann need and order become muddled. Mrs. Treadwell, an essentially sympathetic character, is drawn into Freytag's dilemma the same way — casually, then desperately. It is she who innocently tells her anti-Semitic cabinmate that Freytag's wife is Jewish, not knowing the information is meant to be confidential. Freytag is bitter, forgetting that he has already blurted out the fact at the captain's table in a fit of anger and pride. Mrs. Treadwell wisely points out that his secret should never have been one in the first place. This is odd wisdom; Mrs. Treadwell has a few secrets of her own.

It is from such moral complications that the texture of *Ship of Fools* evolves — a series of mishaps in which both intention and the lack of intention become disasters. The tragedy is that even the best motive is adulterated when translated into action. Need turns people into fools, order turns them into monsters. The *Vera*'s first-class passengers stroll on deck gazing down into the abysmal pit of the steerage — pure need — just as they watch in envy the frozen etiquette of the captain's table and its frieze of simulated order. Even dowdy Frau Schmitt, a timid ex-teacher who cannot bear suffering in others, finally accepts the cruelty of Freytag's dismissal from the captain's table. If she does not belong there herself, she thinks, then where does she belong? A victim, she thus becomes a party to victimization — a situation that is to receive its perfect demonstration in the world of Nazi Germany, which shadows Miss Porter's book like a bird of carrion. Through the need to belong, the whole damaging human complex of fear, pride, and greed, a governing idea emerges from *Ship of Fools* that is rooted in the Prussian mystique of "blood and iron." It is the manipulation of human needs to conform to a version of order.

The flow of events in *Ship of Fools* is based on addiction (sex, drugs, food, and drink) or obsession (envy, pride, covetousness, and the rest). Yet even the most despicable characters, such as the Jew-hating Herr Rieber, seem surprisingly innocent. It is the innocence of ignorance, not of moral goodness. The humbug and misinformation exchanged between the passengers on the *Vera* are voluminous. Each person is trapped in that tiny segment of reality he calls his own, which he thinks about, and talks about, and tries to project to a listener equally obsessed. Not knowing who they are, these marathon talkers do not know the world they are capable of generating. Love is the sacrificial lamb of their delusions, and though it is pursued without pause, it is always a semblance, never a reality. Though they are terribly in need of some human connection, their humanity itself is in question.

Only the Spanish dancers seem to escape this fate. They transform need into a kind of order by subordinating it for financial gain or sexual pleasure, without involvement. They are comically and tragically evil; they have arranged a universe of money around sex and fraud. Consciously malignant, they are outdone by the natural malice of the twins, who throw the Condesa's pearls overboard in a burst of demoniacal spirits. The pearls are a prize the Spanish dancers had planned to steal. The evil of design is defeated by natural evil — a neat point. Even in this closed, diabolical society, in which the emotions have been disciplined for profit, the irrational disturbs the arrangement of things.

At one point, Jenny Brown recalls something she saw from a bus window when she was passing through a small Indian village in Mexico:

Half a dozen Indians, men and women, were standing together quietly in the bare spot near one of the small houses, and they were watching something very intensely. As the bus rolled by, Jenny saw a man and a woman, some distance from the group, locked in a death battle. They swayed and staggered together in a strange embrace, as if they supported each other; but in the man's raised hand was a long knife, and the woman's breast and stomach were pierced. The blood ran down her body and over her thighs, her skirts were sticking to her legs with her own blood. She was beating him on the head with a jagged stone, and his features were veiled in rivulets of blood. They were silent, and their faces had taken on a saintlike patience in suffering, abstract, purified of rage and hatred in their one holy dedicated purpose to kill each other. Their flesh swayed together and clung, their left arms were wound about each other's bodies as if in love. Their weapons were raised again, but their heads lowered little by little, until the woman's head rested upon his breast and his head was on her shoulder, and holding thus, they both struck again.

It was a mere flash of vision, but in Jenny's memory it lived in an ample eternal day illuminated by a cruel sun.

This passage could be the center from which everything in Miss Porter's novel radiates. The human relations in it are nearly all reenacted counterparts of this silent struggle. Inside and out, the battle rages — the devout against the blasphemous, the Jew against the Gentile, class against class, nation against nation. The seemingly safe bourgeois marriages — of solid Germans, of stolid Swiss — are secret hand-to-hand combats. It is no better with lovers, children, and dogs. The dog thrown into the sea by the evil twins is at least rescued by the good wood-carver before he drowns. But on the human level the issues are obscure, the colors blurred; the saint is enmeshed with the devil. Struggling to get at the truth — *Vera* means "true" in Latin — the passengers in *Ship of Fools* justify its title. What truth is there for people who must lie in order to exist, Miss Porter seems to be asking. Against her insane captain and her mad Condesa, Miss Porter poses only the primitive and the remote — an enchanting Indian servant aboard ship, the appearance of three whales, a peasant woman nursing a baby. They are as affecting as a silence in nature.

Miss Porter is a moralist, but too good a writer to be one except by implication. Dogma in *Ship of Fools* is attached only to dogmatic characters. There is not an ounce of weighted sentiment in it. Its intelligence lies not in the profundity of its ideas but in the clarity of its viewpoint; we are impressed not by what Miss Porter says but by what she knows. Neither heartless nor merciful, she is tough. Her virtue is disinterestedness, her strength objectivity. Her style is free of displays of "sensitivity," musical effects, and interior decoration. Syntax is the only instrument she needs to construct an enviable prose. But the book differs from her extraordinary stories and novellas in that it lacks a particular magic she has attained so many times on a smaller scale. The missing ingredient is impulse. *Ship of Fools* was twenty years in the writing; the stories read as if they were composed at one sitting, and they have the spontaneity of a running stream. *Ship of Fools* is another kind of work — a summing up, not an overflowing — and it is devoid of one of the excitements of realistic fiction. The reader is never given that special satisfaction of the drama of design, in which the strings, having come unwound, are ultimately tied together in a knot. Miss Porter scorns patness and falseness, but by the very choice of her method she also lets go of suspense. She combines something of the intellectual strategy of Mann's *Magic Mountain* (in which the characters not only are themselves but represent ideas in human qualities) with the symbolic grandeur of *Moby Dick* (in which a predestined fate awaits the chief actors). Her goodbye to the themes of Mexico and Germany (two subjects that have occupied her elsewhere) is a stunning farewell, but it lacks two components usually considered essential to masterpieces — a hero and a heroic extravagance.

Ship of Fools is basically about love, a human emotion that teeters helplessly between need and order. On the *Vera*'s voyage there is precious little of it. The love that comes too late for the Condesa and Dr. Schumann is the most touching thing in it. But the Condesa is deranged, ill, and exiled; the dying doctor is returning to a Germany that has vanished. The one true example of love — a pair of Mexican newlyweds — is never dwelt upon. We are left with this image of two people, hand in hand, who have hardly said a word in all the thousands that make up Miss Porter's novel. In *Ship of Fools*, every human need but one is exposed down to its nerve ends. Love alone remains silent, distant, and abstract.

The Lonesomeness
and Hilarity of Survival

Losing Battles, Eudora Welty's novel, begins with a rooster crowing and the moon going down "one day short of the full." Although the day is specific — an August Sunday in the nineteen thirties, in the northeastern hill country of Mississippi, near the small town of Banner — the dawn we witness seems more like the first morning of the world. By the time the novel is over, the rich local speech of its characters has managed another note: the sound of a chorus telling its version of the story of the human race. One tale made up of many, layer on layer, the novel advances in a series of rural-comedy scenes that recall the head-on collisions and mock calamities of slapstick farce. But its real action winds downward and backward into the past through remembered incidents, each voice supplying another thread of the tangled story of the Vaughn, Renfro, and Beecham families as they gather to celebrate the ninetieth birthday of Elvira Jordan

Vaughn — Granny. Granny is eventually the center of a throng of people — her grandchildren, her great-grandchildren, babies, friends, neighbors, strangers — and dogs. Surrounding her, the crowd is itself surrounded by a natural world described in deliberately metaphorical terms; the long comedy is suffused by nature, not played against it, and it departs from the natural only through the machine and the homemade (the wreck of a truck, a banged-up school bus, a tin roof, a makeshift wedding dress) — the broken-down engines of poverty and the ingenious charms that ward it off.

Because *Losing Battles* is social rather than psychological, it is focused on the group. None of its characters occupies the stage for long; stage center belongs to the chorus. Its hero, therefore, is a *real* hero, in the theatrical sense, and his arrival is prepared for as carefully as the entrance of the lead in a romantic comedy. Nineteen-year-old Jack Renfro, who has served two years in the pen for trying to rescue Granny's gold ring while protecting his sister's honor, escapes from jail the day before he would have been paroled, in order to attend Granny's reunion. And when he appears, he is everything we expected: charming, undauntable, true-blue — the spunky teenager of the comic strip, the golden boy of legend. Yet in his seemingly competent hands the world continually flies apart. Waiting for him are his orphan-wife and former teacher, Gloria, and the baby he has never seen. As Jack, Gloria, and the baby — the tiny family inside the big one — wander away once or twice to undergo their adventures, a rival center of the story comes to light: an offstage character, Julia Mortimer, the teacher at the Banner school, whose career has spanned the generations. A disruptive force in the impoverished but exuberant lives of the Banner farmers, she is resisted, but her strength matches theirs, not so much in a losing battle as in a battle of equal powers — that is, until hers fail. The day of Granny's reunion turns out to be the day Julia Mortimer dies.

The coincidence is appropriate; Granny and Miss Mortimer, though never in conflict in the narrative, are opposed powers in the novel. Granny, the "source" of the more than fifty people present, hands on the torch of biological renewal. Miss Mortimer dreams of handing on a torch of a different kind; she has a vision of a stream of teachers and students following in her path, the bearers of a tradition of learning and knowledge. Gloria Renfro is the pivotal character between the two older women, the unwitting carrier of a double heritage, for she is both Miss Mortimer's chosen protégée and Jack Renfro's wife, both the mate and the educator of her husband. Lacking Miss Mortimer's sense of commitment and Jack's capacity for love in general, Gloria is endearing and life-size, a game fighter caught between larger forces — and, just possibly, a winner.

Granny's reunion is a day of revelations, each erasing a mystery, only to leave another in its place. When Judge Moody, the man who sentenced Jack, arrives, battle-scarred, after a scene that Harold Lloyd would have appreciated (the Judge abandons his Buick, its motor running, as it dangles precariously on top of a hill, the object of punishing attempts at rescue, including a charge of dynamite), he, too, it turns out, has secret information: a letter scrawled by Miss Mortimer before her death. He reads it as night falls over the reunion. In it Miss Mortimer sums up her life:

"I've had it driven in on me — the reason I never could win for good is that both sides were using the same tactics. . . . A teacher teaches and a pupil learns or fights against learning with the same force behind him. It's the survival instinct. It's a mighty power, it's an iron weapon while it lasts. It's the desperation of staying alive against all odds that keeps both sides encouraged. But the side that gets licked gets to the truth first. When the battle's over, something may dawn there — with no help from the teacher, no help from the pupil, no help from the book. . . . Now that . . . I can survey the years, I can see it all needs doing over, starting from the beginning. . . . I'm alive as ever, on the brink of oblivion, and I caught myself once on the verge of disgrace. Things like this are put in your path to teach you. You can make use of them, they'll bring you one stage, one milestone, further along your road. You can go crawling next along the edge of madness, if that's where you've come to. There's a lesson in it. You can profit from knowing that you needn't be ashamed to crawl — to keep on crawling, to be proud to crawl to where you can't crawl any further. Then you can find yourself lying flat on your back — look what's carried you another mile. . . . And there's something I want to impart to you. . . . It's a warning. There's been one thing I never did take into account. Watch out for innocence."

Julia Mortimer's last and biggest lesson is that lessons come from life, not from books, and she is buried not under the doorstep of the Banner school, as she requested, but in an ordinary grave. Banner takes her in, at last, all too literally.

The small-town values, the Baptist and Methodist sureties that permeate *Losing Battles*, could easily seem remote — a world under glass. Miss Welty transcends the narrow range of its action without shifting focus or underlining a point. From under the comic surface of the novel the vapors of the dungeon rise. Brutality, senility, death, and murder make their appearances, as ominous as the coffin in the back of the gravedigger's truck when he turns up, unbidden, at the reunion. And certain scenes have a startling, primitive intensity. When the mystery of Gloria's parents seems about to be solved, when it seems likely that she has always been a part of the family and is therefore a first cousin of Jack's, she cries out, "I don't want to be a Beecham! . . . I won't be a Beecham!" The gathered aunts, crying "Say Beecham!," throw her to the ground and force her to swallow chunks of watermelon, the juice covering her face and body like blood. The domestic, female world of food, child-rearing, and gossip suddenly takes on the shock of an initiation or a sacrifice. Granny gets up on a table to dance — a macabre bit of theater.

When violence crops up in *Losing Battles*, it is always in scale. The humor, on the other hand, is not; it is outsize, a humor of accordionlike expansion — the slow take, the double take, the take repeated. The long-windedness of Judge Moody's Buick scene is an integral part of what makes it funny: attempts to rise from the dust only fix the strivers more deeply in it. Losing battlers are dogged; they go on and on. The novel is not symbolic, an allegory or a parable, but as its characters stumble into a series of follies, which in turn lead to more, this effect of mistake piled upon mistake, this sense of endless wasted effort, reverberates largely in a book whose basic ingredients are the big ones: birth, love, and death — each leading to the others in endless repetition. In *Losing Battles*, it is effort and resistance that count. The title is ironic; there are no victories other than survival.

As comical and feeling as it is, *Losing Battles* is neither ingratiating nor sentimental. In its large design, human meanness and failure are given their just due. There are no false notes. Because nothing is shirked and nothing is whimsical, poverty never makes a sociological point. It isn't picturesque; it doesn't call for pity. No one in *Losing Battles* is a freak or a statistic. The ties that bind its people together are as necessary as water. Everyone (except Jack's young brother) is a prodigal talker, for the sound of the human voice is a major entertainment and a source of security; it has staying power. The people sing hymns, they listen to a sermon, they talk on through the day and into the night; the way a tale is told has as much value as the truth it tells. The idea that these characters are simpleminded or buffoons or hillbillies or crackers never comes up; Miss Welty is too good and too just a writer. And in the character of Granny she earns our complete confidence. Granny could, in other hands, have been maudlin or idiosyncratic. Here, perfectly poised and funny as hell, she eludes the obvious as well as the eccentric.

Losing Battles is the attempt of people in a history book they can't quite read to tell and reshape their story, to explain how it never was and never could be what it first appears to be. In one splendid passage Miss Welty makes her theme clear:

"And we're sitting here in the dark, ain't we?" said somebody.

"Turn on them lights, then, Vaughn!" Uncle Dolphus called. "Why did you let 'em snake in here and hook you up to current for? For mercy's sakes let's shine!"

Suddenly the moonlit world was doused; lights hard as pick-axe blows drove down from every ceiling and the roof of the passage, cutting the house and all in it away, leaving them an island now on black earth, afloat in night, and nowhere, with only each other. In that first moment, every face, white-lit but with its caves of mouth and eyes opened wide, black with the lonesomeness and hilarity of survival, showed its kinship to Uncle Nathan's, the face that floated over theirs. For the first time, all talk was cut off, and no baby offered to cry. Silence came travelling in on solid, man-made light.

Mostly talk (and what talk!), *Losing Battles* brings to life voices that are individually characteristic and yet archetypal. The folk tale, the metaphor, and the realistic novel have been welded into a single sound. For its author, a pastoral clearly needs farmers. The result is an epic of kin rather than a family chronicle, specifically American in its speech but universal in its poetry, as if Mark Twain and the Shakespeare of *A Midsummer Night's Dream* had collaborated in celebrating three basic human rituals: a birthday, a wedding, and a funeral.

A House Divided

Eudora welty's novel *The Optimist's Daughter*, which first appeared in *The New Yorker* of March 15, 1969, is a miracle of compression, the kind of book, small in scope but profound in its implications, that rewards a lifetime of work. Its style is at the service of a story that follows its nose with the instincts of a good hunting dog never losing the scent of its quarry. And its story has all those qualities peculiar to the finest short novels: a theme that vibrates with overtones, suspense, and classical inevitability.

Known as a "Southern regionalist," Miss Welty is too good for pigeonholing labels. Though she has stayed close to home, two interlocking notions have been demonstrated in her fiction: how easily the ordinary turns into legend, and how firmly the exotic is grounded in the banal. They are subjects only partly dependent on locale. In *The Optimist's Daughter* we are in the South once more, but a South where real distinctions are made between Texas and Mississippi, and Mississippi and West Virginia. And if place has been Miss Welty's touchstone, the pun implicit in the word "place" comes alive in her new novel; its colloquial meaning — caste, class, position — is as important as its geographical one.

When Laurel Hand, a Mississippian living in Chicago, is summoned to a New Orleans hospital to join her father, a seventy-one-year-old judge who is about to undergo a critical eye operation, she clashes with his new, and second, wife, Fay. Laurel is a withdrawn widow still mourning for a husband killed in World War II, and Fay is a childish vulgarian embarked on the one secure relationship of her life. The conflict between these middle-aged women begins a war between worlds hopelessly at odds. Out of the discordant jumble of three lives trapped in a claustrophobic hospital room, a fourth figure emerges — Becky, the judge's first wife.

Because the struggle between Laurel and Fay is a battle of values, it takes place inside Laurel as well; she is forced for the first time in her life to examine what she believes in. The judge, hovering in some twilight zone of pain, immobilized by sandbags, is set upon by Fay, who breaks down under the tension. Though she is not the direct cause of his death, she is implicated in it. From Laurel's point of view, Fay scares him to death. Later, Fay claims that she was trying "to scare him into life." It is a tribute to Miss Welty's skill and fairness that we are able to entertain the notion seriously.

Still, there is a danger in *The Optimist's Daughter* of the case being stacked, of Laurel being too much the gentlewoman, and Fay too harshly the brash opportunist. In truth, Fay is a horror but eludes being evil. Barely two-dimensional, she is saved by being credibly stupid. Naïveté doesn't make her any less destructive but saves her from being malevolent. Laurel is too nice but escapes being a prig. If Fay were a monster and Laurel simply nostalgic, the arena of the action would shrink. What we would have would be case histories. Miss Welty redresses the balance in two ways.

She does something necessary by sketching in Laurel's background in a few delicate strokes. Her childhood days at Becky's mountaintop house in West Virginia, which recall Becky's childhood as well, are the most beautiful pages in the Welty canon, extraordinary passages in an extraordinary book. They yield more than the eye at first takes in. A rural world of innocence comes flying into the imagination as pure as a primary color; its arrival is real, not romantic, and gives genuine weight to a way of life Laurel must eventually abandon. As for Fay, the author does something audacious: she takes on Fay's family. The surprise appearance of the Chisoms — Fay's relatives — at the judge's funeral in Mississippi enlarges the frame of the novel, which is being widened, actually, from two directions: Laurel's past, and the future implicit in Fay.

The funeral itself is macabre and funny, like most funerals. Large emotions center the scene, but somewhere, not too far off in the distance, the edges begin to crinkle; life not being geared to deal with its big moments, comedy sneaks in the back door, a neutralizing antidote to the intensity of the book's strongly felt loyalties and losses.

Though they exist under the shadow of her domination and menace, Fay's relatives make solid claims on life — vitality and endurance — that have to be weighed against Laurel's tradition and understanding. Fay is crude; her family is common as dirt, but they make their point: it takes dirt to make things grow. The difference between the crude Texan and the genteel Mississippian is easy to know but hard to do, and harder to do right. And more than Texas and Mississippi are involved. An onrushing world of shoddy materialism but of attractive energy is set against a vanishing world of civilized values but of special privilege.

Two kinds of people, two versions of life, two contending forces in America collide in *The Optimist's Daughter*. Its small dramatic battle sends reverberations in every direction.

Miss Welty is equally adept at redneck lingo, mountain twang, and the evasions of middle-class speech, but it is her inability to falsify feelings that gives the novel its particular sense of truth. Fay doesn't only represent something; she *is* something. And Laurel takes on flesh and blood as she is slowly drawn back through time into the circumstances of Becky's death. The judge's death is tragic, but there is something more tragic still, the separation of the sick and the doomed from the people who love them. An unbreachable wall, in Becky's case, turns the living into the enemies of the dying and isolates them, on opposite sides, helpless.

An instructive scene that at first seems a digression underlines the moral subtlety of the novel. Four old-lady friends of Laurel's are gossiping in the garden the day after the funeral. Their malice toward Fay is well honed and well deserved, but an uncomfortable question formulates itself: wouldn't any stranger intruding on the provincial bastion of Mount Salus, lovable and loyal though it may be to its self-elected members, get the same treatment? Fay is raked over the coals, yet Laurel, the one person who has reason to hate her, overhears rather than participates in the conversation. She can't stomach Fay, but she can't stomach this ganging up on Fay either. Because Laurel can see two things at once in a world where it's better to see only one, her position is complex but weakened. Her kind of moral strength has, inevitably, its corollary weakness. There's one truth she can't get around: Fay was her father's wife, and she didn't storm the gates of Mount Salus, she was invited in.

In a final confrontation scene, Laurel and Fay meet head-on. In the back of a cupboard, Laurel discovers an old bread-board — a beautifully carved and finished piece of wood made by her husband for her mother — now moldy, scratched, ragged, stained by cigarette butts. As if she still had something to protect, Laurel, in the face of Fay's insults and condescension, finds herself holding the board over her head, a symbol of everything, but now a potential weapon. When Fay tells Laurel that she doesn't know how to fight, Laurel suddenly realizes that Fay doesn't know what they're fighting for, that to win this particular battle, to *want* to win it, is already to have lost it. Fay's victory is to have inherited the house, but its human values, the meaning of the life that has been lived in it, escapes her, as it always has and always will. Laurel's victory is to have those values, finally, so firmly before her. But those values are all she has.

The scene is dramatically climactic but thematically incon-clusive. When Laurel lets go of the breadboard, she isn't thinking of her dead father or her dead mother or her dead husband but, oddly, of *Fay's* nephew, Wendell, a little boy from Madrid, Texas, who attended the funeral without the faintest notion of what he was seeing or hearing. It is because of *him* that Laurel lays down her weapon, relinquishing the past to the dead at last. When she does, the question of whether there is to be a future assumes importance, for a fact that floated behind the scenes becomes apparent at the same moment: she and Fay share a common emptiness; both of them are widowed and childless. No matter who wins, that emptiness will echo across the rooms of what was once the most distinguished house in Mount Salus, or be replaced, ultimately, by new voices.

The best book Eudora Welty has ever written, *The Optimist's Daughter* is a long goodbye in a very short space not only to the dead but to delusion and to sentiment as well.

JEAN STAFFORD

Jean: Some Fragments

I MET her by subletting an apartment in New York, hers and Robert Lowell's, in the early forties. The war was on; I had been hired by the Office of War Information on 57th Street and was looking for a place to stay. Cal was still in jail, serving out his term as a conscientious objector; Jean had finished *Boston Adventure* and was waiting for it to be published. She was going away somewhere for a few months — England, I think — but maybe it was Boston. I don't remember. The apartment, in a brownstone on 17th Street overlooking Stuyvesant Park, was graceful and old-fashioned and full of things Jean loved: Victorian sofas, lamps with pleated shades, deep engulfing chairs, small objects on tables, and books, books, books. Those in the bedroom bookcase were mainly religious; she was a Catholic convert at the time, or at least receiving instruction. She had a weakness for mechanical toys: a bear that turned the pages of a book (named after a well-known critic), a fire truck that turned at sharp right angles and raced across the floor at great speed. When Jean returned from England (or Boston), she would visit me occasionally, always bringing a pint of whiskey in a brown paper bag — either as a matter of scrupulous courtesy or because she felt she couldn't count on my supply — and we would drink and talk. And laugh. A demure quality about her alternated with a kind of Western no-nonsense toughness, and she shed years every time she laughed, showing her gums like a child or an ancient. Funny and sharp about people, she loved gossip. We became friends.

We developed, over the years, a tendency to make elaborate plans that were never carried out. This was particularly true of travel, which we both dreaded. Europe eluded us at least six times. We *did* get to Boston once for a Thanksgiving weekend, but even then something went wrong. We were to meet on the train but never did. We found each other, finally, in South Station, exhausted and bewildered.

I remember seeing a life mask of Jean — Jean the way she looked before the car accident that changed her face forever. (I had known her only since the accident, which occurred while she was married to Lowell.) A handsome woman, she had once been beautiful in a more conventional way, or so the mask suggested. "The Interior Castle" describes the surgical procedure with chilling exactitude; its central conceit is of the brain as a castle probed and assaulted by alien forces. I often forgot that Jean had been through this traumatic ordeal, and the long adjustment that must have been necessary afterwards. That fact, when I remembered it, always made the killing of the girl (rather than the boy) in *The Mountain Lion* more poignant. It also cast a light on Jean's predilection for masks and disguises. She liked to dress up — but in the manner of a child at a Halloween party. Once she came to my house for drinks and emerged from the kitchen wearing a joke mask with a big red nose. Another time I visited her in East Hampton and she answered the door dressed as a cocktail waitress, or something very close.

On her back door, there was a warning sign forbidding entrance to anyone who used the word "hopefully" incorrectly.

A noted hypochondriac, she outdid everyone in real and imagined illnesses. I was waiting for her outside Longchamps at 48th and Madison (bygone days!) when I noticed her suddenly across the street on crutches. It was snowing, I think, a nice, light New York snow. Astonished, I walked over to help her — she was already in the middle of the street by the time I got to her. She was wearing a red plaid cape, very stylish, peculiarly suited to crutches — no sleeves got in the way. When we were safely back on the sidewalk, she said, "Look! Look at these!" and showed me her wrist. Little white blotches were appearing, a sort of albino rash. "What is it?" I asked. "I don't know." She hobbled into lunch. I hadn't even had time to ask about the crutches before she'd been stricken by something new. I never did get the story about the crutches straight. A hypochondriac myself, I was outclassed.

Jean enjoyed medical discussions, symptoms, diagnoses, horror stories, freak accidents, diseases, cures. She owned a

Merck's Manual and a gruesome textbook we would sometimes pore over, looking at the more hideous skin diseases in
color. She was an amateur authority on ailments, including
her own.

Although she was easily influenced, she was the least imi-
tative person I knew. Older women of distinction became
her friends — at least twice — and she would bank her originality in a deference of a peculiar kind, as if a mother with
standards — a woman of impeccable authority — had been
in the back of her mind all the while. But in dress, manner,
and ideas she was independent and crotchety, and about
writers her opinions were her own and unshakable. She
adored cats, old furniture — Biedermeier especially —
books, bourbon, odd clothes. Like the dress she used to
wear that looked like a man's tuxedo and seemed to have a
watch pinned to the lapel. The plaid cape. Fawn slacks and
sweaters. She was a special mixture of the outlandish and the
decorous. She paid great respect to the civilized, but something ingrained and Western in her mocked it at the same
time. Think of Henry James being brought up in
Colorado. . . .

Her favorite cat, George Eliot, used to sit under a lamp,
eyes closed, basking in the warmth. Jean was proud of that,
as if it were some extraordinary feline accomplishment.

In Westport, before she married for the second time, she
had her own apartment for a while. I noticed two typewrit-
ers, one big, one small. I asked her about them. "The big
one's for the novel and the little one's for short stories."

We were going to a cocktail party for St. Jean-Perse. I called for her. We had a drink and then another. Then — and how many times this happened between us! — one of us asked the fatal question: "Do you *really* want to go?" We never got there.

The Met. An opera box. Jean and I turned to each other after the first act of *Andrea Chénier*. This time, the fatal question remained unspoken. We got up and left.

Guilty dawdling became a kind of game between us, as well as a safety valve. If I secretly didn't want to go somewhere, I knew I could always stop off at Jean's and that would be a guarantee of never arriving at my original destination. In any case — or every — Jean was more interesting than anywhere I might be going.

A stitched sampler with the words "God Bless America" hung over her television screen.

She had a dream, a dream in which Arran Island (the one off Scotland, where her forebears came from, not the Aran Islands off Ireland) and the Greek island of Samothrace were historically connected. She paid a visit to Arran Island, and, eventually, she and A. J. Liebling, her third and last husband, went to Samothrace. She began to read seriously in anthropology and archaeology, particularly Lehman on the digs in Samothrace. But I think the broad view of ancient history and mythology required to complete a project mainly intuitive and then oddly confirmed by fact became too complicated and technical for her. What she had started to write with so much enthusiasm couldn't be finished. I stopped asking her about it the way I later stopped asking her about the novel in which her father was the chief character. But one day she let me read what she had of the Samothrace piece — about forty pages — and it was some of the most extraordinary prose I'd ever read. After I'd finished it, I looked at her and said something like, "My God, Jean, if you don't go on with it, at least publish *this*. . . ." I don't know what happened to it. Although Joe Liebling did everything to encourage Jean to write, she was intimidated by his swiftness, versatility, and excellence as a reporter. She shot off in journalistic directions of her own — the book on Oswald's mother, for instance. One day, Joe and I were riding up together in the elevator at *The New Yorker*. I told Joe I'd read the Samothrace piece and how good I thought it was. "I know," he said, "I wish you'd tell her." "I *have*," I said. And added, "I wish I could write prose like *that*. . . ." Joe, about to get off at his floor, turned to me and said, "I wish *I* could. . . ."

She was a born writer, and if certain mannerisms entered her prose later on, there was no question, in my mind at least, that she was one of the most naturally gifted writers I'd ever known. She simply couldn't write a bad sentence, excellence was a matter of personal integrity, the style was the woman. She couldn't stand the half-baked, the almost-good, the so-so. She made her views clear in a series of brilliant book reviews, still uncollected. They are all of a piece throughout, united by a single sensibility and an unwavering intelligence. And the annual round-up reviews of children's books she did for *The New Yorker* were scalpel-like attacks on mediocrity, commercial greed, stupidity, and cant.

One of her qualities hardest to get down on paper was the young girl always present in the civilized and cultivated woman. The balance was delicate and impossible to pin down. Like her conversation, it vanished into smoke. But what smoke!

A strangely momentous occasion: when she and Joe Liebling took an apartment on Fifth Avenue and 11th Street — an elegant, rambling apartment in a house built by Stanford White — before they moved in, Jean and Elizabeth Bowen and I walked about the rooms, talking about rugs, draperies, and so on. One of the rare times in New York City when people were dwarfed by space. Steve Goodyear gave Jean two plants. One, a rubber plant, had leaves that scraped the ceiling — eighteen, maybe twenty feet high.

Jean and I (at Fifth and 11th) sometimes would take out her Ouija board when I came over early for a drink. (This must have been in the late fifties.) The person always summoned up by Jean was her brother Dick, killed in the Second World War. The board would begin to shake, she would become excited by the message she read. . . . But these sessions never lasted long. Joe Liebling didn't like Jean using the Ouija board, and when we heard his key in the door, the board was hastily put away.

The farmhouse Joe Liebling bought in the thirties was first his, then theirs, then hers. It brought her enormous pleasure. She embarked on a long series of renovations, mostly of the interior; each change was a great source of satisfaction, perhaps too much so, for a writer discovers — especially a writer who lives alone — that a house can become a formidable enemy of work. Creative energy is drained off in redecorated guest rooms, expanded gardens, kitchens designed and redesigned to be more practical, new wallpaper, decking, house plants — the list is endless. In Jean's case, off the downstairs dining room she built a new bathroom in one direction and a new study–*cum*–guest room in another; a second new study appeared upstairs. The kitchen was revamped. The thirty or so acres surrounding the farmhouse boasted a particularly beautiful meadow some distance behind her house, a greensward worthy of a château. The shingled farmhouse was ample but modest. Its small living room had a fireplace set at an angle so that no one could ever quite face it. There was a larger dining room and a kitchen and pantry. Farmers didn't waste their money on unnecessary fuel, and, originally, the living room had been a concession to formality rather than a social center. The Liebling-Stafford house had been built for practicality (close to the road in case of a snowstorm), snugness, and warmth. It was a comfortable house and Jean fell in love with it — slowly, I think. It became —in the end — her refuge and her garrison, the place she holed up in and from which she viewed the world. The literal view was pretty enough because, from the front window, across Fire Place Road, you could see the water of an inlet, often intensely blue. There was an apple tree in the backyard, seemingly dead. It developed a new twisted limb and became grotesquely lovely. Behind it, there were many yucca plants with their white desert flowers, and in front of the house a mimosa tree that bloomed each spring.

In spite of a certain reputation for waspishness, the result of a sharply honed and witty tongue, Jean was generous and courageous. When she was accused of being the leader of the supposedly quixotic NBA jury that chose Walker Percy's *The Moviegoer* as the best novel of the year (no one had ever heard of Walker Percy before), she stood up for herself, and for him. And the same thing was true when John Williams's Prix de Rome was withdrawn. She spoke up for anyone she admired. Her nervous but good-natured allure derived from a special combination of the tart and the sweet. She was a surprisingly fine cook, liked entertaining and being entertained (at least for the better part of her life), and, above all, enjoyed good conversation.

She could resist a good writer if she disliked his person, but she was far more open to affection and the giving of it than seems generally known. She put herself out for people she liked and did nothing at all for people she didn't.

Youthfulness of manner was belied by the satiric thrust of her language, the slightly breathless drawl of her speech, the odd sense that she was searching for the next installment of words, another piece of the story, some phrase that would precisely focus what she had in mind — habits of speech cruelly underlined by her stroke, when she became unsure — she, of all people! — of her words. It was unfair and particularly cruel to be stricken at the very center of her being: talk, words, speech. It was not unlike — in the meanness of the affliction undercutting the essential person — Beethoven's going deaf.

She was anecdotal in the extreme, turning everything into a story. This became, later on, and long before the stroke, somewhat edgy. A certain amount of complaining, of being the great-lady-offended had become habitual. Something on the order of "And do you know who had the *nerve* to invite me to dinner last Wednesday?" And so on. But then it would turn out that she had *gone* to dinner, so that the point of the complaint seemed muddled. Once she had taken a real distaste to someone, she refused any invitation, any offer of friendship. And she made enemies easily by being outspoken, opinionated, strict in her standards. Once she took a real scunner to someone, she rarely changed her mind.

She felt abandoned by her friends, sometimes, and they, sometimes, by her. She would forget you for a time and then be hurt and surprised that she had been temporarily forgotten. People I think she liked without qualification: Mrs. Rattray, Saul Steinberg, John Stonehill, Peter Taylor, Elizabeth Bowen, Peter De Vries.

We had dinner together for the last time on July 13, 1978, in East Hampton, at a restaurant called Michael's. I called for Jean. Not being able to drive had once united us; now I had a driver's license. Convenient as it was, I'm not sure Jean approved of it. We arrived — down dark paths to a restaurant on the water. Jean, who had been drinking at home, ordered another bourbon. The question of what to order loomed. No menu came to hand; a young waitress reeled off the available fish of the day. Jean deferring, I ordered striped bass. Then Jean said, "I cannot do striped bass." But she didn't seem to be able to do anything else, either, and, after some confusion, I asked the waitress to give us a few minutes. I went over again what fish were available. The waitress came back. Jean said, "Striped bass." I asked her if she was *sure*, considering that she'd said she couldn't do striped bass, and she said she was *absolutely* sure. But when her dish came, she said, "This isn't what I wanted." I wanted to send it back; Jean said not to. Then she added, "What I really wanted was the finnan haddie." There hadn't been any finnan haddie; it had never been mentioned. And I realized we were in some kind of trouble, though most of the conversation was rational, pleasant, at times funny. Suddenly she said, "What do you think of friends?" I was surprised, but babbled on about how they might be the most important people in one's life, not the same as lovers, of course, but desperately· needed, a second family, essential. . . . Jean said, lighting a cigarette, "Yes, I must give them up. I'm going to give up smoking." And it became clear she had meant the word "cigarettes" or "smokes" when she said "friends." And I suddenly remembered something: years ago, way back, a mutual friend had described cigarettes as "twenty little friends in a pack — twenty friends always available. . . ." I thought: Could there be a memory behind the choice of every mistaken word?

We talked on the phone twice while she was in New York Hospital. I called again on the afternoon of March 26 because I was going up to see my doctor on East 68th Street and thought I'd stop by and see her. The voice on the phone told me she was no longer there. They had no forwarding address, no information. I called East Hampton. No answer — odd, because there had always been a phone machine where you could leave a message. I couldn't figure out where she'd gone. To the Rusk Rehabilitation Center, it turned out later, a special outpost of the hospital. I found out the next day she had died that afternoon.

PART FIVE

The Poet's Voice

How much the reputation of a writer depends on critical attention! And how little attention is paid to writers who are either too popular or too "obvious" to merit close reading or explication. What pleasure is there in writing criticism that reveals what everyone can see for himself? By the nature of the beast, criticism is attached to the enigmatic. And the enigmatic is assumed to be new just as the new is assumed to be important. About certain writers — no matter how good — practically nothing is said. For every piece on E. M. Forster there are a hundred on Virginia Woolf, for every essay on Tolstoy two hundred on Joyce. The plainer the writer the less there is to explain, or so it seems at first glance. "Modernism" has spawned a backyard of critics eager to untangle the intricacies of this or that new phenomenon for an abashed public or admiring colleagues. To imagine a critical establishment with nothing to unravel is like imagin-

ing a processing factory with nothing to process. So the difficulty, the *unavailability*, of a work spawns — in numerical
proportion — interpreters: shedding light, showing the way,
and re-creating the work while creating its reputation. There
are fashions in difficulty as there are in hats. Fashions do not
detract from genius; they merely allow copiers an opportunity for reproduction at bargain prices. Yesterday's avant-
garde — Eliot, Joyce, Stravinsky, Picasso — all seem now remarkably congenial. The process has even been speeded up:
except to a very few, John Ashbery was ten years ago an
inaccessible writer; he may soon be in danger of becoming a
household word.

And so it comes as a surprise to find Richard Poirier, in
Robert Frost: The Work of Knowing, tackling a poet who has up
to now been considered self-evident. Used as a model to
counter the difficulties of Eliot, Yeats, and Stevens, Frost
has been taken for granted as a dispenser of recognizable wis-
doms and acknowledged truths — good, maybe great, but
needing no gloss. Randall Jarrell in two essays, "The Other
Frost" and "To the Laodiceans," began the complicated task
of rescuing Frost from his admirers by examining the texts
in the way they deserved, separating the extraordinary writer
from the public man. Frost played the Yankee rustic deep in
the verities; except in scattered statements on poetry, his critical intelligence was masked. As early as 1917, he wrote in a
letter to Louis Untermeyer, "All the fun is . . . saying
things . . . that almost but don't quite formulate. I should
like to be so subtle at this game as to seem to a casual person
altogether obvious."

Why the notion of Frost as a one-dimensional grand
old man of American letters developed — and why it is

wrong — is Mr. Poirier's subject. In his close reading of representative poems, he sees Frost's work as "a perpetual debate between, on the one side, the inherent necessity for form in language and in nature, which requires a dialogue of accommodation, and, on the other, the equally inherent human need for excursion beyond form." The argument involves method as well as theme: the grand sonorities of traditional English poetry scored against vernacular New England speech, and the idea of "home" — a place of rest, love, and enclosure — in opposition to the desire for flight from it. Frost used Thoreau's word "extra-vagance" to imply more than excess — to stand for the need to go beyond the strictures of the formed, whether they were to be found in the domestication of marriage or in the metrical pattern of the poem itself. Since form was the basic subject and putting it into form the method, a poem became a secret commentary on itself. As Mr. Poirier explains, Frost's speculative "walks" were both real actions and metaphoric devices, the theme of a poem and the way to write it. ("He would have known that 'stanza' means 'room' — so that when he walks out into the woods, he takes his 'room' with him.") Frost often cast himself as a meditative wanderer temporarily off base, searching for freedom yet regretting its restrictive loneliness, or hankering for security only to find it limiting and dull. These two states were not mutually exclusive. Ambivalence enriches implications, and Mr. Poirier discovers unexpected meanings in texts long familiar:

"Stopping by Woods on a Snowy Evening" is about a central human experience — the enchantments that invite us to surrender ourselves to oblivion; "Mending Wall" is about the opposite impulse, which is to fence yourself in, to form relationships that are really exclusions. But at the same time and in the same terms both poems propose that these human dilemmas are also poetic ones, in the one case the possibly destructive solicitations of the sublime and in the other the claustrophobias of mechanical forms. The poems are about the will to live asserting itself against invitations either to surrender or to constraint, and these, it is intimated, issue as much from the convention of poetry as from conventions of feeling.

These might be overreadings if the context were not so intelligent that Frost becomes something altogether new; the effect is like listening to a symphonic chestnut revitalized under the baton of a gifted young conductor. Beneath the easy surfaces of the poems, tensions between speech and eloquence, commitment and rebellion, and heaven and earth struggle for resolution. The frequent use of the words "stars" and "walls" suggests a connection between — and the distance that separates — the earthbound and the sublime. Frost worked in the mine field of the middle ground: a realist who believed in instinct and a rationalist drunk on the romantic. A spokesman for altitude, but only up to "a certain height" — his notion of freedom was hedged in by reservations.

Frost's preoccupation with the natural world overlay two concurrent obsessions: love as a vital force surrounded by mythic rituals (or sometimes merely formal conventions), and poetry as a natural gift in need of shaping and pruning. Nature, love, poetry: a triple strand, each thread spun of something native and something civilized, is interlaced in poem after poem. Mr. Poirier's most original teasing out of inner meanings is in tracing the inherent sexuality of Frost's poems. Frost himself said that the subject of "The Subverted Flower" was "frigidity in women," and only allowed the poem to be published after his wife's death. Yet in spite of this kind of corroboration from his subject, the critic is persuasive but not wholly convincing. Sexuality in Frost may be "a submerged metaphor," but the reticence that led to its immersion in the first place remains a barrier to the reader's experience of it.

Although Mr. Poirier never makes a claim he doesn't try to demonstrate, something in Frost thwarts the complexity of his interpretation, as if the very grandeur and rightness of phrasing the poet achieved in his best poems — "Design," "The Silken Tent," "Home Burial," "Provide, Provide," "After Apple-Picking" — armed them with skins so tough they repel complication. And in his exhaustive technical analyses, Mr. Poirier oddly makes no mention of Frost's use of monosyllabic words — crucial, it seems to me, to his mastery of common speech in formal verse. No other poet I know uses them to the same extent, and often in a final line wholly made up of monosyllables that serves as the dramatic conclusion of an action or the summing up of an idea — "In Hardwood Groves," "Never Again Would Birds' Song Be the Same," "Waiting," "A Dream Pang," etc.

Mr. Poirier makes claims for Frost equal to those made for Yeats and Eliot. And it may be that Frost resists greatness less than readers like myself, brought up under the influence of Eliot, resist his being great. But though there is no lack of emotion in Frost, there is a lack of emotional range — a refusal to be either naked or gorgeous — and the insistent absence of the city narrows the field of vision. Sometimes the scale seems too inhumanly local. Who would ever guess from reading Frost that he was born in San Francisco and spent his first eleven years there? A touch of the borrowed personality enters into the moralizing sageness of his work — possibly the "cuteness" and "smugness" the critic himself so dislikes. No matter: Mr. Poirier has broken fresh ground everywhere, and, in a single book, has repositioned Frost, a writer already considered major, so that he remains in a tradition but is differently placed and more truly seen. A metaphysical cloak has replaced the rustic mantle. To illustrate how a reputation is deserved but developed for the wrong reasons and then to supply plausible correctives is one of the most difficult undertakings imaginable, the kind of rescue operation that artists need from time to time but rarely get. Mr. Poirier has done for Frost what Ralph Kirkpatrick did for Scarlatti and Eliot for the seventeenth-century metaphysical poets. Seen in a new light, the music and the poems were brought back to life. And in Mr. Poirier's wonderfully fresh readings of the texts, particularly of "Home Burial" and "A Star in a Stone-Boat," he has made it impossible to approach Frost again in a simpleminded manner. Moreover, by being a defense in the particular, his book is an attack in general on the notion that only the experimental is new.

The premise of David Kalstone's *Five Temperaments* is simple: poetry reflects life. Therefore: how do five very different American poets manage to use autobiographical material in their work? The poets are Elizabeth Bishop, Robert Lowell, James Merrill, Adrienne Rich, and John Ashbery. Where Mr. Poirier probes, praises, and dismisses, Mr. Kalstone appreciates. We are given the ordered observations and asides of a man who has thought carefully and deeply about his subject, a learned man, but one who is willing to be seduced by the magic of words, casual or mandarin. And always something new turns up. In his essay on Bishop, Mr. Kalstone connects the scream of the mother in the autobiographical story "In the Village" with Aunt Consuelo's scream in the dentist's office in "In the Waiting Room" — a remarkably revealing insight, for the latter poem is the one where Bishop first becomes aware of the unwanted burden of consciousness, of *being* someone:

> *But I felt: you are an* I,
> *you are an* Elizabeth,
> *you are one of* them.

And so we become aware that in Bishop consciousness is directly related to the experience of pain, and that the meticulousness of her perceptions may be a form of wariness. Mr. Kalstone is the first person I know to suggest that the poems in *Geography III*, the poet's last book, are visitations to the earlier poems, as if they were places of travel. In "The Moose," we encounter again the childhood Canada of her first book, *North & South*. And, in the late "Poem," a primitive landscape is drawn by the same great-uncle who "scribbled hundreds of fine black birds / hanging in *n*s in banks" in "Large Bad Picture," a poem from the forties.

In discussing the change of style between Lowell's second and third books, the most influential shifting of gears in the last thirty years of American poetry, Mr. Kalstone lets the author speak for himself:

I was in San Francisco, the era and setting of Allen Ginsberg, and all about very modest poets were waking up prophets. I became sorely aware of how few poems I had written. . . . Their style seemed distant, symbol-ridden and willfully difficult. . . . I felt my old poems hid what they were really about, and many times offered a stiff, humorless and even impenetrable surface. I am no convert to the "beats." . . . Still, my own poems seemed like prehistoric monsters dragged down into the bog and death by their ponderous armor. I was reciting what I no longer felt. . . . I felt that the best style for poetry was none of the many poetic styles in English, but something like the prose of Chekhov or Flaubert.

Mr. Kalstone is particularly canny in spotting key subjects and ways of dealing with them: Merrill's conviction that "life was fiction in disguise," his use of houses — each enclosing the scene of a continuing drama — to fix and transfix the past, his "slides" lit up from within, "as if a poem required a kind of scrim among its resources, before or behind which action may be seen in new configurations as new beams of light are introduced." Mr. Kalstone sees *Divine Comedies* as the culmination of Merrill's interest in narrative and nothing less than a contemporary reconstruction of its singular predecessor — Dante emerging from a Ouija board. Or Adrienne Rich's "burning impatience with the way writing fixes experience . . . her preference for the provisional . . . [her interest] in American life as registered and suffered by those not in power, those not directly responsible for it, and especially women. . . ." Or this, on Ashbery:

A great deal of [his] writing is done in an atmosphere of deliberate demolition. . . . In his images of thwarted nature, of discontinuity between present and past, Ashbery has turned his agitation into a principle of composition. . . . [He] is not simply reminding us that poetry has access to the inner life; he is emphasizing the unique power of language to reveal how much of external life the inner life displaces.

There is in *Five Temperaments* a warmth rare in criticism — Mr. Kalstone enjoys what he's talking about — and one weakness: the list of poets he has chosen to illustrate his argument seems dictated less by his thesis than by taste and, to use his word, temperament. One could make a list of five other poets who might more convincingly demonstrate a link between poetry and biography: Ammons, Merwin, Plath, Ginsberg, and Sexton, say. But it may be that the sometimes strained disparity between the work he admires and what it is meant to demonstrate led to the kind of increased awareness a detective might develop on discovering that his wife is the chief suspect.

In the middle of Mr. Poirier's book, we come upon the following: "Voice is the most important, distinguishing, and conspicuously insistent feature of Frost's poetry and of his writing about poetry. There is scarcely a single poem which does not ask the reader to imagine a human character equivalent to the movement of voice." Taken together, these two books suggest that the poetry of the past fifty years has discovered its central theme, but it is a theme so involved with the difficulty of writing poetry itself that seeing it plain isn't easy. In the pull between speech and eloquence, the low style and the high, gutter talk and the King's English, how to speak in the name of something real without being merely commonplace led to the subject to be spoken about. And that turned out to be: *who is speaking*. The problem of *how* turned into the problem of *what*. The tone of voice became the key factor. The human voice, like the fingerprint, is characteristically identifiable. The major question was one of truth or falsity — or, if not falsity, then the façade that Literature and society and civilization have put in the way of speaking the truth. Art is civilized, we have been led to believe by reading, looking at, and listening to more than twenty centuries of it. How could it be natural? The question was naïve but of absolute significance, for most of the efforts to get around it are visible in thousands of galleries, are whispered or shouted at a hundred poetry readings every night, and can be heard hammered out in our concert halls. The insistence on not being formal, or stuck-up, or mannered, the freedom to use any kind of language, the emphasis on being real and spontaneous are all to the good, but they are also symptoms. People who are natural do not ask themselves how to be natural. Art isn't nature. In the attempt to make it so, more than one artist raced in the opposite direction from the one in which he thought he was heading, like an arrow propelled backward from the bull's-eye to the bow. He adopted fashion where style was required — and by style I mean something as native to the individual writer as it is to the individual person. Marianne Moore, for instance, had style, because the way she wrote was hers alone. And by fashion I mean the sense of the word as it pertains to clothes. Its main feature is its impermanence; in order to exist, fashion must be deliberately changed. The shifting hemline and haircut made Paris, a city of art, into a center of fashion. It was in painting that fashion first asserted itself (because, of all the arts, painting is the most closely allied with money), and it has spread to every art in every corner, so that the distinction between what is truly style and what is merely fashion has become increasingly muddy. In discussing the abrupt shift in method between *Lord Weary's Castle* and *Life Studies*, Lowell explained why "Skunk Hour" — the most famous and characteristic poem in *Life Studies* — is dedicated to Elizabeth Bishop: "Because re-reading her suggested a way of breaking through the shell of my old manner." And, in regard to style and fashion, it is Elizabeth Bishop, in the end, who is the most illustrative and exemplary. She was herself from the beginning.

The First Line

In my case, the first line of a poem is crucial and is usually the given thing that comes out of the blue without conscious maneuvering, when the mind is released from the habitual. Most often it comes when I am in motion, when no fixed mooring allows habit to keep from consciousness what the imagination may be evoking. I mean "motion" literally: in subways, taxis, cars, buses, trains, planes, ships — and in dreams, for I take dreams to be forms of transportation. Lines that come from dreams, however, have to be written down when they occur — they tend to evaporate — or require the use of mnemonic devices in order for the aroused dreamer not to wake up completely, turn the lights on, get out of bed — or all three. Even so, I've lost lines I felt certain I would remember; associative reminders — words, things in the room, colors, clues embedded (you would think) unforgettably — have not been enough to keep them fixed in the mind. What poet hasn't had the feeling, sometime during the day, that a line, an idea, a title that sprang to mind the night before was lost forever? In the moment of knowing it has been experienced, there is also the experience of knowing it is gone. (There are, of course, occasional recapturings.)

The first line may turn out, in the end, not to *be* the first line, and, if it is not, it is usually the last. It can, on rare occasions, be a line in the middle of a poem around which the rest of the poem clusters, but most of the time, it is the opening wedge, the beginning of . . . what? Writing a poem is finding out what the given line leads to, or, to put it another way, what the line has hidden behind it. Sometimes it takes years to discover that; sometimes it follows as the night the day. It doesn't matter whether the poem is written quickly or takes months to revise, as long as the original "gift"— notion, words, phrase, sentence — is spontaneous. Sometimes the line leads nowhere. I call these false poems, like false pregnancies. That is not necessarily the fault of the line. It can be a failure of the imagination, a sickness of will, a bad period in anyone's life that stifles the messages the imagination is sending out. A broadcasting station with no atmosphere through which electromagnetic impulses can travel.

What does a first line do? It can seem to do nothing, be deceptive, like the beginnings of novels that are quiet, that do not arrest the attention very much, in which the lulling voice lures the reader on with a children's story told to a tea table, very quietly, an aside. I will a tale unfold, it says, but you can hardly hear it. "One afternoon, in the year 1889, a young woman got into a carriage in Amsterdam." And we are already launched. So many things are bubbling in the pot. Who is she? Where does she come from? Why is she getting into the carriage? There is the Holland sky. There are, perhaps, cobblestones? Boots? Horses? And a few trees?

The first line of a poem does more than that: it intrigues the ear — some way, no matter how quietly. And how hard it is, now, to think of all those famous first lines being put down on paper for the first time! They intrigue the ear *and* the mind. "April is the cruellest month, breeding. . . ." (The hand is poised above the typewriter? What will come next?) "I wonder, by my troth, what thou and I. . . ." (The pen hesitates?) "Lay your sleeping head, my love. . . ." "The saris go by me from the embassies. . . ." "Each day with so much ceremony. . . ." I would say that the best are musical and contain an embryonic concept: in the Eliot, the paradox of spring and cruelty; in the Donne, questioning and swearing at the same time; in the Auden, asking someone asleep to perform an action; in the Jarrell, being a passive witness to something exotic *and* official; in the Bishop, the implied irony of each day being a ceremonious occasion — yes, maybe, but not in any ordinary reader's life (including the poet's). So the line contains within it a seed of expectation. Or, if it is merely descriptive, it has to have something arresting — something implicitly dramatic, perhaps — no matter how subtly toned down. This can be the drama of syntax: "Anyone lived in a pretty how town. . . ." Or the delayed verb, of which Merrill is a master. Like the opening notes of a musical composition, it has to *allow* for the possibility of going further, of going *on*, has to be a springboard but also to sound inevitable. Who would think, after hearing the announcement of the first theme in the "Pastoral" Symphony, of going on in a different way, a way different from

Beethoven's? The theme has already taken on the authority of nature, as if it were a form found rather than a form invented. One would no more think of revising a rock. Well, if one has a first line like that, one is very lucky. And, of course, first lines arc never *like* that, except in retrospect. Nothing is inevitable until it is concluded. Until the poem is written, the finality of the first line is subject to change; its ultimate absolute shape remains in doubt. It may be the most solid thing around, but still, like ice in spring, it is capable of melting. "On the way to the contagious hospital . . ." Is there any word that could take the place of "contagious"? Supposing (only for the sake of argument) Williams had written "On the way to the courageous hospital . . ." (A clinic in a leper colony hacked out of the jungle?) How wrong it would be, now that we know! How outrageous.

Is the first line — or even the whole poem — dreamwork? Or fancy footwork? Is it the agile cleverness of someone tuned up to receive what the receiver has taken in — and given out — before? It is hard to say. The freshness of certain poets gets lost, even as the skills increase. Yeats and Stevens and Williams got better as they got older. Other poets were not so lucky. Two things are equally boring in art: a lack of skill and too much of it.

Things deepen. Landscapes become engraved. Relationships become richer — or, sometimes, bitter. Either is grist, though I hate to say it, for the mill, because it is intensity that counts in certain poets, rather than the contemplative authority of the voice, its richness and depth.

I'd say there were three modes: the meditative (which includes the elegiac); the intense (which includes the narrative);

and the associative, which includes everything the first two do not cover but is particularly applicable, say, to Spanish and South American poets, who have had such an influence on United States poets. There, the image is central, the originality of the image and the ability to move on with a certain underground relevance from one image to another. Examples: the meditative — Stevens; the intense — Warren; the associative — Ashbery. None of these are pure distillations. I think, for instance, that part of Ashbery's current influence comes from the combination of two modes, the meditative *and* the associative, as if the deep image had found a philosopher.

The story counts for more and more. Openings of plays are clues, provide hints, because they are the precursors of action. In *The Seagull*, the first line is "Why are you wearing black?" The second, "I'm in mourning for my life." And though neither is the actual first line of the play, these are the first lines Shakespeare assigns Cleopatra and Antony — they are almost one-liners:

CLEOPATRA: If it be love indeed, tell me how much.
ANTONY: There's beggary in the love that can be reckon'd.

The whole extraordinary play is there in capsule. They have said, at the beginning, what they will eventually act out.

Think of the first shot in movies. *Casque d'Or* opens wonderfully. The world stays in motion. The long gliding of the canoes under the trees to the river bank followed almost immediately by the contained wildness of the dance — apache. In *Madame Rosa*, the three Hebrew letters on a street sign, casually planted in the opening shot. Who, in recent years, hasn't wanted the opening credits of movies to go on and on?

Often so much more alive, interesting, inventive than what follows.

Is it inevitability or familiarity that makes a first line sound right? To answer that honestly would be difficult. But take five lines with substituted words — words close to the meaning of the originals: "My heart hurts; and a drowsy numbness pains"; "Lay your sleeping head, my friend"; "The dresses go by me from the embassies"; "August is the cruellest month, breeding"; "He was in Venice writing letters home."

The Keats and the Stevens sound more plausible than the others, but in the first the level of discourse has changed. The alliteration lowers the temperature of the grand manner. And, in the Stevens, a canal is not a bay. A great deal hangs on that. "See Naples and die." Not Venice. The Auden switch changes a love poem into something innocuous and hesitant, something on the verge of the ludicrous. The Eliot loses its pathos and irony. August is very conceivably cruel: it's hot, it is the prelude to the end of things, the fall. The very notion that animated the line — spring, a time of joy; cruelty, a thing to fear — is gone. The paradoxical shock is missing. And the Jarrell is completely ruined. Everything magical in a magical poem has been flattened out at the beginning. And is there a better first line, by the way, in the use of sound and ideas working together than "The saris go by me from the embassies"? "Saris" and "embassies" rhyme. And carrying the same sound but, equidistantly isolated from the two- and three-syllabled plurals, is that wan, singular echo, "me." Also notable: with the exception of the repeated "the" and the rhyme words, every vowel sounded is different.

What sounds right may be what we have already heard.

Probably. But I doubt it in the case of poets, because a poet is the one to whom the new first line comes. Echoes, yes. Of what is read, what is lived, what is seen. But the echo is changed by the chamber in which it reverberates, and what brings new speech to birth are words and sounds that can be found anywhere: in books, popular songs, phrases, catch phrases, jazz, overheard speech, signs, menus, the talk of children, instructions in manuals, patent medicine throwaways, etc. And particularly the slightly out of kilter, the verbal connection shaded off. I can't think of a better example than "The Man-Moth," Elizabeth Bishop's poem based on a newspaper misprint of "mammoth."

The more transposable the better. Take a song from *Guys and Dolls*: "The Oldest Established Permanent Floating Crap Game in New York." Then isolate ". . . established permanent floating. . . ." The first line of a poem on the Taj Mahal? New York in certain lights? Monet's water lilies?

Or take song titles, particularly jazz: "Tuxedo Junction," "Avalon," "Big John's Special," "One O'Clock Jump," and those three spondee songs: "Blue Skies," "So Rare," and "Much More."

Poems that come from life come from characters: spokesmen, archetypes, legendary figures, the self. Does it matter whether they start in words or in experience? (And, for a writer, words are experiences.) Eliot saw the proper uses of drama, of dramatic tension, in lyric poetry. He went both ways: he started to write plays and ended up writing string quartets. Perhaps the most beautiful string quartets ever written in the English language. Song should never be downgraded, particularly in relation to first lines. Poetry is, essentially, the use of words to express the nonverbal. Because it uses words in a double way, its closest analogy is music, which uses no words at all, but equally expresses emotion, equally articulates form through sound.

Fantastically good prose can be a launching, like Cobbett in *Rural Rides*, or Sir Thomas Browne in "Urn Burial," or this, from Anthony Collett, which Auden reprints in his commonplace book:

Far and wide through the moors of the northern countries run the dykes and sills of hard black basaltic rock called whinstone. Nature has forced it between softer layers of rock much as cement is driven between the crumbling stones of a cathedral wall. But this volcanic grouting is so much harder than sedimentary rock, and the operation was carried out so many hundreds of thousands of years ago, that the basaltic bonds have outlasted the layers which they compact, and now project beyond them. Dykes are vertical layers of whinstone, which out-top the moor's surface by 20 or 40 feet, like a wall.

Or good critical writing. Like Pritchett's. Or a more romantic version of scientific writing, from *The Ocean*, by F. O. Ommanney:

The barnacle is a small shrimp-like creature which, when the tide covers it, stands upside down in its box made of plates of lime, feathering food towards itself with long curved legs. When the tide recedes it closes its box by means of four accurately fitting valves. In doing so it entraps a bubble of air and enough moisture to keep its gills damp. If you listen carefully just after the tide has left the rocks you may hear all around the whispering talk of the barnacles, a faint crepitation. It is caused by the tighter closing of the valves in millions of little houses whose

inmates are alarmed by the monstrous reverberation of your
bare feet.

The half-seen, the barely glimpsed, if they make an
impression, are more usable, usually, than the familiar.
Though sometimes if the right connection is made, a place
one has been steeped in comes alive. A similarity and a difference, like coming on a seacoast resort like St. Mawes in
England having known Rockport, Massachusetts. A woman
with a jar walking toward the water in Nicaragua. A lamp
swinging in a doorway in Russia. A man settling in for the
night at a pub in Wales. Are they not the old streets of childhood, under a streetlamp, while you skated at twilight? They
are. And they are not. They are real and imagined. One
doesn't have to read Freud to know how the imagined can
become real, or Stevens to understand how the real can become imagined. Memory, the key to everything, brings with
it nostalgia, which must be outgrown. Not to appreciate the
world as objective means that the Nicaraguan woman, the
Russian lamp, and the Welsh pub will never be more than
children's paintings. Wonderful, for their age. And frighten-
ing ten years later.

All things noticed but never set down, or things never
brought to consciousness — the conventional made fresh, the
new brought into being — are the properties of poetry and
the peculiar provinces of first lines. Whether they can be singled out, later, after one knows what comes after — again,
one would have to be equivocal. "Each day with so much
ceremony / Begins, with birds, with bells, / With whistles
from a factory . . ." (How — in the first line — those commonplace monosyllables add weight to "ceremony"!) Eliza-

beth Bishop has a fine Italian hand at first lines. The undertow is felt at the water's edge. The matter-of-fact tone only
adds to the excitement.

It is true some poems escape this particularity of the first
line in a special way. Norman Dubie, say, where one enters
a *terrain*, and slowly, building up, in front of you, is the
detail of the story, the massing of the narrative in objects,
animals, discrete observations, as if one were crawling across
a painted canvas from one side, binoculars in hand, watching
the wonders, the grass, under one's feet, grow. That is different. Because there, the linear travel of the rail-line has become three-dimensional: the future of the poem is being built
in sections, sections of varying thicknesses. And it is different, too, in a Dave Smith poem, where the choral voice
sounds out of the bay, or out of the railway yard, that not-
quite-single-person's voice, which is the voice of the single
person speaking for many. I would say — using these two
poets as unwitting examples — that the more narrative the
poem the less dependent on the first line. But it would be a
mistake to make a hard and fast distinction between the lyric
and the narrative. It is precisely poets like Smith and Dubie
who have brought the excitements of the lyric — that is, of
language sounded for non-prose reasons — into the narrative, and precisely Elizabeth Bishop who has done the opposite. In narration, the onrushing power of the story may
seem to count for everything, but it only counts for half. It
is the voice of the narrator that is equally significant. That is
why detective stories seldom last. There is no voice behind
them.

The first line, then, is the kernel of the poem, however
pared down, embellished, or revised, whether it arrives,

originally, *as* the first line, ends up being the last ("The first shall be last and the last shall be first"), or becomes the nucleus around which the cells begin to construct an organism.

There are three characteristic "first" lines:

1) That line which is, in itself, a complete statement. The poem that follows extends or plays variations on the already-stated theme: "Do not go gentle into that good night"; "They flee from me that sometime did me seek"; "For Godsake hold your tongue, and let me love." There are subjects and predicates, nouns and verbs. And if we had to (we don't), we could accept short rations and make a very tiny poem out of the line itself. (Many people do: they know lines, not poems.)

"Great" first lines retain a relevancy outside the poem, being universal and local, immediate and abstract — the subjects above, being death, abandonment or betrayal, and sexual impatience — and are marked by incongruity, some hidden interest, either in the way the words are sounded, used, or positioned.

In the Thomas, there is the adjective "gentle" in place of the syntactically called-for adverb, the unusual use of the phrase "good night" — both blessed darkness and the familiar words of parting — the playing off of the soft "g" of "gentle" against the hard "g" of "good," and the strangeness of what the words convey: the notion that one can control one's own death. The line is both an admonishment and a declaration of love.

In the Wyatt, the same vowel sounded in "flee," "me," and "seek," the exaggerated drama of "flee," the special twist of "seek" — meaning "seek out"— and, for us, Wyatt's "sometime," a synonym for "once," with more than a slight ring of "once in a while." And though "sometime" is the one word

in the line that is not a monosyllable, it is, really, an amalgam of two monosyllabic words placed side by side. Oddest
of all is the very first word, the plural "They." Why not
"She flees from me who sometime did me seek"? This is
more than a lover's betrayal; this is a wholesale abandonment, which reverts, in the second line, to the singular —
"with naked foot stalking within my chamber." The plural
"They" tells us something about the narrator: is this "foot"
merely one of the many who have fled? So it would seem.
There is an elliptical "all" after "They" and an implied
past tense: "They all have fled who one time sought me
out. . . ."

In the Donne, the invoking of God for the most secular of
subjects, sex. The tongue is both an instrument of speech
and of love, and "hold" brings up two meanings at once — to
refrain and to embrace — as does "tongue," the organ of the
body and the word that stands for language. There's a further complication: The speaker — the poet — is forced into
speech. He cannot love while he is writing. The line is elec-
trified by contradictions.

2) Those first lines in which the second line already holds
sway, in which the thing to come is part of the originally
given words. You might say, these are the first *two* lines, or
three — whatever the case may be. For instance: "Remembering the Strait of Belle Isle or / Some northerly harbor of
Labrador, / Before he became a schoolteacher, / A great-
uncle painted a big picture." I would call the fourth line here
the "first" in the sense I mean it. Because the poem plays off
the central notion of "great *versus* big" in many subtle ways,
and ends with an affectionate, ironic contrast, one that tells
us all: "commerce [big] or contemplation [great]." (And how

nicely the conjunction that ends the first line works! It is secretly repeated three times in the following line.)

Or, for an example of a second line proper, "It is equal to living in a tragic land / To live in a tragic time."

3) The third example is not really a first line though it comes at the beginning of the poem. A syntactical diving board, and necessary, it has no particular interest in itself. Most contemporary poems begin this way, lower than low-keyed, with nothing particularly memorable either in the phrasing or the thought. In fact, it might be said that one of the habits of contemporary poetry is to be *against* the concept of the first line, its grandeur, its operative (and operatic) effect. As if to use words too well might be a sign of falsity, or excellence of phrasing a mark of inflation, of trying to win the reader over with fake enticements. It is a naïve view, but there is a lot to be said for it. Melodrama and sentimentality are the enemies. But sometimes feeling goes by the board as well. Whether the fear of rhetoric has led to the fear of feeling, or vice versa, would require a whole essay in itself. But the kind of line I refer to can begin wonderful poems without being wonderful: "There's a mystery" (David St. John's "Gin"); "A soft wind" (Philip Levine's "No One Remembers"); "With my eyes turned toward the sky" (David Ignatow's "Love Poem for the Forty-Second Street Library").

The writing of poetry seesaws, I think, between the desire to attain the first line and the desire to evade it. For in the first kind of first line there is the threat of the grandiloquent and of stopping — of there being nothing more to be said. In the second, the danger of getting lost in a muddle — too much has been given at once. And in the third, the problem of banality — of drifting into prose.

Once it has arrived, the first line should be revised in only one way: in terms of the ongoing.

Unlike the "foreword" to a literary work, first lines are introductions to worlds that never existed before and also parts of the worlds they introduce. We enter through them, but they are part of the structure, like doorways to houses. A good doorway doesn't exempt itself from architecture. A mystery whose solution falls into place only at the end, a first line is closer to an overture or a prelude, whose purpose is to say "This is a beginning" while being the very thing that has already begun.

The Poet's Story

In Gorky's *Reminiscences*, he tells of having read some scenes from *The Lower Depths* to Tolstoy. Tolstoy wasn't pleased. He said, "Most of what you say comes out of yourself and therefore you have no characters." And that simple statement says more clearly than anything I know why poets attempt to write fiction. For the self — the *I* — is most typically the viewpoint from which a poem is conceived and written. With a few important exceptions — Homer, Chaucer, Browning — *they*, *you*, *he*, and *she* stand outside the poet — the net of reality, a huge temptation. And in time, I think, most poets fall into that net. It takes courage to enter one's own world with any degree of truth. It takes a different kind of courage to enter the worlds of other people — and, for a writer, a different kind of skill. Poets bring to the task one advantage and the defect of that advantage. Though they have learned to search for the truth, because that search has been directed toward themselves, their interest tends to be parochial or narcissistic or limited to the landscape and the psychology of the ego. That tendency must be overcome before a writer can produce poems of dramatic tension, a legitimate dramatic poem, or fiction. If writing could be conceived of as a religious matter, poets would be admired for being devout and scorned for having committed themselves to the wrong faith.

It would be difficult to make a list of fifty poems of this century that exhibit a true interest in character — character as I think Tolstoy meant it and demonstrated it. Psychology, yes — psychology is all over the place. But it is not the same as character. In fact, the very existence of the word "psychology" reinforces the fragmentation of character. Though we use the word so commonly, it was not always at the tip of everyone's tongue. Psyche was a character in a story before she became an attribute of everyone. Psychology can be dispersed: it can ring true in abstract statement, in insights and perceptions, strike home in a passing observation, and even be demonstrated in figures essentially hollow. And that is not only true of the figures in poetry, when they appear at all. A great deal of what passes for fiction consists of puppet plays; yet the puppets may ring true psychologically. The trouble is they don't necessarily ring true any other way. The shadings are off; if they're emotionally believable *and* interesting — almost anyone can be emotionally believable and dull — there's something wrong with their minds; or they don't walk properly; or they don't speak understandably; they can't swim; some of them can't even drive. I'm not speaking here of the mechanics of fiction, or true-to-life fiction, that low order, where the characters are merely accurate and live on streets that have real names and use the right golf clubs and eat the right entrails. No, I mean something like a mystery story where everything is obviously false with the exception of the motives of the characters (themselves false) in it.

Psychology, then, is the key to character but it is not character itself; after all, a key unlocks the door leading to something else. What is it, then, psychology unlocks? I think you might say that psychology is general and that character is specific. The door must be recognizable in order to be opened. But the room it opens on is capable of infinite variation. It is the credibility of each variation — the ability on the writer's part to describe precisely the individual room and to make it felt — that becomes his task and his difficulty. A chair's a chair . . . but *this* one? The wall is blue . . . but what *kind* of blue? The distinctions become increasingly difficult as one moves from psychological abstraction to characteristic experience. This is true not only of the so-called realistic novel but of any novel, for no matter how fantastic the variation or exquisite the conception, the novelist ultimately tangles with personality. The poet has already fought an analogous battle with imagery, having progressed from the general outburst to the specific metaphor. The struggle with character is similar. The amateur poet fails by making experience general. The amateur novelist universalizes character, and displays his not very fine Italian hand by allowing each character a dominant trait: Gloria is angry, Tom is sad, Helga is weatherbeaten.

Yet if psychology is general and character specific, something further needs to be said. General things are diffused; the specific usually has a direct impact. But in the case of psychology, because it is a medical discipline as well as a word that stands for human insight, the reverse is true. Psychology defines, character eludes — you'd think it would be the other way around. Though it categorizes, psychology tends to be increasingly cautious in its definitions. We now know that a word like "schizophrenia" covers more territory than language permits. Hardly meaningless, it nevertheless demands more and more qualification. And it is precisely in art that those qualifications already exist. Character cannot thrive in the abstract. What may be symptoms to a doctor are ways of behaving to a writer. Take Nicole in *Tender Is the Night*. Dr. Dohmler, at the Swiss clinic, makes a definite diagnosis: "Schizophrenia." But Nicole is more than a schizophrenic. Her charm, her anger, her sexuality, her selfishness, her terror are all made manifest despite the label. And in Chekhov's "Ward Six," Ivan Dmitrich is classically paranoid. Dmitrich would have no force or conviction if he were not subtle, penetrating, and masterful in argument.

Fitzgerald's novel and Chekhov's story are less concerned with mental illness than with its effects on other people — and they have certain resemblances. The leading characters in both are doctors dealing with psychotic behavior, and each of them reverses positions with the very character he is treating. Nicole drains Dick Diver. Dr. Ragin ends up in Ivan Dmitrich's place. But these likenesses are superficial. The overtones of the Fitzgerald novel are psychological, romantic, nostalgic, and, to a limited extent, social. The thrust of "Ward Six" is philosophical and political. It profoundly concerns itself with the difference between being a victim of evil and the luxury of rationalizations about it. It takes the enforced incarceration of Dr. Ragin in his own psychiatric

ward to make him see what no amount of learning or training
or observation or thought or imagination has been able to
illuminate before. Evil is concrete and immediate; it is more
than a philosophical abstraction. The sufferings of its victims
are real, and those who do nothing in the face of it abet it.
"Ward Six" opens up an abyss. An attack on the passivity of
Tolstoy's moral theories, and a product of Chekhov's trip to
the prison colonies on Sakhalin Island, it is a work of conscience — the most overtly political of all of Chekhov's
stories.

"Ward Six" anticipates R. D. Laing by almost half a century. Both Chekhov and Laing test common assumptions,
but Dr. Laing is shedding light on a problem Chekhov already understood. It would be false to confuse art, necessarily enigmatic and mysterious — it is always about to utter
the unutterable — and science, which must describe, clas-
sify, and predict. Yet I would still go to Chekhov, who died
in 1904, rather than to Dr. Laing, an expert in the field, to
understand the human dimensions of the problem. The truth
is, I learned more about the unconscious from reading Proust
than from reading Freud.

People who are summed up in a word are people we are
lying about. Art questions that lie constantly, by showing us
how things really happen to people and, on a more profound
level, by its shadings, by the intelligence that fuels its emotional force, and by its range.

Character is elusive not only by being truly reflected from
life, where it is hopelessly enigmatic, but because character
always has something left over, something not used by the
author in the course of the story, novel, or poem. No pool is
truly a pool once it has been drained. And so a character

must exist outside of his framework — before and after the action. If he has no past or future in the reader's mind — no matter how unconsciously — he hasn't registered completely. Stories are read for thousands of reasons, but anyone who appears in a story has a pre- and a post-reality. An author has one limitation any mother transcends: he cannot give birth to a character; at best, he can catch the baby in swaddling clothes. He *can* kill a character off. In which case, he risks, like all of us, immortality or oblivion.

Immortality or oblivion — like ecstasy and glory — were once fairly common words in poetry, at least in romantic poetry. The poet progresses from lines without imagery meant to convey great feeling, like "the sky is full of joy," to something as specific, say, as Eliot's description of the sky as "a patient etherized upon a table." Vague exultation has become no exultation at all. A poet may reverse the process in the way Stravinsky, after *Le Sacre*, embraced neoclassicism — a very sophisticated embrace — but one might note that, for all its oddness, Eliot's image is supported by the most conventional of iambics. Simplifications of style, leanness of syntax, this or that new kind of poetry always point up the inescapable: after all is said and done, the poet is stuck with the image in the same way the novelist or storyteller is stuck with character. For both, memory is the great source; one doesn't set down, even in the present tense, at whatever level of consciousness, something that is not memorable. For a poet, memory connects — the very function of metaphor, where one thing reminds you of another, or rather, one thing *enlivens* another. For a fiction writer, memory accretes and sums up — the function of meaningful action. But because one term of a metaphor must precede the other, and because accretion involves process, memory is a function of time. That would seem obvious, but time is different for the novelist and the poet, for the fiction writer is dominated by the clock and the poet by the metronome. They are just dissimilar enough — metronomes can be sped up, slowed down, or stopped — to provide a fertile field of transaction.

From the beginning of this century, poetry and fiction have borrowed from each other, imitated each other, and in some cases become each other. Whitman and Rimbaud, an odd couple at first glance, are the godfathers of the prose poem. As prose moved into poetry — Ezra Pound and William Carlos Williams are crucial figures — so poetry moved into prose. Whenever poets escape from meter — Marianne Moore comes to mind — they approach the conditions of prose; the metronome becomes almost inaudible and one glances up at the clock. What is syllabic writing but a counting out? Counting out is not the same as measure, where duration and stress are more critical than number. Whenever prose writers depend heavily on cadence or the image, they move toward poetry.

In Cocteau's film *The Blood of a Poet*, the poet is spewed out of a mirror — Narcissus is being ejected by the pool. A mouth opens in the palm of the poet's hand and cries, "L'aire! L'aire!" That plea for oxygen implies a window. As I remember it, the poet breaks a windowpane and sticks his hand out into the air to let it breathe. But he never bothers to look out. His true adventures occur later when he is swallowed up by the mirror and enters "a hotel of follies." Nevertheless, the point has been made. The mirror is the totem of the poet, who looks *at* and *into* himself, who creates himself, as it were. And I would say the window belongs to the fiction writer, who looks *out* and *around*, and is a product of the world. In the love affair that has occurred in this century, the novelist has flirted with mirrors and the poet with windows. The increasing prominence of confessional writing in poetry and the numbers of fiction writers drawn to documentation suggest a new hardening of positions. Attempts to get at the truth, they may also, I suspect, be forms of camouflage. In telling all, the poet frees himself to deal with character — having been merciless toward himself, he is free to be merciless toward everyone. And the fiction writer, finding plot, character, and relevance preempted by clever mystery writers, excellent filmmakers, and exploiters of the topical, is increasingly drawn to the actual. Where is reality really to be found? In the blood and guts of one's own experience? In the external event examined with the same meticulous detail, the same concern for form, often, that one would bring to fiction?

The twentieth century is rich in great writers, but because Proust is as much an epic poet as a novelist, he is, to my mind, its key literary figure. He saw the significance of windows very clearly and the importance of mirrors by implication. Is there any other book that so strangely combines plunges into the interior of the self with so faultless a portrait of the external world — natural and social? It is obsessive in both directions. And it would be hard to explain away the fact that every crucial sexual scene in *A la Recherche* is seen through a window. I include in that grouping two scenes not ordinarily considered sexual: that one where Marcel looks out at the garden through his bedroom window and sees his parents dining with Swann, the first clue to the subject of voyeurism in the novel, and his playing with the magic lantern in his bedroom, which shortly follows. The theme of the voyeur — which is spun for us slowly — as well as the device of the magic lantern, tells us more or less the same thing: for the voyeur, the distinction between windows and mirrors is psychologically nebulous; the outward scene merely activates the inner compulsion of the viewer; what he sees is not the reality of the act but a fantasy implicit in himself. The disturbed psyche mirrors what is viewed through the window; the seeming observation is a narcissistic turning inward. The voyeur doesn't look at people in order to examine, understand, or know them, but because they perform — like marionettes of the unconscious — in a certain way. The *character* of the actors has no meaning, though their physical attributes may be of great significance. And the magic lantern, projecting images of others, is manipulable. Not only can the images be chosen but they can be projected at will, and in Marcel's case, the characters he *thinks* he sees (he later finds out more about them) do not conform to the fantasies they first evoke. Moreover, he projects those images where he pleases: on the door, the wall, the doorknob, and so forth. Through the magic lantern, Marcel sees fragments of the history of France. That is its window side. It also has a mirror side. In its repetition of chosen images that lead to fantasy, its ability to frame a person, an image, or an act (the way a window provides a frame for a voyeur), and by being physically manipulable, it is, by analogy, a masturbatory device.

In Proust, intelligence has emotional force, but the sexual scenes often lack sensuality — Albertine and Marcel seem strangely hermetic, as if the act of going to bed together, the heart of their struggle, had somehow become metaphysical

before it was consummated. Swann and Odette exude a more
gamey flavor. With Marcel and Albertine, we are analyzing
feeling rather than experiencing it. We are being tortured,
but tortured so intelligently that following the argument almost prevents us from feeling the pain. It soon becomes clear
enough that that is what feeling is: pain. Proust was no fool;
the window and the mirror, in the hands of the right magician, are interchangeable. That cup of tea out of which Combray is evoked is a mirror of the past but opens a window
onto the future. What are mirrors and windows but the
glassy fields of dissolution and envy? In the one we watch
ourselves decay; through the other we see those things we
long for and can never attain or become. What Marcel sees
reflected   through   a   window   becomes   his   ultimate
reflection — a word almost too luringly usable in Proust's
case. In the end, the dirty pictures become focused: Marcel
turns out to be as sexually compulsive as Mlle. Vinteuil,
Swann, and Charlus.

Using the images that Cocteau and Proust provide as
clues, I would say that the distinction between fiction writers
and poets is becoming obsolete, that it might be more useful
to think of authors as mirror-writers or window-writers. In
the same way that liberal members of opposing political parties may be closer to each other in thought and spirit than to
the conservative members of their own parties, so certain
prose writers are closer to poets than to each other.

In America the two schools stem from two major figures,
both poets, who may be viewed as their source: Emily Dickinson, the mirror, and Walt Whitman, the window. If it is
confusing to have a poet — Whitman — stand for the generic prose writer, one can at least say that Whitman brought

the devices of biblical prose into poetry: repetition, cataloguing, and cadence. It would be hard to find, in any case, another figure who so clearly illustrates what I mean.

Take two superb poems: Dickinson's "Because I could not stop for death," and Whitman's "When lilacs last in the dooryard bloom'd." They have in common the subject of death, but it would be inconceivable for Emily Dickinson to have written an elegy on the death of a public figure, an event external to her life, and a theme whose magnitude derives partly from the power and importance of the subject it mourns. The Dickinson poem, in spite of its intensity, reflects a smaller world. It is measured, literally and figuratively, it is compressed, whereas Whitman's poem is expansive and comes to include, finally, the entire United States. Both are poems of great feeling, perfectly true to themselves, and typical. Whitman's poem, for all its length, is organized around a few images: the star for Lincoln; the lilac for seasonal rebirth; the hermit thrush for Whitman himself. In the course of the poem, Lincoln's body is moved by train across the country. The Dickinson poem uses a similar idea, a carriage ride, sufficient to its scope, and the figure of Death is appropriately a courtier or suitor.

Who is a window? Who is a mirror? Proust may seem too much a mirror, but then one thinks of the party scenes, those gargantuan satires on middle-class and upper-class social life, and a window opens. Chekhov has a house full of windows. Strolling around, one becomes aware that two or three of the panes are mirrored. And in our time, Nabokov is a fine example of both. In spite of being the master depicter of motel life in America, he is essentially a mirror writer. He said: "Time is a fluid medium for the culture of metaphors." Norman Mailer, despite the obvious egotism, is a window writer. Can one imagine Nabokov — or Emily Dickinson — covering a moon launching, the conventions, or a prize-fight? It is not inconceivable, though, to think of Whitman in the role of the evangelical journalist. Good writers hover, like angels caught in a magnetic field, between the mirror and the window.

Some writers hover between, and some are caught between. The poet may decide that not everything can be got down in poetry. And he begins a story or a novel. It would be interesting to make an anthology of the beginnings of poet's novels, especially the unpublished ones. (Unpublished *novels*, not unpublished poets.) I would make a fairly safe bet that the first two pages consist of description in ninety percent of the cases.

We are at a railroad station in Malaya and the sky is turbulent and suffused. In fact, it is raining. It keeps on raining for a long time because the poet is afraid — with good reason — to begin the action, to introduce the inevitable character. Sooner or later, he has to, and Malaya pales before the all-too-recognizable instructor's wife, editor's lover, or professor's mistress. There she is, at the bar, in the hotel, at the counter, and little falsehoods begin to pile up. Some of them are merely the plague of fact. She says she has just had her hair done. Where would she get the hair rinse? The travel book informs us that there are no hairdressers in Malaya, and customs specifically forbids the importation of hair rinse. Or she has just finished a lemon ice. The latest issue of the *National Geographic* tells us that lemon ices have never been introduced into Malaya. But the real difficulty is that she is obviously not the person she is supposed to be. She is either too recognizable or not recognizable enough. Either she changes from minute to minute, or she is hopelessly consistent. Just as conversation is not automatically dialogue, people are not necessarily characters. Who *is* she? She is redheaded and envious. Then she is more envious. And her hair seems to get redder. Later, she is in an absolute rage of envy and completely rubescent. We find out, finally, that she is basically kind. We leave Malaya.

The Malayan novel has not been published — I hope. But poets' novels *are* published, and they stand a better chance than most of ending up at one end of the spectrum or the other. When they're bad, they couldn't be worse, and when they're good, they're superb. Fitfulness and experiment aside, the inner urgency that can lure a poet to prose can, paradoxically, produce work that closely resembles poetry itself. William Faulkner, Malcolm Lowry, Herman Melville, D. H. Lawrence, and James Joyce all started out as poets. Giving up poetry's official title, they continued on its secret missions. Are there really significant differences in the originality of conception, the play of language — the bolt of the imagination in general — between *Moby Dick* and *The Cantos*, between *Ulysses* and *The Waste Land*?

But Ernest Hemingway, Willa Cather, and Muriel Spark started out as poets, too, and in their work, the parting of the ways between fiction and poetry is clearer. The interest in words stays steady, but the language is stripped down, or at least grows sparer; a concern with dramatic structure develops and becomes individual. The metaphor ceases to be central, though the motif may take its place — that doublethreading of language and concept that grows significant by repetition. (It is of interest to note how often motif is expressed in metaphor in the titles critics give to their works: *The Hovering Fly* [Tate]; *The Wound and the Bow* [Wilson]; *The Double Agent* [Blackmur]; *Stewards of Excellence* [Alvarez]; *Masks and Mirrors* [Bewley]; *A Sad Heart at the Supermarket* [Jarrell]; etc.) In Muriel Spark's *The Girls of Slender Means*, the words "slender means" take on a double meaning. During a fire, those characters slim enough to squeeze through a tiny bathroom window have the best chance of survival. The title *A Farewell to Arms* says goodbye to two things at once, love and war. But they crop up again in tandem in *For Whom the Bell Tolls*. What is unique in each of these writers, so different from each other, is the unmistakable sound of a voice. Words exhale temperament. We expect that individual voice — we demand it, in fact — in a poet. And though great fiction writers develop who are not poets to begin with — Proust, James, Tolstoy — they all have two qualities we assign to poets: a singularity and an authority of the imagination. Great novelists may be visionaries or enigmatic or focus on a social sewer; yet they must do two things at once: produce a recognizable world and create one of their own. The ability to make the official document personal is the true link between the novelist and the poet, for each stamps experience uniquely. A literary convention is a passport but, like the real thing, it can bear only one signature. When people say that something is Chekhovian or Proustian, it is odd, when you think about it, that they don't say, "That's pre-Revolutionary Russian" or "That's pre–World War I French," the stigma of long-windedness aside. They don't say it because that is not quite what they mean, though what they mean may certainly include the historical perspective and the period flavor. The social, political, economic, and military worlds of Russia and France are documented in many places. It is Chekhov's version and Proust's version that are so telling. What those worlds once were, the very sense of what it meant to be alive in them, has been re-created for us, yet belongs, in each case, to a single writer. It belongs to him because he has transcended it. We don't read Chekhov or Proust only for glimpses into worlds at a remove; we read them for glimpses into ourselves. No one is as egotistical as a reader.

There is the poetry *of* fiction, that quality of magic that comes from the demands of the medium itself, and there is poetry *in* fiction, two very different matters. The latter is an inferior brand if what is meant is merely "poetic prose." Hundreds of writers are labeled "poetic" for the wrong reason — a gift for description. It consists often of being partial to adjectives. At any rate, a gift is not an art. It is the mastery of a theme, a viewpoint, and a language that makes a superb writer. Poets may come to fiction for any number of reasons, but poets *of* fiction, as well as writers who come to it *through* poetry — window or mirror or both — invariably have one thing in common: they have style.

With the exception of those stories in which a poet deliberately turns his back on his usual subjects and methods, and consciously focuses on the classical ingredients of fiction — plot, character, and suspense — stories written by poets have a tendency to mythologize or to symbolize. They bear the mark of the fable.

In John Berryman's story "The Lovers," for instance, a passionate adolescent love affair is shadowed by an older ambiguous relationship, that of the narrator's mother and a stranger who mysteriously keeps turning up at the house. What becomes obvious to the reader is not obvious to the adolescent boy: the man is in love with his mother and she is not in love with him. We know practically nothing about the stranger, yet he achieves an extra dimension. His character is not to be one. His is the fate the narrator unwittingly suffers, the fate of the enchanted lover who, in order to save himself, must remove himself from enchantment. The stranger carries the knowledge the narrator is on the verge of learning, and, as such, he has something of the function, though none of the qualities, of the serpent in Eden. He is the unwelcome tarnisher, experience's bitter messenger. It is not *because* of him but *through* him that the narrator comes to the end of innocence. At the end, we realize that the story's title refers not to the two young lovers at its center but to the two hopeless men, who love and are not loved back.

The boy in the tree in Richard Wilbur's "A Game of Catch," who pretends to will and control each movement of two other boys playing ball, is an uneasy, painful Cain, striking out at others from a desperate isolation — the awful brother, the outsider whose only way of joining is to gain attention by being hateful. In Jean Garrigue's "The Snowfall," only the dead and the rejected finally embody the perfect realizations of love. Like the mother and the grandmother in Mona Van Duyn's "The Bell," the characters in poets' stories often seem larger than life — by their oddness, the glancing intelligence by which they are perceived, the undertow of metaphor that waits in the shallows. Transmutations of one kind or another extend their meanings. The two nameless lovers in James Schuyler's "Life, Death, and Other Dreams," for instance, seem less like characters than archetypes. In the story's small coda, where the lovers lie side by side in their graves, it is significant that the narrator suddenly makes himself evident. Is he warning us — or himself — against the pretensions of art in an attempt to preclude falsity? Is he simply admitting, through his "characters," that he hopes this story will be read? Self-consciousness is subverted by being included, like the stage manager's asides to the audience in a Chinese play — as much a part of the convention as the action. Using awareness of the medium in the medium itself can result in parody — like bad movie music signaling the action ahead — but in Schuyler's story, I take it to be a form of ironic honesty, like saying "dear reader" to a reader one almost holds dear.

Objectifications can teeter between confession and materialization. In Elizabeth Bishop's "In Prison," the heroine's one fantasy and desire is to be imprisoned. That fantasy tells us not at all who the narrator is but very clearly the kind of person she'd like to be, and allows the writer extraordinary moments of landscape engraving, imaginative leaps — the description of the walls and the courtyard — leaps that seem more daring in a story so obsessed by confinement. And there is that moment, too, in Kenneth Koch's "The Postcard Collection," when the narrator suddenly breaks the thread and says to an offstage character we don't know, "I love you" — a break that both undercuts and highlights the speculation the postcards give birth to. In that switch of viewpoint, something about life and art is being said in the simplest and yet most complicated of ways. For the utterance itself is banal and direct, as if the author were saying, "Enough of all this artifice and theory — the plain truth is 'I love you.'" Yet the postcards, created by artists of a kind — there are little poems on the reverse sides — are sent by, and to, real people whose stories the writer is trying to reconstruct from the stained and defaced messages. The writings on the postcards are artful communications within an artful communication; they are at the heart of the story the writer is writing — a piece of artifice in itself. The postcards may be artifacts, the story may be a work of art, but the writer makes one thing clear: *he* is real. And there is that moment in James Merrill's story "Driver," when the protagonist, after a mystical revelation that reveals very little, reveals a *real* mystery to us: he is sixty years old.

There are other mysteries. The one that pervades the way of life of the mountain people in W. S. Merwin's "Return to the Mountains" — every detail is presented realistically, it seems, and yet with that shimmer, that discreet secrecy, which lets us know that what might seem obvious is not quite within our grasp. When the animals turn, like natural compasses, and point in one direction, and the narrator comes upon the strange balletlike action of old women sewing cauls — we are moved by . . . what? The venerableness of the symbols? The secret of life withheld from the narrator, as it may well be from us? The strange mixture of the exotic and the mundane that gives the story its flavor? Like Merwin's poems, "Return to the Mountains" is visionary in the most literal sense in that the use of the eye is the paradoxical key to what cannot be seen. It makes us aware that there is more than we can see, the revelation of which can never be final. The significant figures in Merwin's story are not characters but a chorus, and it appears with the force of a vision at the end.

Stories written by poets usually take place somewhere between the window and the mirror — stories of revelation objectified to a point, but not to the point of realism. They bear the poet's particular badge: the mysterious and the real held in suspension. You know more when you finish their stories than you can say. If they could have been reduced to statement, there would have been no point in writing them.

ACKNOWLEDGMENTS

"Notes on Fiction," copyright © 1966, first appeared in *Wisconsin Studies in Contemporary Literature*.

"All Praise" copyright © 1966 by Kenyon College. Reprinted by permission of *The Kenyon Review*.

"Three Sisters," copyright © 1978, first appeared in *The Hudson Review*.

"Jean Stafford: Some Fragments," copyright © 1979, first appeared in *Shenandoah*.

"Early Chekhov" and "Good Poems, Sad Lives" (originally titled "Poets in Their Youth") are reprinted with permission from *The New York Review of Books*. Copyright © 1982–83 Nyrev, Inc.

"The Poet's Story" first appeared in *The Poet's Story* edited, with Introduction, by Howard Moss. Copyright © 1973 by Macmillan Publishing Company. Reprinted by permission.

"A Candidate for the Future," "Great Themes, Grand Connections," "The Poet's Voice," "The Lonesomeness and Hilarity of Survival," "Going to Pieces," "Interior Children," "One Hundred Years of Proust," "No Safe Harbor," "A Thin, Curly Little Person," and "The Long Voyage Home," copyright © 1981, 1977, 1978, 1970, 1974, 1979, 1971, 1962, 1967, and 1985 by Howard Moss, originally appeared in *The New Yorker*.

"Whatever Is Moving" and "The First Line," copyright © 1981 and 1978, first appeared in *American Poetry Review*.

"Goodbye to Wystan," "A House Divided" (originally titled "The Optimist's Daughter"), "A Pinched Existence," "Reversing the Binoculars" (originally titled "A Poet of the Story"), and "Hingley's Biography," copyright © 1975, 1972, 1980, 1965, and 1976, first appeared in *The New York Times*.

"After *Madame Bovary*," copyright © 1982, first appeared in *The Washington Post*.

"The Canada-Brazil Connection," copyright © 1977, first appeared in *World Literature Today* published by The University of Oklahoma Press in 1977.